NEVILLE CHAMBERLAIN

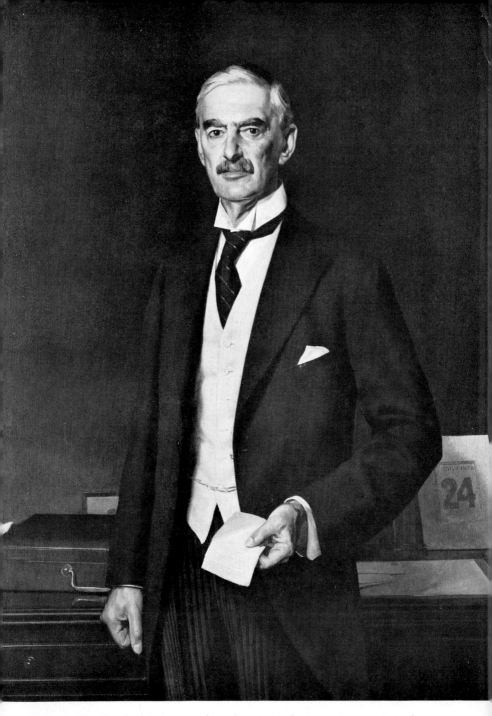

Neville Chamberlain in 1938, from the painting by James Gunn, R.A. in the
Carlton Club

NEVILLE CHAMBERLAIN

by

IAIN MACLEOD

FREDERICK MULLER LIMITED
LONDON

FIRST PUBLISHED IN GREAT BRITAIN IN 1961 BY
FREDERICK MULLER LIMITED
PRINTED AND BOUND BY
HAZELL WATSON AND VINEY LTD.
AYLESBURY AND SLOUGH

To my Mother

ACKNOWLEDGEMENTS

For permission to print extracts from their unpublished letters to Neville Chamberlain, I am particularly grateful to the Earl of Avon, Viscount Hailsham, and Sir Alexander Cadogan.

Mr. R. J. Topping has very kindly allowed me to print an unpublished memorandum to Chamberlain by the late Sir Robert Topping, and the Director of the Conservative Research Department to quote from private files in the Department.

I am obliged to Dr. John Masefield and Lady Namier for permission to quote copyright material, and to the Controller of Her Majesty's Stationery Office for leave to reprint extracts from Hansard and Official publications.

I have also to acknowledge with thanks permission to quote extracts from works, cited in my footnotes, which have been published by Messrs. Cassell & Co. Ltd., Wm. Collins Sons & Co. Ltd., Constable & Co. Ltd., André Deutsch Ltd., Rupert Hart-Davis Ltd., William Heinemann Ltd., Hutchinson & Co. Ltd., Macmillan & Co. Ltd., Methuen & Co. Ltd., Frederick Muller Ltd., Ivor Nicholson & Watson Ltd., Odhams Press Ltd., and the Oxford University Press.

The Gunn portrait of Neville Chamberlain is reproduced as frontispiece by the kind permission of the Chairman of the Carlton Club.

CONTENTS

LIST OF ILLUSTRATIONS

PREFACE

I NEVER met, indeed I do not think I ever saw, Neville
Chamberlain. I can remember hearing his voice only once:
when he broadcast on the declaration of war. I played no
part at all in politics until the war was nearly over, and I rarely
felt myself intellectually or emotionally involved in the political
issues of the 'thirties. When they began I was at school, when
they ended I was in the Army. But after the war, when chance
took me into politics, I found myself constantly taking up work
which Chamberlain had pioneered. He had been the founder and
inspiration of the Conservative Research Department where,
under R. A. Butler and David Clarke, I worked from 1946 to the
end of 1949. I was, as Chamberlain had been, Minister of Health
for a long time. I was concerned as Minister of Labour with the
ending of National Service, he in the First World War had been
its first Director. And from the study I made of earlier social
legislation I began to form of this man I never knew a mental
picture that seemed to me utterly different from the public image
which all but his friends seemed to accept. This is why, when one
by one I stopped playing the games I loved so much, when I no
longer had time or opportunity for shooting or fishing, and when,
hating as I do gardening and walking with an equal fervour, I
decided to try to write in the occasional break I had from work,
I wanted to embark on a life of Neville Chamberlain.

This would not, of course, have been possible without the
free and full use of all his private letters, papers and diaries. I am
deeply grateful to his family, especially to his widow, to his
sister Miss Hilda Chamberlain, and to his daughter Mrs. Stephen
Lloyd, for all the help and encouragement that they have given
me. I owe a special debt of gratitude to Mrs. Lloyd who has com-
piled the Index for this book.

Many people have been kind enough to discuss different parts
of the book with me, but of these Mr. Peter Goldman is in quite

another category. From the beginning he has helped me to plan the book, he has undertaken much basic research, and I have found his historical sense and political judgement invaluable.

Anyone undertaking a new biography of Neville Chamberlain has the additional benefit of Sir Keith Feiling's pioneering work, written during the war.

Even so, I have inevitably taken a very long time to complete it. For the last eighteen months in particular it has been the rarest of pleasures to have a quiet week-end and sometimes a few days in a Parliamentary recess.

Inevitably Neville Chamberlain's name was and will be linked with Munich. Yet it is important that his story should not be overweighted with Munich. Munich and the months that followed were not the natural fulfilment of his life and career in the sense, for instance, that Dunkirk and the months that followed were the crown of Winston Churchill's. Chamberlain was through everything and at all times a radical social reformer. He held to this course in local and in national politics. He sought to sustain it at the Exchequer and at Ottawa. And whatever the verdict on his foreign policies, his aim was always to create conditions in which the wealth of nations should enrich life and not destroy it. Those whose views on Munich and on Chamberlain crystallized long ago are perhaps unlikely to alter them radically because they have read this book. But at least they may now have a better understanding of the man.

IAIN MACLEOD

London
1961

1

THE CHAMBERLAINS

BETWEEN the two world wars three Conservatives, Bonar Law, Stanley Baldwin and Neville Chamberlain, became Prime Minister. There is an obvious link between the iron-master from Glasgow, the iron-master from Worcestershire and the industrialist from Birmingham. Those who followed them, Churchill, Eden and Macmillan, had their links not with them but with their predecessors Balfour, Salisbury and Disraeli. There was, too, an obvious sympathy between the interwar Conservative premiers. Bonar Law's regard for Neville Chamberlain was such that when on his retirement from the Premiership in 1923 he was asked by the King's secretary whom he would suggest consulting about the succession, he thought first of Chamberlain, then, realising he was too junior to tender advice on such an issue, Lord Salisbury the Lord President of the Council. Neville Chamberlain too had no qualms when Baldwin succeeded Bonar Law. "After all," as he confided to his diary, "he is a business man himself." They were all Victorians. Chamberlain the youngest of them was already in his thirties when Queen Victoria died. And they represented a new and important element in the Conservative Party, the well-to-do middle class. They were men of property. They were as solid as their silver. And so the Chamberlains had been in London and in Birmingham for many generations. They come marching down the years from their original home in Wiltshire, through the century of respectable but not very profitable business as shoemakers in Milk Street until Joseph Chamberlain the second, who was the father of Joe

Chamberlain the Colonial Secretary, moved to Birmingham and the great days of the family began.

William Chamberlain, son of Daniel Chamberlain, maltster, of Lacock, who was the first of the family to come to London, or perhaps to return to London, for it seems possible from the records that the family left London for Wiltshire at the time of the great plague, was first apprenticed to his uncle, a confectioner. But soon he was taking up a second apprenticeship as a shoemaker and was admitted to the Cordwainers Company in 1733. William Chamberlain had nine children, but only his two elder sons, William and Joseph, survived to manhood. Both went into the family business; both were Masters of the Cordwainers Company. From Joseph (born in 1752) the first of his name, six Joseph Chamberlains descend in unbroken line to this day. The business at Milk Street was established somewhere about 1755 and was carried on from there for rather more than one hundred years. In that hundred years, six Chamberlains became Masters of the Cordwainers Company and for all but a few months of that hundred years a Chamberlain was on the Court of the Company. The family link with the Company was only broken with the death of Sir Austen Chamberlain in 1937. Because they were men of property the Chamberlains were Churchwardens of St. Lawrence Jewry. Because they were Unitarians they worshipped at Carter Lane Chapel in the City. They were described in a letter of 1829 as "the highest sort of tradesmen, plain, honest and sincere". Pudding before meat was served at their dinners and the dinners themselves were formidable. So ran the unremarkable record of this respected family from the middle of the eighteenth to the middle of the nineteenth century. And in London the Chamberlains might well have remained. But John Sutton Nettlefold took Joseph Chamberlain, his brother-in-law, into partnership and the firm of Nettlefold and Chamberlain screwmakers in Birmingham was formed.

It was necessary to find a representative in Birmingham for the new venture and, reversing the Whittington story, a young man was found to turn his back on the City of London and seek his fortune in the provinces. Joe Chamberlain had left school at the age of sixteen in 1852 and had had two years' experience in the

Milk Street business. He and Birmingham grew up together. Birmingham young, ambitious, thrusting, disrespectful, was already becoming conscious of future greatness. And so was Joe. Unlike Joseph Chamberlain and Sons, where profits were always on a modest scale, Nettlefold and Chamberlain after a hesitant start prospered exceedingly. They were vigorously attacked and as warmly defended for their acquisitive methods. Smaller firms were swallowed up and others reorganised. The grumbles and the slanders grew and indeed later pursued Joe Chamberlain in his political career. But the truth was that Nettlefold and Chamberlain, in what was then an inefficient industry, were vastly efficient. Helped by their shrewd purchase of the English rights of an American patent for improved machinery, their product was cheaper and better than their rivals'. They achieved something near a monopoly of the business. For this Joe Chamberlain was chiefly responsible. He had an immense zest for life and an infinite capacity for hard work. He loved the business struggle as he loved the Parliamentary fight. And he was master of both.

That the man and the city matched and inspired each other is not to be doubted. But one searches for something more than a change of city air to help explain the sudden eruption of a worthy pedestrian family into business success and political brilliance within a generation. Joe's father, Joseph Chamberlain, is a shadowy figure. All the now familiar virtues are there. Like all the earlier Chamberlains he was reserved, sincere, zealous, rigid. His interests were bounded by his business and his Chapel. He was, of course, Master of the Cordwainers and a Churchwarden. The beadle of the Company recollected him as "An immovable man. Nothing could turn him if he had made up his mind. Pleasant and quiet in manner but not to be moved from what he had said by anybody—you could see it in his face." He belonged to Milk Street rather than to Moor Green. Yet his son was an eagle. It is always tempting, with the advantage of hindsight, to look back at a man's ancestors and to attribute to this or that forgotten relative some strong influence on those who came later. There has been no temptation yet to do this: while they were in business in London the difficulty lies rather in distinguishing the Chamberlains from each other. But it is perhaps not fanciful to see in

Caroline Harben, wife of the second Joseph Chamberlain, mother of Joe and grandmother of Austen and Neville, a new and gayer spirit. The Harbens were probably an old Somerset family who had come to Sussex in the seventeenth century. Like the first Chamberlain, the first Harben of whom there is firm record was a maltster. The history of the Harbens is a rather more colourful and chequered one than that of the Chamberlains, and indeed Caroline's father Henry Harben broke away from the rest of the family in protest against the rogueries of his elder brother. Moving to London he established himself first as a brewer and then as a provision merchant. Caroline, who was born in 1808 and died in 1875—the same year as Florence Kenrick, Neville Chamberlain's mother, died—was one of eighteen children. She is the first of the Chamberlain wives to come alive from the records and letters and memories of the family. "It was to her," records Sir Austen Chamberlain in a family history, "that their children owed the chief part of their intellectual tastes." She loved flowers and beauty and the gentle pleasures of a large Victorian household. One of her daughters, later Neville's "Aunt Clara", recalled that their Birmingham home, then on the edge of the countryside, was a centre for family excursions "to the daffodil fields—which stretched from Northfield to the Lickey, to Weatheroak for primroses and sweet violets, and to Earlswood for primroses, and in the summer to all the neighbouring lawns for wild roses". Among the cherished possessions of the family is a tiny silver thimble placed in a grave of cotton wool with this epitaph in her handwriting:

"Here rests from her labours a faithful servant after seventeen years and half of constant devoted usefulness to one mistress. This thimble was given to Caroline Harben on her fourteenth birthday by her grandmother, Mrs. Woodgate, and had she continued Caroline Harben might still have been in her service. But her little son Joey (more ruthless than Time) stamped upon its worn frame and finished what the Old Destroyer might have spared much longer.

It was here laid to repose January 17, 1840, by its grateful friend and mistress."

No wife of one of the earlier Chamberlains could have written anything so frivolous.

18

Joe was the eldest of her nine children. Married at twenty-five to Harriet Kenrick, he was twenty-seven when she died giving birth to Austen. Five years later he married her first cousin, Florence Kenrick, and Neville Chamberlain, their first child, was born on March 18th, 1869. But in 1875 and again in childbirth Joe Chamberlain's wife died. He was not yet forty. But his unquiet spirit was driven all the harder. Success in business alone did not satisfy him. He was always drawn as a Chamberlain must be drawn to public service. And for him public service began in his business life. In Nettlefold and Chamberlain he founded first a social club, then a night school for the employees: the order is perhaps significant and, if it was unusual then, would be approved by a social reformer today. He himself was lecturer-in-chief. He was a regular Sunday-school teacher for the Unitarians. Via the Birmingham and Edgbaston Debating Society, where his first recorded speech was against the motion that "the character and conduct of Oliver Cromwell do not entitle him to the admiration of posterity", he reached the City Council in 1869. A glittering Mayoralty in 1873, was repeated in 1874 and 1875. By now he had sold his business interests. All his works and dreams were of politics. To Southbourne and later to Highbury, the house Joe Chamberlain built in Moor Green, came the Liberal leaders, first of Birmingham then of London. Here with Schnadhorst was fashioned the ruthless efficiency of the caucus, here the Radicalism that was to split the Liberal party was fostered. Here the new Birmingham was charted, and an even newer concept of Empire born.

This was the home Neville Chamberlain knew. But it was a home without a mother and because of that a home from which the father sometimes retreated. Neville was six years old when his mother and grandmother died in the same year. Beatrice and Austen, the children of the first marriage, were thirteen and twelve. Too old to be playmates: too young to be guardians. Neville was the eldest child of the second marriage. Ida was five years old, Hilda three and Ethel eighteen months. First Caroline and then, when Caroline married, Clara Chamberlain, Joe's two youngest sisters, took up the complex double task of hostess to the statesman and foster parent to his six children. Aunt Clara was too young and perhaps too obstinate to be wholly successful. Certainly Neville did not find in her the affection that all his life he needed from his family. Coming home rejoicing to be free of the hated Rugby at the end of his first term, he hurled himself into his Aunt's arms, and always remembered the only reply he got—"Neville, your cap's crooked"—and his private vow that he would never kiss her again. But he was never unhappy for long at home. He was the natural leader of a whole platoon of younger sisters and cousins, the children of Arthur Chamberlain, Joe's brother, who had married yet another Kenrick, Louisa, the twin of Neville's mother Florence, and of William Kenrick, brother of Harriet, who in turn had married Mary Chamberlain, Joe's sister. Only a genealogical table enables one to find a way through the maze of Chamberlains, Kenricks, Pagets and the other Unitarian families who were Neville's ancestors. One example will suffice. Three sons of Joseph Paget of Ibstock married three daughters of the Reverend John Byng, Unitarian Minister of Tamworth. The daughter of William Paget and Mary Byng became Mrs. Archibald Kenrick, the mother of Harriet Kenrick, who was Joe Chamberlain's first wife: the daughter of Thomas Paget and Elizabeth Byng became Mrs. Timothy Kenrick and mother of Florence Kenrick, Joe Chamberlain's second wife. The Kenricks came from North Wales, and their background of solid Unitarian respectability was very like that of the Milk Street Chamberlains. They came to Birmingham at the end of the eighteenth century. Archibald Kenrick, father of Timothy Kenrick, who was Neville's grandfather, was apprenticed to an iron-founder in Birmingham, and after an unsuccessful venture into the manufacture of shoe-buckles returned to the safer business of an iron-founder in West Bromwich. Here he made money quickly and spent it generously. The Kenrick family, like the Chamberlains, found the winds of moneymaking and philanthropy, civic duty and social reform, independence and nonconformity which were blowing through the new city exactly to their taste. The Kenricks were worthy but not dull. Sir Keith Feiling, in his biography of Neville Chamberlain, wrote "By the evidence of all who knew him best Neville's strongest characteristics came from the Kenricks." Certainly from the Kenricks came a love of music

20

and of nature and a quick sympathy with suffering. Typically Kenrick too was the small head (the "wrong shape" Lloyd George called it) and the spare frame. But in much he was Joe's son. The narrow sloping shoulders, the forehead and the firm jawline are much the same in photographs of father and son. Under bushy eyebrows Neville's eyes were brown, and his hair and later his moustache thick and black and only tinged with grey in his last years. He is as much Kenrick as Chamberlain, and once more it is from the mother's side that much of the spirit comes.

Maria Paget, Neville's grandmother, who married Timothy Kenrick of Edgbaston, was remembered as "full of vitality, bright and lively and fascinating". She had eleven children and Florence Kenrick, Neville's mother, was born with her twin sister Louisa in 1847. Florence Chamberlain was only twenty-eight when she died. Of her four children only Neville was just old enough to have more than dream memories of their mother, and there is little to record of her young life. She was serene and happy and extremely intelligent. If she had lived the children would have been much closer to their father in their early years, and Neville would have been less reserved and less ready to shut the door on the outside world and retreat to his private temple.

The Chamberlains had large numbers of children, and the tribe played together as comrades and cousins. In part no doubt the reason for their exclusiveness was because of their Unitarian beliefs. Persecuted over the centuries the Unitarians found in Birmingham and elsewhere that there were still barriers social and political, as well as religious. Not that in radical Birmingham the chapel families looked up to the church ones. On the contrary. The new aristocracy of Birmingham were the great families of the Unitarians or the Quakers rather than those who belonged to the Church of England. But there was another and perhaps simpler reason for their self-sufficiency.

They liked their own company. No table talk seemed ever as satisfying as that of the household at Highbury, especially when the great ones of the political and journalistic world were matching their wits with Joe Chamberlain. No projects seemed more worthwhile than the slum clearance drive, the campaign against drink, the provision of new schools and hospitals in Birmingham.

And to the children no playmates were as gay or as inventive as their countless cousins. They were withdrawn, but in no way a sombre and unhappy crowd. All the family stories of Neville Chamberlain's early life are full of laughter and in most of them Neville himself takes the lead. But outside this close family circle where he knew he was safe and loved Neville Chamberlain was much less happy. When he first went away to a small school in Southport at the age of eight, he was content enough. But he hated the preparatory school he was later sent to, and he hated Rugby. Not for any of the obvious reasons. He was good enough at games, head of his house, successful if not outstanding at work. If he was unhappy and unfortunate in his relationship with Jex-Blake, the Headmaster, and with his Housemaster, the true reason for his deep and abiding dislike of Rugby was surely a deeper one. He was away from his family and his clan. He was alone, and he had not yet achieved an understanding and a conquest of loneliness. Neville could always rejoice with his closest friends and share simple jokes and happiness. But even so only his family ever knew the true man. His family life was his private citadel. Here he was secure whatever storms raged outside. Here he could relax and find new strength. At home Aunt Clara had gone; Beatrice, his half sister, at twenty-two, some six years older than Neville, was in charge, and happiness was back again. And later on in 1888 when Neville was nineteen, his father, now fifty-two, married for the third time, and Mary Endicott, younger even than Beatrice, came from New England to Birmingham to bring peace and happiness to the father and an even greater sense of unity to the children. Now, as far as it could ever be, the hurt of the earlier tragic deaths was healed. Neville was never, when he was young, wholly at ease with his father, and for Austen he felt respect rather than deep affection. But all through his life he had the closest ties with Ida and Hilda, the two sisters to whom he confided all his doings and hopes in long weekly letters from the days of his Lord Mayoralty until the autumn he died. He did not marry until he was past forty and when it came his marriage was the crown and the joy of his whole life. It was a love story always. His children Dorothy and Frank had with him none of the reserve that he had felt for his father. To them he was friend and companion as well as father. These two faces of Neville Chamberlain, the stiff and reserved face that was so often turned to the world and the gay, simple, happy side of his private life are part, an essential part, of the man. Even those who knew him well found him difficult to understand. His physician, the first Lord Horder, said of Neville Chamberlain, "I was very fond of him. I like all unlovable men."[1] But Horder was wrong. It is impossible to read Neville Chamberlain's diaries, or his letters to his family and theirs to him, without knowing that he could not have been unlovable, for he was dearly loved.

[1] The Countess of Oxford and Asquith, *Off the Record* (Frederick Muller, 1944), p. 81.

2

SISAL AND FAILURE

(1890–1896)

SIR AMBROSE SHEA was an enthusiast. He had come late into the Colonial Service and when he was appointed Governor of the Bahamas in 1887, he had already behind him a successful business career in shipping in Newfoundland.

For the moment Sir Ambrose's enthusiasm was sisal growing. The sisal plant was probably introduced to the Bahamas from Yucatan in 1845 by Mr. Nesbitt, then Colonial Secretary of the Bahamas. In his garden at Nassau the plants thrived and multiplied. But in spite of not unfavourable reports from London on the quality of the fibre specimens submitted to them no encouragement came from the Nassau merchants. On sponging, on fruit, and on a primitive agriculture and fishing, what little prosperity the islands had was thought to rest: a new fibre industry was seen as a threat to the cheap labour which was readily available to them. So Mr. Nesbitt plodded on with his lone idea, distributing plants all over the inhabited islands of the Bahamas and remaining obstinately faithful to his theory that a rich source of revenue, sorely needed by the poverty stricken Bahamas, was to be found in the dark green leaves of the Agave Rigida looked on now by the natives as a weed. In due course to Nesbitt's doubtful legacy Sir Ambrose Shea succeeded. The *Pall Mall Gazette* of July 23rd, 1894, at the height of the brief sisal boom told the romantic story of its rediscovery.

"His Excellency had not long been in the Colony when one day a man came into his office carrying a bundle. Sir Ambrose, who evidently possesses an observant eye, fastened it not so much upon the contents of the bundle as upon the rough piece of rope with which it was tied. Unless all his shipping experience was betraying him, the rope was manilla. So he asked the man where he got that cord from. 'It grew in my garden Your Excellency' was the reply. . . . Greatly surprised at this news he allowed himself to be conducted into the grounds, where the sisal plant was pointed out to him. Upon examination of the leaves of the plant, he at once detected its fibrous appearance. He took a few leaves indoors, scraped off their surfaces and picked out from them beautiful long fibres five or six feet in length. . . . Sir Ambrose could see that this plant was going to be a genuine Aladdin's lamp to the colony, a source of endless wealth."

The shallow soil that barely covered the coral rocks of the Bahamas gave little nourishment to ordinary crops. The score of inhabited and the countless uninhabited islands and cays, surface protuberances of the Little Bahama and the Great Bahama oceanic banks, were thickly covered with pine-barren and scrub. Only the cutlass and the axe could hack a clearing from the poor vegetation of the low-lying islands.

It was from the water rather than from the land that the natives wrested their precarious living. For a time it seemed that sisal would alter all this. Sir Ambrose Shea was not alone in his enthusiasm. In the most extravagant terms—"a fitting chapter for the Arabian nights": "the great sisal industry . . . backbone of our prosperity": "recognising in a despised and rejected plant a source of enormous wealth"—the citizens of Nassau with the Legislature of the Colony combined to give a dinner to Sir Ambrose, to "commemorate the beginning of the period of prosperity". The chickens were being counted and indeed sold in advance, for the first fibre yield from the sisal plant is normally in the fourth year. The story of the Bahamas sisal bubble is best told by the Annual Reports from the Governor to the Secretary of State for the Colonies.

1890. "Steady progress continues to be made in this industry, with increasing faith in its value and permanence . . . it will ever be the main export and it is difficult to see how it can fail to pay present investors handsomely."

1891. "It would be difficult to assign a limit to the future advance of the Colony from the growth of this remarkable industry."

1892. "I can confidently assert that none of the investors would, if they could, withdraw from the enterprise and there is no diminution of the confidence with which it was undertaken."

But

1896. "The prospects for this new industry are now becoming more defined and although it has absolutely failed to fulfil the anticipations once formed for it there seems to be less reason to fear that it will die out altogether . . ."

1897. "Very low prices ruled in the American and English markets, and the new industry was in danger of a complete collapse. Two of the most important enterprises wherein very large capital had been invested came to a termination. . . ."

This last information was scarcely news to the Colonial Secretary, Mr. Joe Chamberlain; for one of the "important enterprises" was his own in which nearly £50,000 of his capital had been sunk.

The story goes back to Montreal in the autumn of 1890. Shea, then on the prowl for men of substance to bring capital to this industry in which he had such faith, found himself staying in the same hotel as Joe Chamberlain, who with his third wife Mary and his son Austen, had been on a visit to his in-laws and had extended his tour to Canada. Shea arranged a meeting with Mr. Chamberlain. He was fortunate in his timing. Joe Chamberlain, when he sold his business interests in 1874, had turned his back on business, even insisting on withdrawing the name from his old firm Nettlefold and Chamberlain. He was still comfortably enough off, but politics was an expensive occupation, and the idea of making a second fortune in the Colonial Empire had a natural appeal to him. Moreover he was on the look-out for a suitable occupation for Neville. Austen was already being launched in politics and was soon to become an M.P., Neville must earn his living. Leaving Rugby at the end of 1886 he had had a spell at Mason College, Birmingham studying, with little to show for it, science and engineering design. There followed a successful apprenticeship with a firm of chartered accountants. It was an orthodox approach to a business career in Birmingham and in 1890 Neville was ready to launch out. But a wire came summoning him urgently to meet Austen in New York. They were then to go with all speed to Nassau. Shea's sales talk had convinced Joe Chamberlain that he must investigate sisal, and on the shoulders of Neville Chamberlain, a youth of twenty-one, was to be thrust the task of relining his father's and his family's fortunes.

The two brothers moved with all speed. The need for this had been insisted on by their father. Like Shea he had become convinced that a new gold mine had been discovered. If this were so then soon the prospectors would pour in and the price of sisal begin to fall. The aim was to move in quickly, produce as soon as possible and sell out before the market began to droop. By the 10th of November the brothers had reached Nassau. As always with the Chamberlains long letters began to flood back and forth between Highbury and the exiles. Letters from both of them to their father on the history of the Bahamas and of sisal, letters with minute and perhaps dangerously precise estimates of the capital that would be needed, letters faithfully recording their search for suitable land. And to Mary and to their sisters letters about the people and the scenery, the flowers and the animals. The sisal industry was of course still in its infancy and no firm report of possible profits could yet be made. Sir Ambrose was reluctant to provide even a rough basis for his claim that "the first crop (i.e. in the fourth year) will repay all moneys expended in its production, leaving the gross price of future crops less the current expenses at clear profit". The brothers dismissed this as "altogether extravagant" and set out to collect their own information. But their own laborious calculations began to show much the same result. Austen wrote this to his father:

A.C. to J. C. 22.12.1890.

"The capital required for the cultivation of 1,000 acres is then £12,000 and the cost per ton of fibre in London will be £11.10.0. Assuming £20 as the selling price of the fibre, this leaves a profit of £8.10.0 per ton after all expenses including 7½% interest on capital have been paid—that is a profit of £8,500 on a capital of £12,000 or over 70%. . . . These results are so fabulously good that they appear almost impossible . . . if we are right, Bahama hemp cultivation is nearly as good as the Governor thinks it."

In searching the islands for a suitable tract of land the intricate calculations went on. The estimates were modified and defended

27

against memoranda of criticism from London. The conclusion was that even allowing for only three-quarter ton to the acre a 50 per cent profit could be realised. Of the possible sites Mayaguana was the one the brothers favoured even though it was a very long way from Nassau and no white people lived there. There was just time to obtain a provisional lease of the island on favourable terms from the Governor, and by the end of January 1891 the brothers were back in the family circle at Highbury. There were long discussions but they were only on details, for Joe Chamberlain was determined to plunge and not even Arthur Chamberlain's weighty arguments against the venture prevailed. By April, Neville Chamberlain just twenty-two years old was on his way back, this time alone, to the Bahamas.

Within two days of his arrival he had found his land: "I am confident that I have secured the best site available in the Bahamas." It was not in Mayaguana, but in the north of Andros Island and Neville's confidence is in odd contrast with the brothers' report in January of the same year. "We had now satisfied ourselves that the North of Andros would not do for us." No doubt the nearness of Andros, the largest island in the Bahamas, to Nassau was a decisive factor—no more than twenty miles at the nearest point from New Providence Island. Perhaps even Nassau society, for all Neville's expressed contempt for it, and even the presence three miles from Mastic Point of a grumpy red-bearded Scot, Mr. Keith, weighed in the balance against the loneliness of Mayaguana. Whatever the reasons may have been, a week's tough prospecting on Andros Island, which exhausted his two companions, Michael Knowles who was to be his manager, and Forsyth a surveyor, but not Neville himself, decided the matter. Andros Island for the next five years was to be his home. Terms were easily agreed with the Governor. The newly-formed Andros Fibre Company was to have an option on 20,000 acres in Andros. For the first 10,000 a price of five shillings per acre was agreed with an option to be exercised on the remainder at 16s. 8d. per acre at the end of ten years. Moreover the Governor agreed to build a wharf at Mastic Point of which the Chamberlains were to have free use, and only to sell up to 100,000 acres of Crown lands in all the Bahamas for sisal growing in order to confine the market.

These were good terms, so good that later they attracted a good deal of criticism. Neville, who drew up the agreement, drove a hard bargain while Sir Ambrose was very anxious to secure the prestige of the Chamberlain name in the new industry. Both were satisfied.

There was everything to be done on the land. Houses to be built for Knowles and himself, a garden to be fashioned, roads to be torn out of the ground, the pine-barren to be cleared and cut and weeded, a store selling goods for the native labour to be stocked and managed; later, plants to be bought and sown, machines to be ordered for stripping the fibre, even a railway to be planned and built. And all the time accounts to be kept for his impatient father, in as much detail as if Andros was Birmingham From the beginning Neville knew exactly what he planned to do. Writing from Nassau after the agreement had been made and on the eve of his departure for Andros—

N.C. to Beatrice 7.6.1891.

"Next week I intend to return to Andros and live in a negro's house which I shall hire until I can get my own put up which will not be for two months at least. Books and such luxuries I should not care to have until I am installed but linen and such like necessaries I would be glad to have at once. Now I must tell you a little bit about my future home. The house is to be just half way between Pye Point and Mastic Point, about a hundred yards from the shore on a little hill about thirty feet high. At present it is covered with coppice containing some very fair trees (for the Bahamas) of mahogany, madeira, mastic, gum aloe, stopper, etc. These I mean to leave in their places only taking out the undergrowth. Then if I can get some grass to grow under them they will be very shady and pleasant in summer. I mean to get some ornamental trees and shrubs from Nassau to make a garden with, and I shall also plant fruit trees. Oranges I think I shall import from Florida and perhaps bud or graft them on wild orange trees in the woods. They then should bear a few oranges in two years. I also have a mind to try grapes. Cocoa nuts already are on the spot, planted by squatters. . . . Andros is no place for riding at present but when I get some land cleared I think a pony will be practicable. Sheep, cows and pigs will come in their time . . ."

Most of this came to pass, but it needed some imagination to conjure this settlement out of the rock and coppice that were his heritage. His days were long and laborious. Six o'clock saw him up and about:

N.C. to Ida 20.9.1891.

"First of all I had to count lumber for several hours. Then after twenty minutes for breakfast I hurried out to the pineyard to measure out a lot of ground before paying wages at noon. I hadn't been there an hour when down came sheets of rain which soaked me in my thin clothes in an instant. I would not go in however and continued measuring for three mortal hours in the hardest rain I have ever experienced. About 3 o'clock I paddled back to the store to find Knowles still counting lumber and the people all waiting for the wages. From 3 to 7.30 I sat in a through draught, paying wages till my limbs were cramped and my nails blue with cold. Then I gathered myself up and stumbled home, cold wet hungry and tired in the pitchy darkness."

The store, selling everything from coffee to corsets, although it was a necessary investment to keep and support his erratic labour force, took far too much time.

N.C. to Ethel 16.8.1891.

"Yesterday was pay-day . . . altogether we took £15 over the counter yesterday but it was very hard work. We began at six in the morning and went on till ten when I rushed home for a badly cooked and scanty breakfast. After this I rushed back and never stopped serving and paying till 5 p.m. All I had to eat was two biscuits with nothing to drink and last night when I got home I was pretty tired. Even then I had to sit up till 10 doing accounts and writing letters."

The store, however, proved profitable and in time rather more than one-third of the wages bill was recovered from it.

He was monarch of all he surveyed. It is hard sometimes to remember or even believe that this assured competent leader was only a year or two away from his hesitant teens. Arming himself with an opinion from the Attorney General, he organised opposition to defeat the opening of a grog shop: when the Resident Justice of Andros was dismissed, "I have successfully used my influence to get Forsyth appointed in his place": when Knowles his manager once had too much to drink, "I told him that it was a very serious thing, that a person who allowed himself to get into that state could never be fit for the position we intended for him and that I no longer place the same confidence in him as before": anticipating the Birmingham Municipal Bank, he started a savings bank with 2 per cent. interest offered. He ruled his native labour sternly and won from them an affection that lasted for many years after his enterprise had foundered. Indeed to this day he is remembered there. On his first Christmas Day a round robin was presented to "Mr. Chimblin":

"We do feel already that your presence here has caused as it were a new light to shine among us. Accept our hearty thanks for the indefatigable exertions you have made here."

He could send too with his voluminous first year accounts a good report to his father. By the end of 1891, 650 acres had been cut, 580 of them cleared and 320 of them planted. By May 1892, the first year's target of 1000 acres cut had been reached with a month to spare. He had to put up with a good deal of back-seat driving from Austen who was full of ideas, often impracticable, for speeding up the clearing and planting, and from his father to whom he rendered a weekly progress report, a fortnightly or monthly rough balance and full annual company reports. Joe was a fierce overseer. This in reply to criticism of Neville's book-keeping:

N.C. to J.C. 10.12.1891.

"The agents commission is therefore very difficult to distribute as it is on plants, duties paid, goods for store, provisions for self, little articles for buildings etc. If you wish it however I will attempt to split it up as strictly should be done.

Carriage and Freight.

This includes freight of goods for store, plants, lumber and sundries. It shall in future be divided up and the a/c as it stands shall be apportioned as accurately as possible if you wish. . . ."

All this for a salary of £200 a year which Neville refers to in a letter to Austen without irony as "my absurdly large salary".

So it was a cheerful exile with a good tale to tell who returned in July 1892 for what was to become an annual three months' leave. Austen returned with him for a brief visit in the autumn, and then Neville was alone again. But now his house was finished, "as good as any in Nassau" and a flood of gifts streamed from his sisters and cousins to help furnish it. Not all of them were equally suitable: "the tablecloths especially fill me with apprehension as to their fate at the wash . . . by the way what is the especial use of 'tea towels'?"; but he had hewed for himself a comfortable enough oasis in what had been wilderness. There was the garden with coleus and vincas, roses and hibiscus, gloxinia and golden rod, and even water orchids in a vast tank. Every possible vegetable and fruit grew and most of them flourished in the kitchen gardens from the seeds sent regularly from Highbury. From his huge flagpole waved the Union Jack or his Lion Standard (made by Hilda) to proclaim that here was a truly British enclave. He had stabling for his horses and mules, and the beginnings of a farm. He had his sailing boats *Beatrice* and *Lola*, and his schooner *Pride of Andros*. Above all he had his library now with him from Highbury. Not that he worked any the less hard because he was not now living in wretched surroundings. In the field he worked harder and longer hours than Knowles or than the native labour corps. And in the evenings he toiled on into the small hours making up accounts, studying German, and reading Carlyle and Romanes, Green and Mahan.

The Andros Fibre Company had reached the moment of decision. The family were still confident of full success although early in 1893 the first anxiety came with Neville's report.

N.C. to J.C. 5.1.1893.
"Both confirmed what I had had unpleasant rumours of before *viz* that our plant poles in 7 years from time of setting out. This only gives 3 years cutting and . . . if this proves true I fear it will knock off a very large percentage of our profits . . ."

Joe Chamberlain visited Andros Island in the autumn of 1893. It was a brief visit and during it he was plagued with every sort of ailment. For most of his fortnight's stay he remained in the house. But he gave orders for pushing on with the railway and with new roads, for more mechanization and more building. All this was bound to add greatly to his capital expenditure which was already formidable. When he returned to England he decided on a debenture issue to raise the capital. It was not a prudent decision, when the success of the enterprise was still unproven. He was

advised to turn the business into a limited company, but he was
also advised by Mr. Lescher of Lescher and Co., whom he had
consulted, that what he proposed might well furnish ammunition
for his political opponents. Mr. Lescher was right: the debenture
issue became an election issue at the "Khaki Election" of 1900
along with other attacks on Mr. Chamberlain's business holdings.
It also led at the same time to a libel action against the *Star* Newspaper Company in which Neville Chamberlain was the successful
plaintiff, being awarded £1,500 damages and costs.

Mr. Chamberlain brushed aside these objections and the issue
went forward. The capital of the Andros Fibre Company was
put at £100,000, and the debenture issue, described as the first of
a series, was for £20,000. An unusual provision was the insertion
of a guarantee of the principal and interest of all the debentures
for a minimum period of three years while the enterprise proved
itself. The issue was a private one and not advertised or sent out
to the public. As soon as the £20,000 was privately subscribed the
issue was closed.

The problem of capital for the moment was solved. Neville,
who had paid a brief visit to Cuba to study the machinery used on
the island's sugar plantations, drove himself all the harder. He had
pleaded with his father not to bring him home for the usual spell
of leave in the summer of 1894, but Joe Chamberlain, partly
because of his concern for Neville's health, partly because he
wanted Neville home for the discussions on the debenture issue,
had insisted. Neville's main task now was the construction of the
railway track, but as usual he had a hundred other things to see to.
Knowles could take little of the burden from him; his wife had
died suddenly in premature childbirth and his strength was gone.
Neville's letters too at this time begin to show an understandable
weariness. The battle with the weeds became a nightmare. The
price of sisal fell and fell again. His lovable and erratic labour
force needed now a supervision that he alone could not give. The
first real hint of failure comes in a report to his father.

N.C. to J.C. 17.1.1895.

"I wish I could give a satisfactory account of the growth of the plants.
They certainly are not doing what they ought in many places. . . .

I have convinced myself at last that even in A.1 pineyard such as we are cutting now plants won't grow as fast as in good coppice."

Still—but now perhaps obstinately—he advised his father to push on.

Mr. Chamberlain was himself torn between the fear of going on, and the financial calamity of admitting failure. Order and counter order resulted. The plans for additional managerial help for Neville were cancelled, and all further clearing stopped; but the railway construction was finished, a baling shed and more labourers' houses built and Neville continued to buy vast quantities of plants.

In November 1895 he returned from England. His first reports carried a little hope with them, but it was soon extinguished. In Christmas week a disastrous fire razed the new baling shed to the ground and with it all the carefully hoarded bales of fibre were destroyed. The samples of fibre sent to New York were too stiff and harsh. Knowles' health began again to give way. Neville's letters at this time to Mary and his sisters tell nothing of the slow sense of failure that was gripping him. He wrote still of flowers and insects, of books and his house. But his letters to his father are eloquent of the conflict in him. Knowing in his heart he had failed he still refused to admit failure: plans for the future read oddly beside his frequent black moods. It was a bitter disappointment to him not to succeed better than the other plantation managers of whose inefficiency he had been so scornful, and he was beginning to feel a deep desire to get away from Andros and start again on something else. His letter at the end of February is typical.

N.C. to J.C. 27.2.1896.
"I am not quite certain whether I thanked you in my last for the very kind present of books you sent me in the midst of your labour. They are a capital selection and are most welcome to me.

I was very much disappointed in not receiving the corrugated iron for my warehouse this mail . . . the press too which I expected will not come till next mail and I foresee now that I shall just get everything in working order as I reach the end of the crop. It is very disheartening.

I have heard from the [company] again. This time they say that they find that in order to introduce Bahama fibre a very choice article is required. . . . I think the upshot of this is that in order to satisfy them we must go to the expense of washing the fibre . . . and whether the extra $\frac{1}{4}\%$ will repay us for this is a question. I rather think that in the end it would pay to produce the very best article although more expensive at first . . . of course any extra expense is hard to put up with at first, but I think I could still see my way clear to a good profit if only I could be sure of a supply of leaf. But the plants don't grow and I am again feeling very low and despondent about the whole concern. I find I have not been able to crop so large an area as I had hoped; I don't see how we can possibly last out longer than the end of March and then we must wait till the plants are ready to cut again. How long this will be is hard to say: a few plants might be cut now in the front but I put the wait at two months. Meanwhile everything will be disorganised. All the order and discipline that I have worked up will be lost, all the people will go away, for I shall have nothing for them to do and I myself shall be at a loose end. I should not mind so much if I could see any prospect of a speedy increase in the leaf supply, but I do not. . . . In spite of all that you and Austen said before, this is my failure. I can't bear to think of it only it is impossible to shut one's eyes to probabilities. Meantime I find it very hard to work with energy and enthusiasm while I have this ominous outlook before me all the time. . . ."

At the end of April Neville reported the results of his final survey:

N.C. to J.C. 28.4.1896.

"It seems to me that there is only one conclusion to be drawn from it which I do with the greatest reluctance and with the most bitter disappointment. I no longer see any chance of making the investment pay. I cannot blame myself too much for my want of judgment. You and Austen have had to rely solely on my reports but I have been here all the time and no doubt a sharper man would have seen long ago what the ultimate result was likely to be."

Plans were discussed without much conviction for starting again on new land, and for continuing with a smaller project at Mastic Point. They came to nothing. Neville returned home to confer and the decision to abandon the enterprise was taken. Neville returned early in 1897 to wind up the Company but only a few hundred pounds were salvaged by the sale of equipment and property. It may have been true that a "sharper man" would have seen the final failure a little earlier, but the truth is probably that Neville went on when he knew himself he should retreat. From the beginning the venture was unwise. The Bahamas were not Birmingham and Joe Chamberlain knew too little and found out too little before he plunged. He was unwise too both in the method he adopted of raising capital for further expansion and in his obstinacy in chasing his losses. The Andros Fibre Company deserved to fail, but no one could have done more to make it succeed than its resident Managing Director. To this enterprise he gave six years of his young manhood. He gave it his single-minded attention and devotion. The Andros Fibre Company may have failed, but he did not. Andros strengthened him, and he left it a man instead of a youth, wiser, more self-reliant but also more tolerant. In his early letters home few people escape his scorn. His criticisms have all the arrogance of youth and also an acid quality which is not attractive. No one came under the lash as often as his neighbour Mr. Keith. Contempt for his intellect, scorn for his incompetence, disgust for his slovenly appearance are regular ingredients of Neville's earlier letters. Four years later suddenly one comes on this:

N.C. to Ethel 15.5.1894.

"Keith came up on Sunday and spent the night here as usual. I have got over the irritation I used to feel at his oddities and even have a gentle liking for him."

It wasn't Keith who had changed in those years.

3

MAN OF BIRMINGHAM
(1896 – 1916)

EVEN more than his father Neville Chamberlain was a man of Birmingham. In Birmingham he achieved the modest fortune which had eluded him in the Bahamas. In Birmingham he steeped himself in the local government, the social service, the community life to which his upbringing and his sense of duty were bound to lead him. From Birmingham, when Lord Mayor, he was called by Lloyd George at the crucial point of the First World War to the post of Director of National Service.

The Birmingham to which Neville Chamberlain returned in 1896 when the Bahamas venture foundered was busy consolidating her position. The thrusting years of Joe Chamberlain's mayoralty were behind her, the adventures of Greater Birmingham still ahead. In 1884 Birmingham became an Assize town, in 1888 a County Borough, in 1889 a city. The first Lord Mayor took office in 1896 and there followed the University, and in 1905 Charles Gore came from Worcester to Birmingham as the first Bishop of Birmingham. The impulse to social reform in the city came from the chapels. From Dale at Carr's Lane Chapel, Crosskey at the Unitarian Church of the Messiah, Vince at Graham's Street Chapel. These men were preachers and politicians, filled with radical as well as religious fervour. The practical application of these theories fell to the earnest efficient business men who were the core of their congregations. Liberal politics, nonconformist principles, private money, these were the driving forces behind the men, with Joe Chamberlain at their head, who

37

made Birmingham the "best governed city in the world". Inevitably there was tension between church and chapel, between Conservative and Liberal. Gore's coming did more than anything else to heal the first division: Byng Kenrick, Neville's double first cousin, told me—"Till Gore came we never thought much of the Church people, but you couldn't ignore Gore. He was too big a man." The political division had been complicated by the decision of Joe Chamberlain to leave the Gladstone Government in 1886 over the Home Rule question. Birmingham followed its leader. But it was to become as much an economic as a political division, although neither Joe Chamberlain nor the town saw it clearly then. Already by the end of the '70s the hold of the Liberal caucus on Birmingham was less secure. With growing uneasiness the city watched the tariff walls in Germany, and later in the United States, rise higher. The swift boom of the early 1870s had been followed by a longer period of trade depression. In the General Election of 1885, with Lord Randolph Churchill leading the onslaught by challenging John Bright in the Central Division, the Liberals only just staved off the Conservative threat. All seven seats were held, but in two of them, including Central Birmingham, the majorities were less than a thousand votes. "Fair Trade" was part of the Conservative case and the slogan had a strong appeal to the small manufacturer and the artisan. The Home Rule schism came just in time to hold back the tide of Conservative advance in Birmingham. With typically fierce energy Joe Chamberlain swept most of the old Liberal Association into his new National Radical Union. But Harris and Schnadhorst remained faithful to Gladstone, and between Liberal and Liberal Unionist the fight was on. From this the Conservatives might have expected to profit. They had now an efficient organisation, and their industrial and economic policies were beginning to find echoes in a Birmingham growing restive and suspicious of Free Trade policies in the face of Protectionism on the Continent. But Joe's thoughts were moving towards a greater imperialism and in this he had begun to see the Tories as his natural allies. He was right, but in this at least he did not lead Birmingham. Rather did he follow.

Joe Chamberlain still thundered against Free Trade and Fair

Trade, but the position became steadily more difficult to hold. Conservatives won seats from Gladstonian Liberals in municipal elections in Birmingham and by 1891 had nineteen seats on the Council, while there were twenty-nine Liberal Unionists and twenty-four Liberals. In 1889, when John Bright died, only Lord Randolph Churchill's quixotic decision not to stand allowed the Liberal Unionists to hold on to the seat. Something had to be done. From now on Joe Chamberlain pressed the two parties together. Slowly the suspicions were overcome. An agreement was reached about ward representation and the right to nominate the parliamentary candidate for the Edgbaston Division ceded to the Conservatives. The alliance was sealed by unity over the fiscal question in 1903. But the different names remained, and it was not until 1918 that both wings took the simple name "Unionist." And at that meeting Neville Chamberlain was in the chair. Joe's achievement was complete.

This then was the Birmingham to which Neville returned. He was twenty-eight. His father was Secretary of State for the Colonies, his brother Civil Lord of the Admiralty. Once again as in 1890 Neville had to start to earn money. A Directorship in Elliott's Metal Company at Selly Oak did not satisfy him, and he bought for himself the firm of Hoskins & Son in Upper Trinity Street, Bordesley, forming under the old name a private company of which he became chairman. Hoskins' fitted exactly into the picture of the Birmingham at the turn of the century—a city of small firms, of old-fashioned engineering shops, of skilled men with a close sympathy between employers and employed. The firm's main business was the manufacture of ships' berths, a tiny industry wholly concentrated then in Birmingham. Its main advantages over its two competitors was the patent held for folding berths for emigrants, so that cargo could be loaded for the homeward voyage. Minor activities included the making of ammunition racks for warships. The firm has survived change. Neville's son-in-law is today chairman and his son was until recently a director For the most part the machinery is still as it was when Neville had finished modernizing the plant. To-day beds for the National Health Service rather than for ships are the main product. Otherwise the years have passed Hoskins' by.

It is easy to walk through the building today and see it almost as
Neville must have seen it in the '90s. He was living at Highbury,
about two miles from Upper Trinity Street, and daily he used to
cycle to and from the works, hanging his bicycle high on the wall
of the loading bay when he arrived. At its peak, employment in
the firm was no higher than two hundred, and often less than half
as many There was no great gulf between the skilled craftsmen
and the small owner, and Neville was always close to his men.
As his father had done, he pioneered in welfare work in the firms
he was connected with and, again ahead of most of Birmingham,
recognised and encouraged Trade Union development among his
men. His outside interests continued to grow: he became chairman of Elliott's and joined the board of the Birmingham Small
Arms Company. But it was to Hoskins' that he gave most of his
time, and he found a deep satisfaction in proving that on his own
he could succeed. In these years the failure of Andros was forgotten.

Until he had proved himself in business he felt he could not
take up politics either at Westminster or on the Council. In any
case, there seemed no room for a third Chamberlain. But inevitably he was drawn swiftly into local politics, although he continued to decline invitations to stand for election. When Parliament was in session he was often the only Chamberlain at Highbury, but his kinsmen still loomed large in Birmingham affairs
and there was much to be done. Besides, he had a true relish for
the robust political atmosphere of the city. He had made his
maiden political speech at the General Election of 1895 in support
of the Unionist candidate at Newcastle-under-Lyme; it was
"very warmly received". In the General Election of 1900 he
was again active and the *Birmingham Daily Post* announced
"on excellent authority that Mr. Neville Chamberlain intends
to come forward as the Unionist candidate for Dudley at the next
election". In fact he had no such intention. It was to be business
first.

All the same, his commitments multiplied. He was on the
council of the University which had grown out of the old Midland Institute and the newer Mason College. Joseph Chamberlain
in 1896 was the first President of the University College and the

first Chancellor of the new University in 1900. Sir Oliver Lodge was its first Principal, and Neville became his close friend and supporter.

It is never easy to persuade the ratepayers of any city of the need for a civic university, and Neville canvassed hard for the funds and support needed. But the idealism of the '70s had not vanished, and besides it suited Birmingham's pride to have its own University.

Neville at least had a clear idea of the University that should be built in Birmingham: "We cannot compete—we don't want to—with the older universities round which cluster the venerable traditions of centuries, and perhaps some of the cobwebs of centuries too. We think there is open to us a different and wider field of usefulness. We do not despise any branch of learning . . . but the essential point of the University must always be science, pure and applied." Birmingham manufacturers could see the advantage to them and to the city of such an institution and, with the success of the appeals assured, the University was opened. Again the combination of civic zeal and business contributions had triumphed.

Closely linked too with his father's work before him was Neville's deep and abiding interest in hospital work in Birmingham. In time this led to the decision in 1924 when Neville was Minister of Health to establish the Birmingham Hospitals Centre on a site given to the city by Cadburys at Edgbaston near the University. Here were grouped the medical school and the new hospital known as the Queen Elizabeth. Of this great advance which once more and in another field brought Birmingham to the leadership of the provincial cities, Neville was the true architect. In 1906, the year when Joe Chamberlain's health broke down and he became little more than a patient till his death in 1914 at Highbury, Neville became Chairman of the General Hospital. Founded in 1765 it was re-opened in new buildings in Steelhouse Lane in 1897, as modern as any hospital of its time. The city was proud of its many and varied voluntary hospitals, and true to her tradition Birmingham raised through Hospital Sunday and Hospital Saturday Funds massive sums for their maintenance. The Hospital Saturday Fund, with which the Chamberlains were closely associated, sought to raise funds by working class collections in firms and factories.

The other health field in which Neville was particularly active in these years was that of the General Dispensary, founded in 1793, of which he became Treasurer. He waged a long campaign, against a good deal of opposition, to relieve the crushing burden on the out-patients' department at the hospital by diverting many of the applicants to the dispensary. At his first annual meeting as Chairman at the General Hospital he put forward his views:

21.3.1907. B.D.P.[1]

"They had first rate and expensive apparatus, they had trained nurses, and they had a highly-trained and experienced staff of physicians and surgeons; but to put these men to deal with those trivial cases which might equally well, or better, be dealt with at a dispensary, was like putting a cabinet-maker to chop wood. He thought that the out-patient department of a hospital should be as far as possible a consultative institution. He did not think any new cases ought to be turned away without being attended to; but, having had the benefit of the opinion of the staff at the hospital, and having had first aid, cases which could be equally well treated elsewhere should be sent elsewhere."

Two years later he was citing the minority report of the Poor Law Commission in support of his scheme which was by then in operation. To take some of the strain of the 65,000 cases that were passing each year into the out-patient department of the General Hospital Neville turned to build up a new Birmingham and District Provident Dispensary, of which he became President. The scheme "was not intended for those who were well able to pay medical fees and did not comprehend those who were too poor to pay anything at all". The entrance fee was a shilling per member, and the subscription 5*d*. per month, with a reduction for large families. Over a hundred medical men joined the staff of the Provident Dispensary, and consultant care was available at half the normal fees. Each member of the Provident Dispensary could choose and change his doctor. Drugs were dispensed not by the doctor but by chemists or at the dispensaries. The assistance of the General Dispensary, who placed all their buildings at

[1] *Birmingham Daily Post.*

42

the disposal of the new venture, meant that a wide coverage was obtained throughout the city. It was essentially a scheme for the decentralisation of medical relief. Neville secured the general support of the medical profession, the voluntary boards running the hospitals and the Hospital Saturday Fund. All the same, his Provident Dispensary had a short life. Lloyd George's National Insurance Act, with its panel of doctors, had too many features similar to the voluntary dispensary scheme for the latter to survive. But it was well in the Birmingham tradition to pioneer in front of state legislation.

Yet it was neither Education nor Health that brought Neville at last in 1911 to the City Council. Town Planning was the lure, and the creation of Greater Birmingham the opportunity. The development of the tramway system and the coming of the motor car enabled both working man and employer to live further from the crowded centre of the city. As demand for services in the near suburbs grew, so the problems of administration increased. Birmingham, even after the extension of its boundaries in 1891, was too small for the efficiency that its city fathers pursued so faithfully. The most ardent advocate of expansion was J. S. Nettlefold, who became Chairman of the Housing Committee established in 1901 and the Boundaries Commission established in 1908. Naturally there was opposition from the districts—Aston Manor and Handsworth in particular—which were recommended by the official report in 1909 for incorporation in the City. But there was also a great number of ratepayers, with an eye on the advantages of a wider area. The public inquiry by the Local Government Board pronounced firmly in favour of Birmingham, and although there was some vigorous opposition in Parliament (in which Stanley Baldwin in the capacity of a Worcestershire County member played a full part) the Greater Birmingham Bill became law in May 1911. Birmingham was to become for a time at least the second city of the Empire. A local paper announced:

10.11.1910. B.G.[1]

"We have the authority of Mr. Chamberlain for stating that should the Greater Birmingham Bill pass into law . . . he will come forward

[1] *Birmingham Gazette.*

43

as a candidate for municipal honours. In such an event his election is already a foregone conclusion for he is extremely popular and his business capacity has already been proved in several directions."

In September 1911 he was adopted as Liberal Unionist candidate for the All Saints' Ward in his father's constituency of West Birmingham, and was elected in November. At local election meetings he put forward his policies.

25.10.1911. B.D.P.

"Those who advocated the extension of the city boundaries did not do so because it would be wiser to be bigger . . . it was better government and not bigness that they were after. He had himself felt that the opportunities in Greater Birmingham were so great that he should not like to remain outside, and he had determined that he would have a try.

They wanted a forward and progressive policy. They wanted to tackle some of those social problems on which the happiness of the people so largely depended. . . . What they had to do to distinguish themselves from other towns was to set a new example in town planning. In that word he included for the moment housing, because although the improvement of houses in the old city was in one sense not a part of a town planning scheme, the great objects were the same, the health and happiness of the people."

In January of the same year, 1911, at St. Paul's, Knightsbridge he had married Anne Vere Cole. He was forty-two and his wife in her late twenties. For some years now Neville had begun to grow a protective shell of bachelorhood round him. Not that he was ever a hermit, but his social life was almost entirely confined to the close-knit circle of the cousins and the clan, and at their dances and parties he was more often than not an unwilling victim. There was nothing of the Chamberlain in Anne Cole, but it was a Chamberlain link that led to their meeting. Alfred Cole, Anne's uncle, had married in 1907 Lilian the widow of Herbert Chamberlain, Joe's younger brother, and it was when visiting her aunt at Cannes in April 1910 that Anne Cole met the Joseph Chamberlains and Beatrice. A few months later in London Beatrice plotted a dinner and theatre party and invited Anne to meet Neville. The Chamberlain sisters had decided to try their hands at matchmaking. They could scarcely have hoped for such swift success, for Neville fell in love at once with the lovely Anne Cole and she with him. They saw each other at friends' houses, met again in Birmingham and in London, and in a few weeks the engagement was announced. Neville had a formidable stint of public speaking to carry out at the General Election in December and then he was free.

The Coles for many generations had been Norfolk farmers and small squires. William Cole, Anne's grandfather, had left the family estate at Pulham and become a successful merchant in London. With his money he had bought West Woodhay in Berkshire, a lovely Inigo Jones country house built on the site of an ancient manor house. William's elder son, William Utting Cole, Anne's father, became a soldier, while the second son Alfred carried on his father's prosperous exporting business and became a director and then Governor of the Bank of England. There were three daughters.

Anne's mother, Mary de Vere, came from an old Irish family which had distinguished itself in war, in the hunting field and in the arts. Anne Cole's father died of cholera in India in 1891, when he was a major in the 3rd Dragoon Guards. She was only nine years old. Her grandparents' home at West Woodhay became her childhood home and there are charming snapshots of her in Mary McClintock's delightful book *Portrait of a House* about the memories the cousins shared of West Woodhay.

The Chamberlains were delighted with the engagement, but the Coles and the De Veres less enthusiastic. They liked Neville well enough, but a rather precise, earnest Birmingham business man seemed hardly suitable. The backgrounds were very different and heads were shaken at West Woodhay and in Ireland. But they themselves never had any doubts. From their honeymoon in the sun of Algeria and Tunisia they came back eagerly to Birmingham.

They made their home at Westbourne in Edgbaston, a solid, comfortable house on high ground looking out over fields to Kings Norton and the University. Here with orchids from Highbury, roses from Ireland, wild flowers from their gleanings in North Africa, with vines and flowering shrubs, Neville was able to build for himself the garden he loved. On Christmas Day

1911 their daughter Dorothy was born, and two years later a son Frank completed their family. All through their married life Neville Chamberlain delighted in paying tribute to his wife. The small triumphs of Birmingham municipal life, success in the House of Commons and as a minister, the achievement of the Premiership—for them all he had the same proud explanation: "I'd never have done it without Annie." For him more than for most men his family was his sanctuary as well as his joy. It was an ideally happy marriage, and from it Neville was always able to draw strength and fulfilment and peace.

When he was elected to the Council in November 1911 he became at once Chairman of the newly established Town Planning Committee. The old firm of Nettlefold and Chamberlain was in business again. The Committee was new, but there was already an established Town Planning tradition in Birmingham. The Calthorpe estate in Edgbaston had long been carefully planned as a model residential area, and George Cadbury's Bournville scheme had been for years an inspiration to those who practised the then infant art of Town and Country Planning. Neville tackled his new task swiftly and with enthusiasm. Presenting his first report as Chairman of the Committee to the City Council in May 1912 he brought forward schemes for Quinton, Harborne and Edgbaston. These were the first schemes in the country to be approved under the 1909 Housing and Planning Act and when he stood for re-election as councillor Neville was able to boast:

16.10.1913. B.D.P.
"They not only had to show the way in Birmingham, but to the whole country, so much so that the Local Government Board refused to consider other people's schemes until Birmingham had got hers through."

These years as a councillor were full, happy years for Neville. Although his main interests were the Town Planning Committee and the Public Health and Housing Committee, he was active in every aspect of the city's life. He took a special interest in his work as Chairman of an *ad hoc* committee appointed to study the housing conditions of the poorest in the city. He found in all his social work an ardent lieutenant in his young cousin Norman Chamberlain, who had become a councillor in 1909, and whose death in action in December 1917 affected Neville even more deeply than his own father's death had done, and sowed in him the seeds of his life-long hatred of the futility of war.

A year later, in November 1914, he was elected alderman and the following summer was offered the Lord Mayoralty. Three years as a councillor, one as an alderman, matched his father's swift rise to the same post. Five of his uncles, ten of his kindred had been Lord Mayor. He was forty-six years old.

It was certainly Neville's ambition to be Lord Mayor. But to be Lord Mayor in war time meant that his most cherished ideas had to wait. In his speech to the City Council on assuming office there is a passage which calls down the years to his struggle for peace when he became Prime Minister.

10.11.1915. B.D.P.

"He had hoped that he might bring the influence and authority of the Lord Mayoralty to bear upon that noble and fascinating ideal, the transference of the working classes from their hideous and depressing surroundings to cleaner, brighter and more wholesome dwellings in the still uncontaminated country which lay within our boundaries. . . . Among the many crimes which lay heavy on the head of the German Emperor and his advisers not the least was that by their wicked ambitions they had stayed the march of progress and had set back for an indefinite period reforms that might have bettered the lot of generations to come."

He turned his restless energy to war work. Much of it was routine, no more and no less than other civic heads were doing. The work of recruitment and entertainment for the forces, presiding over the tribunal to consider exemptions from military service, providing crèches for the children of mothers who worked in munition factories, helping to organize hospital work and the City Aid Society, these and a hundred other problems filled his days. But there were also more personal contributions. He seized the opportunity of the Hallé concert in Birmingham in March 1916 to advocate a contribution from the rates to a municipal orchestra, and one of his most cherished dreams came true when in 1919 the City Orchestra (again the first of its kind) was set up with municipal support. When in January 1916 the first of three abortive Zeppelin raids was made on Birmingham—it was of course out of range of enemy aircraft—Neville organized a conference of Midland mayors to improve air raid precautions, and produced his own scheme for the Home Office to mull over.

The lasting memorial to his time as Lord Mayor was the setting up in 1916 of the Birmingham Municipal Savings Bank. For those who had the habit of thrift many opportunities for saving were open. Neville looked beyond this class to the working men and women, many of them earning high wages in munition factories. If now part of these wages could be put away, then the days of adjustment, when the munition factories turned over after the war to civilian production, would be easier to bear. Long before the National Committee on War Loans for small investors issued their report with its plea for local action, Neville, working with the Citizens' Committee and making full use of his friendly relations with Labour leaders and the local Trades Council, had prepared an outline scheme. It was simple enough. The employee was given coupons by his employer to the amount, in multiples of a shilling, that he wished to save. These coupons were stuck by the employee on a card and when the coupons reached the sum of £1 the card was deposited in the bank and began to earn interest at $3\frac{1}{2}$ per cent. Capital and interest were guaranteed by the Corporation. Withdrawal was made easy for the depositor and the Corporation planned to recoup its running expenses by investing most of the money deposited in Government securities. Neville canvassed his scheme so successfully in London that it was adopted as the basis of a national scheme, and Mr. E. S. Montagu, the Financial Secretary to the Treasury, introduced a Bill to the House of Commons in April 1916 to implement the main points of the Chamberlain proposals. Success seemed assured until without warning a double blow fell. The Government capitulated to the opposition in the House of Sir Frederick Banbury, who spoke for the Joint Stock Banks, and withdrew their Bill. At about the same time, the local trade union secretaries expressed hostility to the proposal, although the Labour councillors stayed, now a little warily, in support. The main objection was that the employer would know the amount of a man's savings and could use his knowledge in a wage claim or an industrial dispute. Arguments that, as the rate and amounts of withdrawals were secret, the employer could make no reasonable estimate of savings did something to reduce but not remove this traditional suspicion. Neville was in despair.

N.C. to Hilda 14.5.1916.
"I'm beat and the Savings Bank is dead. The selfishness of the Banks and the apathy of the Treasury together make an impenetrable entanglement, but what makes it impossible to carry on the fighting is that I have been taken in the rear."

His black mood did not last long. Within a few weeks a new Bill was introduced and before the end of August it was law. In deference to the bankers' opposition only boroughs and cities with a population of over 250,000 (50,000 in the original Bill) could establish Municipal Savings Banks, and they had to be wound up within three months of the end of the war, while the control of investments was given to the National Debt Commissioners. But the bank was floated and its success ensured its continuation after the war. In July 1919 the Birmingham Corporation Act secured permanent powers for its operation. Neville Chamberlain believed that "if after the war 50,000 would have saved £5 each through the bank then Birmingham would have again showed the way to the country". These figures were easily exceeded. (It may be noted that in 1961 there were nearly three-quarters of a million accounts with a total credit balance exceeding £85 million.)

He had, then, made at last a brilliantly successful debut in local politics. It was also natural that, whether he liked it or not, Liberal Unionist politics were bound to claim more and more of his time. Honorary Secretary in 1899 of the Association, and Treasurer later, his father's illness and his brother's emergence as a national political figure, left him as the standard bearer of the Chamberlain tradition in Birmingham. Although he rejected many invitations to stand for Parliament, and his letters are full of his protestations that politics were not for him, his speeches show an increasing enjoyment of the rough and tumble of the hustings. He was always ready to provide the strong meat demanded by the crowded public meetings before the glamour of films and television melted political audiences. In the 1900 General Election

President Kruger and Mr. Steyn provided easy Aunt Sallies, and a storm of hisses and boos followed every mention of their names. After the Liberal triumph in 1906 the targets were at Westminster. At Selly Oak:

18.1.1907. B.D.P.

"A Government of hurry and humbug. Having won an election by false pretences they were trying to rush through legislation to satisfy their discontented supporters. The Government had placed at the head of the Colonial Office a feeble peer whose only claim to distinction was that he had made a failure of his Indian Viceroyalty, and the Colonial Office was represented in the House of Commons by a bumptious youth (laughter) who thought he could harangue those great self-governing states as if they were a parcel of schoolboys and he, forsooth, their schoolmaster. (Applause.) The sooner Lord Elgin retired to decent obscurity and Mr. Winston Churchill was sent as an Ambassador to Timbuctoo the better it would be for the country and the Empire. (Applause.)"

Or in more kindly mood at the Annual Meeting in May:

11.5.1907. B.G.

"Sir Henry Campbell-Bannerman seemed to his supporters to be a knight paladin setting out on a crusade to reward the deserving poor and punish the wicked lords. (Laughter.) Mr. Asquith was a magician at whose touch everything was to turn to gold: Mr. Birrell was a sort of fairy in spectacles: and Mr. Winston Churchill—(ironical laughter and hisses)—well, I think they took him for a benevolent sprite. (Laughter.)"

But this was only the seasoning for his speeches. Most of them were closely knit, well-reasoned arguments for Tariff Reform. Neville in Birmingham made the cause that his father was too ill and his brother too busy to proclaim his own. It was a popular cause in Birmingham, and increasingly Neville began to link his advocacy of Tariff Reform with his views on social policy. He was never a Liberal in the Gladstonian sense of the word. Indeed, it is doubtful if Joe Chamberlain ever was. Joe's Radicalism had far more in common with the Tory Democracy of Lord Randolph Churchill than the more clinical approach of the Gladstonian Liberals. If not on Home Rule then on either an imperial or an economic issue, Joe Chamberlain would surely have left the Liberal Party. The whole pull of Birmingham interests and his own political development would have ensured it.

Neville missed no opportunity of plugging his belief that in Tariff Reform lay the true answer to the country's discontent. By the "country" he meant, as Joe so often had meant, "Birmingham". But his vision in the social services, although it started from and often returned to municipal politics, was never parochial. In many fields, as with his Provident Dispensary, he was not only in front of Birmingham but in front of Westminster. More remarkable still were his speeches on industrial relations. Here he was talking nearly half a century ago a language that is still only half understood and teaching a lesson still only half learnt.

18.12.1912. B.D.P.

"If a workman by working harder himself can save the firm money, then the firm ought not to grudge him any wages he can make. There is no more stupid blunder and none more common made in business than to suppose that a bargain for you cannot be a good bargain unless it is a bad bargain for somebody else. In my opinion, a piecework rate once fixed should never be reduced."

To a meeting of Labour Unionists in Birmingham:

16.2.1914. B.D.P.

"He believed they would like to see themselves represented in Parliament by a Unionist working man—(applause)—who would be in touch at first hand with their needs and would be able to give the leaders of the Party the benefit of his advice through his knowledge and experience. He must admit that he did not think the Unionist Party had treated them as well as they might in this respect. It was no use talking about anxiety to see working men in Parliament if they never gave them a chance of fighting a seat. (Hear, hear.)"

That this is a gospel that still needs to be preached in the Conservative Party can be illustrated by a similar, but more recent quotation. Speaking at Brighton on October 11th, 1957 to the Conservative Party Conference the Minister of Labour and National Service said:

"It is an illusion to think, and it is an impertinence to talk, of ten million trade unionists as if they were all devoted followers of the Socialist Party. Three million of them vote Conservative. And whether people like it or not—and I for one like it very much indeed—that is one of the central and one of the dominant facts of British political life to-day. Even in 1945 our trade union vote was numbered in millions. It is quite true that those millions are not represented yet on the benches in the House of Commons as we would like to see them and as they will be. (Applause.) I hope those who clap will do something about it, too, because it is in your hands."

To Neville, Tariff Reform had become the basis of Social Reform:

11.3.1914. B.D.P.

"The more he [Councillor Chamberlain] saw of the conditions of the poor the more he came back to this fact, that if they could not have more money they could not have better health and could not afford to have better houses. It was all very well to talk about providing a minimum wage. It was no use giving a man a rise of five shillings a week if at the same time he had to go on short time. What was wanted was steadiness of employment."

Particularly in the war years Neville's thoughts turned more and more to the partnership between masters and men in which he saw the cure for the friction and bitterness that existed between them. The speech that he made as Lord Mayor to the T.U.C. meeting in Birmingham in 1916 shows more clearly than any other how his mind was moving:

5.9.1916. Morning Post.

"Nothing that can happen at the Trades Union Congress this week can exceed in interest and importance a striking speech delivered by the Lord Mayor, Mr. Neville Chamberlain in welcoming the delegates to the city this morning. He broke all precedents in the way of civic welcomes, and seized the occasion to make a most valuable and statesman-like contribution to the problem of national reconstruction after the war. As he stood addressing the Congress from the platform of the Town Hall, many who in years gone by had been privileged to hear his father speak from the same place could almost imagine that the great Imperialist was with us again. The speech was one of singular courage at such a time to such an audience, but as the Lord Mayor proceeded it was obvious that he was taking the Congress a long way with him and that the delegates realized that they were listening to a pronouncement that was much more than a welcome; that in fact here were proposals for a coming together of Capital and Labour that will be discussed a long way beyond Birmingham for a long time.

'The workers,' he said, 'will demand three things. A greater share in the distribution of the wealth they help to produce, regularity of employment, and improved conditions in the factory and in their homes, so that they could preserve their health and spirit and bring up their children in cheerful and healthy surroundings.' "

This, although few employers would then have regarded it with any enthusiasm, was safe doctrine. But he went on to a much more startling proposition. "Trade Union leaders," he argued, "should on occasion be admitted to the councils of employers, and be allowed to see a little more of the game from the inside." True, this is now pure orthodoxy, even if the point still needs to be hammered home, but in the middle of the First World War it must have seemed strange doctrine to come from a Unionist and a businessman. Neville was ready to explain and expound his ideas still further:

10.9.1916. Sunday Chronicle.
"Some working men want to have some voice in the control of the policy of the business; they want to see the work from the inside. I am inclined to think that a good purpose might be served if that privilege were afforded them; the information would throw a good deal of light upon matters which at present seem to perplex them, and to draw from them criticism of the management . . . personally, I should have no objection to the men having a representative on the board of directors, but I know many business men who would object to such a proceeding."

So they would to-day.

Neville emerged then from his "Birmingham" period as a Tory Democrat, although he would not have recognised the term. He had clear, robust views on foreign and imperial policy, and a radical approach to social problems. Everything in the end for him turned on social reform.

By example in his works, by precept in his public speeches, by the compelling strength of his dedication to social reform, he became, as his father had been, the mainspring of progress in

Birmingham. The standing gibe against Neville Chamberlain has always been that he was provincial. So he was. It is not a term of abuse. No man has ever been Prime Minister who had knowledge to compare with his of health and housing and education and town planning, and all the other provincial aspects of administration. For him always *Salus populi suprema est lex.*

But his horizons were wider than Birmingham, just as Joe Chamberlain's had been. In these years meticulous travel diaries record his impressions of India and Burma, Algiers and Egypt, Italy and France. Besides, there can have been for the young Neville few better schools than Highbury for the study of imperial and foreign affairs. It was by Neville's deliberate choice that in these years he was a provincial, and his lines seemed cast in Birmingham. But in fact he was about to take his place on a wider stage.

4

DIRECTOR OF NATIONAL SERVICE

(December 1916 – August 1917)

BY December 7th, 1916 the political intrigues and counter-intrigues were, for a time, over. Asquith was out and Lloyd George in. The Chamberlains were delighted. Neville had not yet acquired the distrust of Lloyd George (a mutual dislike) which was to colour so much of his political career. Any change was for the better.

N.C. to Ida 9.12.1916.
"Well, apparently the crisis is over in the political world. Like you, I heartily rejoice at the disappearance of Squiff [Asquith] and Grey and, although I am very sorry that Montagu and Runcy [Walter Runciman] have gone when they were doing good work, when I think of Lulu [Harcourt] and Crewe and McKenna I feel it is well worth while. I should have been content if Walter Long had remained at the L.G.B. [Local Government Board] but to put him at the Colonies and A.B. [Balfour] in the Foreign Office shows conclusively that Ll. George did not feel himself strong enough in the H. of C. to do what he would have wished. I don't know what to say about Austen. He seems so tired that I can hardly wish that he had a more active post. . . . Some time ago he said to me, 'None of us would serve under Ll. George.' But of course circumstances alter cases."

The Chamberlain sisters had a simple test of the new administration. If Lloyd George gave Neville a post they would approve it. Otherwise not. Certainly there was no reason why the new Prime Minister should do anything of the sort. Already with

Austen as Secretary of State for India he had the Chamberlain name in his Cabinet: Neville was a worthy, successful Lord Mayor of Birmingham, whose only national appointment in wartime had been from 1915 as a member of the Liquor Control Board. Equally certainly, Neville had no thought of being brought into the administration, and noting—high praise—as "business like" the lists of ministerial appointments, he returned content and indeed with a new confidence to Birmingham's affairs.

But Lloyd George was finding one post difficult to fill. He had decided to try to solve the chaotic manpower problem by creating both a new Ministry of Labour and a Department of National Service. To the first post John Hodge, a leading Labour M.P., was appointed. The second was offered to Edwin Montagu, Minister of Munitions in the late Government. Either because he did not wish to serve under Lloyd George in a less important post than the one he had held, or because he saw the hopelessness of the task, Montagu declined. Austen, who had for three months been Chairman of the Manpower Board, suggested Neville's name to Curzon and to Milner, and both of them spoke to Lloyd George. So it was decided.

N.C. to Ida 24.12.1916.

"I had gone up to a conference on municipal borrowing in U.S.A. on Tuesday morning in response to a telegram from the L.G.B. I had got everything I wanted to the delight of L.G.B. who said, 'This is due to you: Birmingham is leading again,' and was returning triumphant when fate in the person of Mr. Wilson appeared at Paddington."

Neville was taken to see Austen at the India Office, and then almost at once to the Prime Minister, who wanted to announce the appointment without delay and was impatient with Neville's reluctance. Neville's dismay at leaving his Birmingham work half done was unfeigned, but he did not really doubt that he must accept. The Prime Minister in his speech to the House the same day outlined the task.

Rt. Hon. D. Lloyd George, M.P. Hansard 19.12.1916.

". . . it is proposed to appoint at once a Director of National Service to be in charge of both the military and civil side of universal national service. The civil and military sides of the directory are to be entirely separate and there shall be a military and a civil director responsible to the Director of National Service. The military director will be responsible for recruiting for the army and will hand over to the War Office the recruits obtained . . . As regards civilian service, it is proposed that the Director of National Service shall proceed by the scheduling of industries and of services according to their essential character during the war.

"Certain industries are regarded as indispensable and the Departments concerned will indent upon the Director of National Service for the labour which they require for those services. . . . Labour that is set free from non-essential and rationed industries will be available to set free potential soldiers who are at present exempted from military service. . . . This labour will be invited to enrol at once and be registered as war workers on lines analagous to the existing munitions volunteers. . . . If it is found impossible to get the numbers we require—and I hope it will be possible—we shall not hesitate to come to Parliament and ask Parliament to release us from pledges given in other circumstances, and to obtain the necessary power for rendering our plans fully effective.

"We have been fortunate in inducing the Lord Mayor of Birmingham (Mr. Neville Chamberlain) to accept the position of Director-General under this scheme. It was with very great difficulty that we induced him to undertake this very onerous duty. . . . He will immediately proceed to organise this great new system of enrolment for industrial purposes, and I hope that before Parliament resumes its duties in another few weeks we shall be able to report that we have secured a sufficiently large industrial army in order to mobilize the whole of the labour strength of this country for war purposes."

This sort of speech usually does, and this one did, go down well with the House of Commons, who dispersed for the Christmas recess confident that the problem of manpower was to be solved by the time they returned. The Press was no lesss enthusiastic. But the Prime Minister should have known—indeed, for he had been both Minister of Munitions and Secretary of State for War, must have known—that he was dressing an empty shop-window.

N.C. to Ida 25.12.1916.

˅ "I have never had even a scrap of paper appointing me or giving me any idea of where my duties begin and end. I don't know whether

57

I have Ireland and Scotland as well as England. I don't know whether I have munition volunteers. I believe I am to have a salary but I don't know what."

To understand the position in which Neville was placed it is necessary to begin at the beginning. Before the war broke out three departments concerned themselves with different aspects of labour problems. The Home Office administered the Factory Acts and had responsibility for safety in mines, and for the supervision of the hours worked in factories by women and young persons. The Home Office was also the responsible Ministry for Workmens' Compensation and the Shop Acts. The Local Government Board (later the Ministry of Health) was responsible for the administration of the Poor Law. The Board of Trade, starting with its concern for the welfare of sailors, had gradually infiltrated into manpower problems. Before the turn of the century the Board of Trade had become the Ministry most concerned with problems of manpower. Gradually they extended their authority. In 1911 the Department of the Chief Industrial Commissioner was set up as a department of the Board of Trade. It was followed by the Department of Labour Statistics in 1913, and by the Labour Exchanges Department, which administered the Labour Exchanges Act of 1909 and the payment of unemployment insurance under Part II of the Act of 1911. There was no co-ordination of manpower problems, except that the three Ministers were all members of the Cabinet. The Admiralty and the War Office did their own recruiting in peace and war, subject to Treasury control. There were plenty of cooks.

Britain as usual was unprepared for war, especially for trench warfare. Her traditions were of the sea and a small professional army. The citizens' army needed to fight the First World War had to be improvised. Not that the volunteers were lacking. In their millions they came from farms and the foundries, the factories and the shipyards, the offices and the mills. And naturally it was the best and the most skilled who went first—and were killed or maimed. But the vaster the army the greater the home productive effort needed to support it, and the needs of the forces and the factories began to conflict. A system of badging those munition and other workers engaged on essential work was introduced.

There were indeed two systems, one operated by the Admiralty, one by the War Office, although in both systems the actual responsibility for selecting those to be badged was given to the employer. In July 1915, with the creation of the Ministry of Munitions, there was for the first time one badging authority. Almost at once the machine had to go into reverse. Too many men, protected by the Government's pledge not to introduce compulsory military service, were now in the factories, too few in the forces. Too few anyway for the grinding, bloody campaigns of slow annihilation that the Generals were directing in the First World War. So de-badging had to start, while badging itself was actually still being extended. At last in October 1915 the Reserved Occupations Committee began, at official level, the survey that should have been ordered a year or more before. For the 1916 campaign 1,500,000 men were needed. The survey showed that the men were there, but not coming forward. Still, Britain, now the only one of the principal belligerents to struggle on without compulsory military service, hesitated. Or rather, the Liberal Government did. With the agreement of the Trade Unions, one more last voluntary appeal was decided on and in October 1915 the Derby scheme was launched. The Derby scheme met with a fine response, but the final figures were conclusive. At least a million unmarried men of military age had not presented themselves. Voluntaryism was dead and on January 5th, 1916, Mr. Asquith at last introduced the first Military Service Act. Tentative and incomplete as it was, it provided the only possible basis for the future. A few Liberals led by Sir John Simon, the Home Secretary, who resigned from the Cabinet, opposed the Government, but the Conservative Party was vastly relieved and the long controversy between the two great parties on compulsion was stilled.

But although now it was decided to compel it was not yet clear who was to be the central authority that would direct compulsion. A Cabinet Committee was set up in March 1916, but it had neither executive authority nor was it closely linked to the war-planning machinery of the Government. It produced little or nothing and gave way in September 1916 to the Manpower Board under Austen's chairmanship. Again, and again of course fatally, it had no executive authority. All the same, it did produce quickly a scheme for the immediate de-badging of men under the age of 26. But this was too violent for the leaders of the Trade Unions and the Labour Party, and so to the accompaniment of growing industrial unrest the tortuous compromise of the Trade Card Agreement was reached in November 1916. By this the Trade Unions themselves were to issue cards of exemption.

It was at this point, with the Trade Card Agreement still in being, that Lloyd George in the first days of his Premiership created the Ministry of Labour and appointed Neville as Director of the new National Service Department.

This was a great advance on the Asquithian ditherings. Lloyd George took the first steps towards the combined Ministry of Labour and National Service which worked so efficiently in the Second World War. The National Service Department's greatest —indeed, its only—virtue was that it was an executive authority. But, unhappily, only in theory. The other Departments still pursued their own separate paths. The infant Ministry of Labour fought bitterly with its brother. The new Director had no seat in the Cabinet, or even in Parliament, no effecive link with Government policy, no local organisation. When Neville resigned in August 1917 his successor, General Sir Auckland Geddes, became head of the new Ministry of National Service. He became, too, an M.P. and a member of the Cabinet. He was given exact written instructions from the War Cabinet, and under General Smuts a small War Priority Committee of the War Cabinet, of which Geddes (but not the Minister of Labour) was a permanent member, was established. He was given, as Neville was not (in spite of Lloyd George's blue-print), control over both military and civil recruiting. Bulk release from exemption, the use of age classes, the use of a Schedule of Protected Occupations—these, after long and careful study, were the solutions that Geddes put forward. But they had been urged months before by Neville. Even to the end the dreary, frustrating story goes on. Not till February 1918 did the Military Service Act, taking powers to withdraw by Order bulk exemptions for certain age groups, become law. The final list of Reserved Occupations was issued on September 26th, 1918.

Too late for the last push, and just in time for the Armistice. Four years had passed.

The handling of the manpower problem was the worst administrative failure of the First World War. The hesitation of Asquith's leadership, the timidity and suspicions of the Labour Party and the Trade Union leaders, the clinging for so long in a professional war to Britain's amateur status, the puerile warfare waged in Whitehall between the Departments, all these contributed to the blunders and the failure. At least the lessons were learnt for 1939, and Ernest Bevin, commanding the allegiance of a Trade Union movement and a Labour Party devoted to the success of the struggle, with brilliant civil servants, notably Sir Thomas Phillips as Permanent Secretary and the two Directors of Manpower, Sir Godfrey Ince and Sir Harold Emmerson, and closely linked to the driving leadership coming from Winston Churchill, was able to direct and inspire the Ministry of Labour and National Service.

We must return to Neville and December 1916. To assert that he was given an impossible task is not to argue that he himself was free from blame. He made serious errors, most of them out of an ignorance of the ways of Whitehall, surprising in one whose knowledge of Local Government was so complete. By Christmas Day, instead of bemoaning his lack of clear instructions, he should have been banging his fist on the table at 10 Downing Street. And he should have taken his resignation with him. A Minister, particularly the head of a new Department, is never so strong again as in his first few weeks of office. His resignation, which in a few short months may have become just a "little local difficulty", is not to be thought of when he has just been selected for a new post. If he had been obstinate at this point he could have secured for himself most, perhaps all, of what was given to his successor in August 1917. Certainly at least he would have retained some control over military recruiting without which his work was shadowy. But this was kept in the grip of the War Office, where General Geddes was entrenched as Director of Recruiting. Emboldened, other indenting Departments began again to put their own demands for labour without reference to Neville. If he protested he had little support from his colleagues, and none from the Prime Minister. He was already defeated.

Again, in selecting his Deputy and his personal staff Neville showed poor judgement. Lloyd George suggested in turn as Deputy a Mr. Walker (of a whisky firm), Stevenson from the Ministry of Munitions, Kennedy Jones, a journalist, and even Geddes, Neville's eventual successor. But Neville, who had already taken Mr. Collins, the Birmingham City Treasurer, as Chief of Staff, and other Birmingham worthies, including Mr. Hill, the President of the Birmingham Business Club, to form the nucleus of his staff, still hoped to persuade Mr. Hiley, who had recently resigned from being Town Clerk of Birmingham to go into business, to join him:

N.C. to Hilda 31.12.1916.

"I went next morning to see him and ask him if he'd come. I gave him the day to think it over as he was dining with me that night, but in the evening he said he felt his experience was too narrow and he didn't consider he was equal to the job. I didn't press him. . . ."

That should have been that. It would have been in any case bad tactics to staff a new Department with his own men, who were only fully at home in the local government world of Birmingham. Neville toyed with the idea of not having a Deputy at all to control civil recruiting, but Lloyd George (rightly) insisted and the protesting Dr. Addison was forced to disgorge Stevenson from his Ministry as a "temporary" appointment. Within a few days it was clear that Neville and Stevenson were ill-matched. Again Neville asked for Hiley and this time (as a result of the Prime Minister's personal appeal to his firm) Hiley agreed. This appointment was no more successful and in a few months Neville was writing cryptically:

N.C. to Hilda 27.5.1917.

"Hiley has resigned but as I have intimated his departure will not make any difference now so long as Ll. G. doesn't hear of it and begin his tricks again."

These were Neville's errors. But the crowning blunder (apart from the absurdity of the plan itself) came from Lloyd George. Whether by accident or design, the scheme for the Directorate of National Service ignored the House of Commons. Probably by accident. There was little case for making the new Department of inferior status in wartime to the Ministry of Labour, whose field covered only seven trades and some four hundred Exchanges. Indeed, it seems clear from the offer of the post to Montagu that Lloyd George's first intention was to put the two appointments on the same level, for Montagu had held a key post in Asquith's Cabinet. Either, then, the Prime Minister changed his mind, or the conditions were re-jigged to suit Neville's circumstances. He, on his appointment, had said to the Press, "The Cabinet do not think it necessary—or even desirable—for me to have a seat in the House of Commons, so the question of entering Parliament does not arise". Nor even was he sworn of the Privy Council, which would have given him some standing as a Departmental Chief. Presumably the argument was that it would be easier to schedule unessential industries and the other disagreeable tasks that were to be undertaken by the Director if he were insulated from Parliamentary pressures. But the House of Commons would never accept this position. Indeed, it was only likely to acquiesce in such tremendous decisions if the man who took them could be made answerable to the House in the House. There is some evidence that the Cabinet, disturbed no doubt by the hostility in Parliament, wished to go back on its former decision and that now it was Neville who resisted.

Rt. Hon. Sir George Cave, M.P. Hansard 13.3.1917.

"The present Director-General does not for the moment desire to sit in Parliament. Personally, I hope that before long he may reconsider his decision, as I am sure we would all like to see him here."

But by this time it was almost certainly too late. When Parliament reassembled after the Christmas recess the nagging questions had begun. There was not even a Parliamentary Secretary to reply, for the Bill authorising the appointment was not yet ready. All sorts of Ministers took in turn the onus of trying to satisfy the questioners. Even the Vice-Chamberlain of the Household was pressed into service. "I have been asked to reply"—the traditional preamble when an answer is given on behalf of a colleague—was followed by the reading of the answer Neville had prepared. But to the supplementaries the replies had to be, "I will inform the Director

of that point," or, "I am sure the Director will note that."
The House growled impatiently. By the time the Ministry of
National Service Bill was introduced on Second Reading by the
Home Secretary (Sir George Cave) on February 22nd, 1917, the
House had already made up its mind.

Mr. Tyson Wilson, M.P. for Westhoughton. Hansard 27.2.1917.
"I am absolutely amazed at the blind confidence the Government
seem to repose in any one man they have appointed to control or
direct a certain Department. I take it if that one man is not a Member
of this House and he fails in his mission or the work he undertakes,
the Government will put all the responsibility on that man, and they
will escape altogether. I say without hesitation that no-one should
have the control of either men, women or material to any extent
unless he is directly responsible to this House."

Mr. Dillon, M.P. for East Mayo. Hansard 27.2.1917.
"If Mr. Chamberlain were an archangel, or if he were Hindenberg
and Bismarck, and all the great men of the world rolled into one,
his task would be wholly beyond his powers."

The first schedule of essential industries came in for fierce attack. Cotton had been omitted and Lancashire Members were up
in arms. Those who represented the industries which were
deemed inessential feared the loss of labour and the closing down
of firms. When the Bill finally became law in March 1917,
Stephen Walsh, a Labour M.P., was appointed as Neville's Parliamentary Secretary, but he carried too few guns to cope with his
persistent critics.

Neville's Department was established at St. Ermin's Hotel, and
there, with Hiley and Collins and a motley crew of advisers and
advisory committees, he laboured on a scheme which was already
under attack before its final details were known. The plan was
announced at a public meeting at the Central Hall, Westminster,
on February 6th, 1917. The Prime Minister, Henderson and Hodge
also spoke. In essence, the scheme was to be to the factories what
the Derby scheme had been to the forces—a last attempt with industrial compulsion in the background, to secure the men needed
by a voluntary appeal. Men between the ages of 18 and 61 in non-
essential occupations were to be invited to become National Ser-

64

vice volunteers to replace men withdrawn from the key industries for military service. The volunteers in their new jobs were to receive either the negotiated wage or 25s. per week, whichever was the higher rate. The non-essential trades were to be rationed in labour and materials, and were invited to pool their resources of plant and manpower. Part-time National Service was to be encouraged. Women were to be invited to volunteer at a later stage and Mrs. Tennant and Miss Violet Markham were appointed to take charge of a woman's branch of the Department. Usually the Employment Exchange was to be the place of enrolment, and local recruiting committees were to be set up with the help of the Local Government Board.

The idea, then, was to collect round pegs and place them in the vacancies that were to be created. But that turned out to be the snag. The other Ministries did not play their part. The men were not winkled out of the key industries, and so there were no holes for the pegs. Nor was there yet any one central authority. The Department fought not only with the Ministry of Labour, but with the Ministry of Munitions for this position. Inevitably it was out-gunned. Neville had no wish to take over the Employment Exchanges, nor even to work through them. There was some reason for this; for the Exchanges, poorly staffed and housed, were in the early years unpopular, not only with the employers but with the unions as well. But his own solution of local substitution committees loosely linked to the Exchanges proved equally unsatisfactory.

Neville embarked on a series of speeches and appearances to publicise the scheme. Within a very short time he had spoken in practically all the great provincial cities, adding to these burdens talks to Members of Parliament, a Conference of Trade Union leaders, the Stock and Baltic Exchanges, the Church and the Stage and the Insurance profession. The reports both in the national and local papers of these meetings tell exactly the same story. Always he was "very warmly received": always the speech was "enthusiastically applauded": always there was a "fine response" from the audience to the appeal for volunteers. But Neville was not deceived. He knew that in politics as in chess forays to the wings, even successful ones, are of little value if the centre is not secure. And it was in Whitehall that he was being defeated. His dispute with Hodge and the Ministry of Labour was referred to Henderson for judgement. Henderson's report, approved by the War Cabinet on March 23rd, 1917, laid down that "the primary function of the Department was to collect labour for National purposes . . . the primary function of the Ministry was to place labour for National purposes". But as Henderson added that the Ministry should also carry out the "Process of substitution as part of its ordinary business of placing labour and all officials engaged on that work should be under the jurisdiction of the Ministry of Labour" his report was in practice a charter for Hodge. Probably Neville would have been wiser to resign now. Milner and Austen were his only allies, and with a hostile Press, a suspicious House of Commons, and a complete lack of support from the Prime Minister, Neville's disappearance from office was only a matter of time.

Northcliffe—largely because he wanted to see a compulsory instead of a voluntary scheme—kept up in his newspapers a rain of criticism on Neville and the Department. Neville in fact would himself have been glad to abandon the voluntary appeal. Indeed, from the early days of January, he had argued with an unresponsive War Cabinet for the policy of the "clean-cut"—the cancellation of all exemptions, including the Trade Card Agreement, for the younger man. But he was bound by the Prime Minister's terms of reference on his appointment and also by the pledges given to Labour leaders against industrial compulsion. So he toiled on with a scheme in which he had ceased to believe.

N.C. to Hilda 1.7.1917.

"This last eventful week has pretty well brought my affairs to a climax too and in all probability this is the last letter I shall write to you as D.G.M.S. . . . Now I hate the idea of resignation under present circumstances; you know I like to stick to things even after there seems no chance of success, but when I have made up my mind that the thing is hopeless I generally cut the loss with rapidity and determination. Now I am in a position that reminds me of the Bahamas when the plants didn't grow. With all the Departments against me and a chief who won't help, I see no chance of success, and if so it would be folly to let slip an opportunity of getting out on a principle. . . ."

It was at this point that Austen, although in no way responsible for the failure of the medical arrangements revealed by the Mesopotamia Commission, thought it his duty to resign as Secretary of State for India. Neville's sense of isolation inevitably grew stronger.

Neville, then, was looking for an opportunity to resign. For his part the Prime Minister had already decided to let him go, and appoint General Geddes in his place. Indeed, from January this was clearly the only sensible solution. As Neville could not become a General, Geddes had to become a civilian. But even his decision that Neville was expendable does not excuse Lloyd George's rudeness to him in the final weeks. Without a word to Neville the Prime Minister replaced Stephen Walsh by Cecil Beck as Parliamentary Secretary to the Department. Neville protested in angry terms, and an apology duly arrived. But on the next day Lloyd George invited Hodge and Beck to breakfast, again without a word to Neville, and having listened to Hodge's outburst against the Department instructed Beck to draft a memorandum in reply. This reply was to be considered, again at breakfast and again without Neville, in a week's time. There was a further protest and a further apology, but clearly the breaking point had come. A memorandum by Neville on the future of National Service, although it was also signed by Derby, Rhondda, Walter Long and Hayes Fisher, was ignored by the War Cabinet. Neville sent his resignation in to become effective on July 20th, but agreed to delay it on the Prime Minister's request, while a report submitted by Geddes was considered. There were last-minute flurries, and as usual a variety of compromises suggested. Neville's Labour Advisory Committee sprang to his defence. A letter to the Press signed by all its members, headed by J. H. Thomas, Tom Shaw and Ben Tillett asserted flatly that the Exchanges were incompetent and unpopular, that the National Service Department had secured full co-operation from both the employers and the employed and that the bitter attacks on Mr. Chamberlain were "evidently inspired and one-sided". But in any event it was too late. Lloyd George was determined to have Geddes, and on August 8th Neville resigned. The letters exchanged were purely formal. Neville said that he had lacked support, and Lloyd George denied it. Nevertheless, a bitterness had grown between them that was to last for the whole of their political lives. Lloyd George and Neville Chamberlain had little respect for each other, and it was never likely that they would work successfully together. Yet for all the obvious differences between them they shared a background of dissent and social reform. If there had been no personal antagonism between them the scheme, for all its follies, might have been recast and have been a success, for even admitting the failure of both men in this field, they saw clearly enough between them what needed to be done. Still, something was gained from failure. Given the inhibitions of the Liberal Government and the Labour movement in the early years of the war, the period of the National Service Department was probably an inevitable stage in Britain's progress towards becoming a nation in arms. It was Neville's misfortune that he was called on to lead a crusade to nowhere.

A pleasanter note was provided by the presentation to Neville of a parting gift subscribed to by the Department. Presentations in Whitehall to Ministers, even after years of successful service, are rare enough, and it was a remarkable tribute to his leadership that after a few months he should have earned such a tribute from a Department that must at the time have been feeling defeated and dispirited.

The bare statistics of the appeal for National Service volunteers make cheerless reading. Some 350,000 applications were received for enrolment, about three-quarters of them through the Exchanges. Of these 8,842 were placed in employment, 2,267 of them being placed as ordinary applicants for employment. This, of course, was a reflection of the fact that men had not been withdrawn from industry for the forces to create the vacancies on which the whole scheme depended. As Neville put it later in a speech to the Birmingham Unionists explaining his resignation:

19.12.1917. B.D.P.

"The mistake about National Service was fundamental. What was wanted was not a campaign for volunteers; what was wanted was a careful and thorough survey of the whole resources of the nation in manpower and woman power, followed by a decision of the Cabinet as to the best method and the best manner in which those resources should be allocated."

The only permanent mark was made on agriculture, where about 100,000 persons were found work on the land, and where for the first time a minimum wage was established for the agricultural labourer.

To this heritage Sir Auckland Geddes succeeded. That, in spite of his increased powers, the problems of manpower still continued, has already been noted. But one should mark too his tribute to Neville on the introduction of the Military Service Act:

Rt. Hon. Sir Auckland Geddes, M.P. Hansard 14.1.1918.

"I should like to pay a sincere tribute of respect to Mr. Neville Chamberlain. Much misunderstanding still exists with regard to his position and actions. The problems of National Service are varied and manifold, and Mr. Chamberlain's personal contributions to the solution of the manpower problem were solid and valuable. To him, I think, is due the credit of finally convincing the country of the need of a Ministry to work out the problem of the strategical use of man-power. . . ."

And the postscript may perhaps be best given by the leader of the Conservative Party, who was at the time Lloyd George's closest confidant:

Rt. Hon. A. Bonar Law, M.P. Hansard 13.2.1918.

"I have no special friendship with Mr. Neville Chamberlain, but I think he had under the circumstances a hopeless task, and I listened with the greatest pleasure to what was said in this House as to how hard he had worked and how difficult his duty was."

5

WESTMINSTER BEGINNINGS

(August 1917 – October 1922)

EVEN if failure had been inevitable, the sting of failure
remained. But his immediate, almost instinctive, reaction
was to fight again. The Chamberlain family spent little
time consoling each other, and less in bewailing what was done.
Within a few days his sisters opened fire. A letter from Ida, after
a long and meticulous account of the sedate adventures of a railway journey to Newquay, suddenly erupts:

Ida to N.C. 18.8.1917.

"The more one thinks of it the more one feels that it must be public
work of some kind, and that the only avenue to it is to go into
Parliament. I gather from conversation with Mary that this is her
view too and that she has told you so, and as the family has a great
tendency to think alike on these matters I think it probable that by
this time you have come to the same conclusion. I can't say that the
immediate prospect is particularly inviting, but your experience
shows you what a handicap it is to be out of Parliament and consequently out of the political swim . . . of course then there is the
question of a seat, and if you decide to go into Parliament it *must* be
a Birmingham seat, but surely if it were known that you wanted to
go in someone might make room for you."

Hilda added her thrust in the next letter.

Hilda to N.C. 24.8.1917.

"Your letter makes me feel even more strongly, if that were possible,
that Parliament is the next step for you. I don't suppose that A.
[Austen] ever will be in a position to form a government, because

one knows how often such things are anticipated and how constantly things turn out otherwise, but if you have already made up your mind that in those circumstances you could not become a member of it without having been in Parliament, why, the sooner you are in the better. However, I need not labour this point for I feel pretty sure that almost from the first you have seen this as a necessity, and at bottom have known that it must be, much as you dislike the idea of it. . . . You *are* a natural born leader of men . . . and I believe you will shortly be recognised as such. I don't mean that you will be P.M. for many things may open or bar the way to such a post, but that you will be a leader with a devoted following before long I am sure. . . . However, as I say, I feel pretty sure that you *do* mean to go into Parliament in your inner mind, and have known it for some time, however much the outward man protesteth. You could never be content to sit down to make a fortune for yourself and the children, and Annie is not the woman to accept such a decision! You are neither of you extravagant people, and certainly would not be happy leading aimless lives, however rich you might be. Even the amelioration of the lot of your own particular workpeople is not a nearly big enough field for you, whether they are hundreds or thousands. No, public service claims you, and you recognise its claims."

Neville capitulated:

N.C. to Hilda 27.8.1917.
"Your letter was abominably clear sighted and brutal in pulling off all the clothes under which I had crawled. I suppose I have had a sort of uncomfortable feeling all along as to how things would turn out, but I have tried to avoid coming to a decision even in my own mind. But the fact is as you say, I could not settle down to make money, much as I should like to be rich. . . . I suppose therefore that really and truly I have what you may call made up my mind to go into the House and last week I wrote to Vince about it."

Neville recognised clearly the cardinal error that he (and Lloyd George) had made during the period of the Department of National Service. The House of Commons had defeated him once. He was determined not to underestimate it a second time:

12.9.1917. B.D.P.
"My experience in London has shown me that the House of Commons does possess more real power than previously I had been dis-

posed to attribute to it. . . . Now I have decided to embark on a political life I do not want to wait an indefinite time—until a General Election—before going to Parliament. Naturally I would like to represent a division of Birmingham. I am quite satisfied of this—that if I am to be useful in the reconstruction work that has to be done I must be in the House of Commons for some little time in advance, in order to get adequate experience of Parliamentary life and procedure."

It was less than tactful to put his claims as bluntly as this, but Neville, having determined on his course, was impatient of delay. Powerful though he was in Birmingham affairs, it was asking much of the city's Unionist Members that one of them should retire at once to make room for him. And with one consent they began (not surprisingly) to make excuse. The autumn months dragged on while Neville at first feverishly and then doggedly pursued his new ambition. Jesse Collings in Bordesley was now eighty-six and failing fast. But a prospective candidate was already in the field there and unwilling to withdraw. In any event, the present constituency boundaries were to be redrawn for the next General Election, when Birmingham's seven seats would become twelve and there would be places to spare.

There was in any case much to do. He had returned to the control of Hoskins' and Elliott's, and rejoined the board of B.S.A. There was the Municipal Bank to be encouraged, the first concerts of the new municipal orchestra under Sir Thomas Beecham to be supported, the University to be maintained in strength. He had gone back to the Council and was Deputy Mayor. His garden as always demanded his time and affection. And he delighted above all else in the sanctuary of his home and the company of his children. He should have been happy but he was not. The smaller affairs of the City Council had become tedious to him, and the months seemed dreary and endless as he waited for the General Election, which in turn waited for victory. Both seemed far away. Besides, the hurt of the National Service fiasco was too recent and too deep:

N.C. to Hilda 7.10.1917.

"You show your usual sympathy and understanding of other people's feelings in your comments on the difficulties of my position here. I do feel it intensely—so that I often think I should like to flee away and hide myself in a South Sea island. Of course people naturally don't suspect how sensitive one is and in fact I do my best to prevent their seeing it, and the consequence is that they unintentionally tread most unmercifully on one's corns. Even the sympathy which is fully and freely expressed hurts like the devil."

Only by success in Parliament could the slate be wiped clean. No other solace would do:

Diary, 27.12.1917.
"Last night I received a letter from the P.M. saying that the King had approved his recommendation that I should receive the honour of a G.B.E.
"To-day I declined it."

1917 was not to pass without one more numbing blow. The war to Neville had been something to be fought whole-heartedly, but he had not felt himself personally involved in its tragedy and waste. Now in December came the news that Norman Chamberlain, son of Herbert Chamberlain, Joe's younger brother, was missing. Two months later his body was found in No Man's Land. Norman Chamberlain was fifteen years younger than Neville, but actually his senior on the City Council which he had joined in 1909. In the years that led up to Neville's Lord Mayoralty they were together in every scheme and project. Neville's leadership was followed unquestioningly by his young cousin, but Norman had a flame of life and eagerness in him to which the older man responded. Norman, a true Chamberlain, was a born social reformer with a thoroughly practical approach which revelled in the Committee work of the Council, the preparation and study of papers on the problems of unemployment amongst young people and the personal supervision of the lads in the Youth Clubs he started in Birmingham. Norman Chamberlain's death stunned Neville. He had always expected that after the war they would resume their partnership. He set himself the task of collecting Norman's letters and papers and the only book Neville ever wrote, *Norman Chamberlain, A Memoir*, was the result. It is an unremarkable book, for Neville could never bring himself to make public what he felt. But his diary and letters show his distress:

Diary, 10.2.1918.

"Somehow I had always associated Norman with anything I might do in the future. He was like a younger brother to me."

and

N.C. to Hilda 23.2.1918.

"I feel frightfully depressed over his loss and sort of discouraged too. I was counting and depending on him more than I realised and he was in fact the most intimate friend I had."

Neville's abiding hatred of war was born of the death in action of Norman Chamberlain.

The first few months of 1918 were the most frustrating period of Neville's life. He had no prospect of reaching Westminster now until the General Election came, and as the war scene darkened the chance of an election receded. His wife was often ill in these months, his children had their fill of childhood's infectious diseases, he himself had chicken-pox, gout, sciatica and then gout again. He suffered as much from the strenuous "cures" as from the afflictions. Norman was dead and Neville was weary of the struggle and apprehensive of the future. In France the German offensive, mounted in March, rolled forward with grim and frightening momentum. In Parliament the Government faltered as the disgruntled Opposition seized on the dismissal of General Robertson from the post of C.I.G.S., and the sensational charges of General Maurice, to make their own onslaught on the conduct of the war. And then, at last, both the fortunes of war and Neville's own prospects began to improve. The German assault faltered and ground to a standstill. Haig's thrust on August 8th near Amiens was the trumpet call for final and overwhelming victory.

And for Neville too the dark days were over. He was fit again, and illness had passed from his family. His political future at last was settled. He could not obtain the reversion of Bordesley, but Sir Edward Parkes, the sitting Member for Birmingham Central, announced that he would retire at the General Election, and the

74

new constituency of Ladywood, carved out of the Central Division and part of West Birmingham (Joe's old seat) adopted Neville as their prospective candidate. He turned down a suggestion that he might return as Lord Mayor in November. It was to be Westminster or nothing. Now it was urgent to look to the political organisation of the Birmingham constituencies, grown rusty in the years of war and political truce. Neville took the lead in this:

N.C. to Hilda 3.8.1918.

"To finish London. I went in the afternoon to a meeting of Birmingham M.P.s and candidates in Austen's room. I had called the meeting to consider proposals put forward by the fused Management Committee of which I am Chairman for a new method of organisation. In effect this was centralisation. All subscriptions to go to a Central Fund, and all organisation in Divisions and Wards to be done from the centre. I am sure it is right and will lead to increased efficiency and economy, incidentally forming a splendid training school for young professional agents, but it is not the method hitherto followed and some people think they can run their constituency better themselves than by entrusting it to a central office. However, the older Members very warmly supported me and in the end I got a practically unanimous agreement and acceptance. Of course, as I am Chairman (Steel-Maitland is associated with me but he doesn't come) this decision practically places the direction of Unionist politics in my hands. I am not sure whether all those present perceived this; I didn't mention it!"

There was one short-lived political flirtation during the months of waiting. Neville's favourite theme at the time was the need for an alliance between Capital and Labour after the war, and he hoped to see Unionist working-class candidates standing in Birmingham. He was attracted then to the manifesto of the British Workers' League, which he regarded as representing the true feelings of the Labour movement against the insidious doctrines of MacDonald and Snowden.

N.C. to Hilda 17.11.1917.

"I wonder if you read the British Workers' League programme? Many of the 'Planks' are somewhat vaguely expressed and are capable of various interpretations, but there is hardly one which could not be interpreted in such a way that I could accept it and it is difficult to see what there is to divide the B.W.L. from the more progressive section of the Unionist, and for aught I know the Liberal Party too. Subject to a talk with Austen I have arranged for the annual meeting of the Birmingham Lib. Un. Assn. early next month, when he and I would be practically the only speakers and I should like him then to make some careful allusion to the B.W.L., expressing sympathy with their ideas."

But the conservative Austen was cool and Central Office disinterested, and although Eldred Hallas, the Labour Councillor who had been lieutenant to Neville in the struggle to establish the Municipal Bank was adopted in one of the City seats with Unionist support, and Victor Fisher representing the National Democratic and Labour Party had Neville's support in Stourbridge, this shaky alliance did not long survive the Election.

Neville, although Lloyd George and Bonar Law sent him their support, did not use the "coupon" at the General Election in December 1918. He had a more potent weapon. Kneeshaw, his Labour opponent, had made in September a speech calling for Peace by Negotiation, which had been denounced by Labour Party Leaders. W. J. Davis, of the National Society of Amalgamated Brassworkers, Chairman of Neville's Labour Advisory Board during the period of the Directorate of National Service and a former Chairman of the T.U.C., wrote to Neville a letter which—reproduced as a pamphlet—was quickly circulated in the constituency. It contained this sentence:

"I trust that you will not only be returned, but that the result of the Election will give you a very large majority, especially as your opponent did all he possibly could to incite the people to harass and obstruct the various Governments in their struggles against the foulest foe the world has ever known."

In the jungle atmosphere of the post-war election nothing else was needed. A third candidate, Mrs. Corbett Ashby, an Asquithian Liberal, appeared, but the result was never in doubt. Even with the poverty that darkened so much of Ladywood, Chamberlain was sure to win. From his speeches, orthodox in the main in support of Lloyd George and the Coalition programme, only his views on housing are distinctive enough to be isolated:

76

22.11.1918. B.D.P.

". . . the speaker turned to the housing problem. The shortage, he said, was so great that we must put aside all old ideas and prejudices. In his opinion the proper way to deal with the question was for the State to take it up, to provide the money, and announce at once to the people a great programme of national housing—not to be undertaken by the State itself, but to be carried out by the local authorities which alone knew the conditions, could provide the sites and could collect rents in trust for the State. That would convince the people that the Government were in earnest and not tinkering with the whole question."

At the height of the campaign Neville's half-sister Beatrice, the beloved Auntie Bee of the whole Chamberlain and Kenrick clan, died after a short illness from influenza.

Diary, 22.11.1918.

"She was a wonderfully gifted woman of brilliant intellect and the highest moral character. She had the warmest heart and her love for children and genius for amusing them made her always a favourite. It is an awful gap in our family circle. I cannot write more now."

Neville flung himself the more fiercely into the closing stages of the campaign. He hated now, as he always did, the showmanship and salesmanship inseparable from an Election:

N.C. to Hilda 7.12.1918.

"I do wish speaking didn't make me so unhappy beforehand. About teatime I begin to feel unwell—by dinner my appetite has completely gone, and if I have an exciting meeting I can't get to sleep for ages afterwards."

The Election took place on December 14th and a fortnight later the votes were counted. The Ladywood result on a 40 per cent. poll was:

Neville Chamberlain	..	..	9405
J. W. Kneeshaw	..	..	2572
Mrs. Corbett Ashby	..	..	1552
	Majority		6833

All the Birmingham seats were won and Neville could boast, "Once we used to say 'We are seven.' Now we can say, 'We are twelve.' Or rather, eleven and an ally." So Neville entered the House of Commons in the first post-war Parliament—that Parliament cheerfully described by Lloyd George as the Trades Union Congress facing the Associated Chambers of Commerce. He was almost fifty years old.

He took his seat at Westminster early in February 1919. By the time the House rose for the recess six months later he had established himself. The brief tale of his contributions to Hansard in this short session is well worth study. He made his maiden speech on March 12th in Committee of the House on the Rent Restriction Bill. His speech was judged by the *Birmingham Post*—a friendly critic, of course—"an admirable performance, good in substance, in form and in delivery". He spoke for ten minutes without notes in support of an amendment providing that the proposed increase in rent of 10 per cent could not be obtained by the landlord unless he produced a certificate certifying the house fit for human habitation. The Attorney General, who had already rejected this point, rose again to undertake to put words into the Bill to meet Neville's argument. Few maiden speeches achieve anything, but this was a promising start although he got into dire trouble with the Birmingham Property Owners' Association. Within a week (almost an indecently swift return for a maiden speaker) he addressed the House again on the subject of Canals and Waterways—an old love of his. In July during the Committee stage of the Electricity Supply Bill, he defeated the Government, carrying an amendment of his to a new clause proposed by the Home Secretary. Finally, early in August, he took a leading part in the debate on Treasury Control in a speech described by Winston Churchill who followed him in the debate as "a very important and helpful speech." None of these speeches is worth resurrecting from Hansard, cogent in each case though the argument is. But this is a record of humdrum successful application with which a backbencher of many years' experience might well be content.

He had, of course, in one sense a flying start. His name at West-minster was his passport. His father's memory was still green: his half-brother Chancellor of the Exchequer. This last Neville regarded as something of a mixed blessing. Too much, he thought, would be expected of him, and besides Austen might thwart Neville's housing schemes and blight his hopes for the continuance of the Birmingham Municipal Bank. After a stormy interview with a tired Austen, who had had little time and probably little inclination to study Neville's elaborate memorandum on future housing policy:

N.C. to Hilda 4.1.1919.

"The fact is I always said that if I went into the House we should differ and we are bound to do so because our minds are differently trained. He thinks me wild and I think him unprogressive and prejudiced."

This was written in anger, and Neville repented of his outburst. But Austen would certainly have thought "wild" Neville's radical views on the mining industry and industrial unrest at the time of the Sankey Report. Joe would, however, have approved.

N.C. to Ida 22.3.1919.

"The announcements made this morning do, I think, show that the strike has been averted, but the miners have won a fairly complete victory. Some people take it rather hard but I confess I think they have deserved it so far as the merits of the case go, and it must be admitted that if they had not taken drastic steps they would never have got the public enquiry. But it is difficult to estimate the effect on other industries which I am inclined to think will be widespread. On the whole, I am disposed to look upon the affair as a good thing for the community. Many people have been sceptical about the suggestion that there was to be a new England and many others have never intended that it should be very different from the old if they could help it. If they had had their way I think we might have drifted into a revolution, but this is a real change in our industrial system. I am referring not to what is given now but to what is contemplated for the future of the industry. Whether it will be nationalisation in the sense that the State owns and works the collieries, or whether, as is more likely and I think more practical, some State control will be exercised, the workmen having a voice in the direction and a share of the profits, it is a long step from the system hitherto followed. I expect railways will probably adopt a similar plan and then we shall see an agitation for the extension of the movement to other industries. Evolution by steps is the only way in which any fundamental change can be brought about without disaster, and so I regard the future with comparative equanimity."

When his first short Parliamentary session ended Neville was sure enough of his future to resign his Aldermanic seat on the Birmingham City Council. Parliament was becoming a whole-time occupation. Besides, even if he had made a solid mark in his first few months, he was over fifty now and he had to move fast if Parliamentary honours were to come to him. As a Member with some experience of the ways of Ministries, and a deep and intimate knowledge of local government, he was inevitably in great demand for the numerous Committees that proliferate in Whitehall. In his first year as a Member he became Chairman of the Unhealthy Areas Committee set up by Dr. Addison, the Minister of Health, Chairman of a departmental Committe on Canals and Waterways, a member of the Colonial Development Committee, of a Committee on the Salaries of the Ministers, of the Health Advisory Committee and of Committees on Licensing and anti-dumping. All this apart, of course, from the ordinary toil of Standing Committee work in the House. "I seem," reported Neville, "to be the handyman of the House as far as Committees are concerned." Ministers usually appoint Committees for one of two reasons. Either because there is a genuine interest in the out-come, or because it is a convenient way of containing, for a time at least, inconvenient pressures. And the value of this last expedi-ent is all the greater if one can immure the critics of one's policy in the Committee. "Most Committees," as Sir Winston Churchill once observed during his second Premiership, "are to Govern-ments as the inky discharge is to the cuttlefish. They do no good, but they obscure the issue." And certainly some of the Commit-tees with which Neville lived laborious days and nights in his early days as a Member were of this type. But the Unhealthy Areas Committee belonged to the first category. Its task was "to con-sider the principles that should be adopted in the clearance of slum areas", and, this, together with the provision of new housing for the people, were the great post-war tasks that challenged the in-fant Ministry of Health. The two reports of this Committee were Neville's own:

N.C. to Ida 6.3.1920.

"I am beginning to shape an interim report dealing with London only which will I think contain some novel ideas. The recommendations I have in mind are to set up a new authority with jurisdiction over a wide zone including London and the area lying beyond it for purposes of town planning, transport and finance so far as that is necessary to allow the authority to decide on future developments, e.g., they might wish to have one part wholly residential, another mixed and another chiefly commercial . . . then I want the local authorities to be able to define congested areas within which houses could not be pulled down nor factories extended without a licence. And I want the L.A. to be able to buy up unhealthy areas."

And of the final report with its major recommendation that local authorities should be given powers to buy and to improve slum areas, paying little more than site value compensation to the landlords:

N.C. to Hilda 12.3.1921.

"I had a very successful meeting of my Unhealthy Areas Committee on Wednesday; I had spent a lot of time going through the report, re-drafting and adding to it, and the Committee simply opened its mouth and swallowed everything at a gulp. . . ."

Neville's position as an influential backbencher is seen most clearly in his early election to office in the Reconstruction Committee. This Committee was the successor of the wartime "Ginger" Committee of Unionists and the parent of the 1922 Committee which still today is the accepted forum of backbench opinion. At the end of October 1919 he formed, with a natural satisfaction, one of a deputation of four who saw Lloyd George and Bonar Law to protest against the P.M.'s long absences from the House and his habit of dealing with large policy issues over the heads of his colleagues and of Parliament. They were received with evasive politeness, but obtained some assurances for the future; these, however, probably owing more to a Government defeat on the Aliens Restriction Bill (Neville being one of the rebels) than to their arguments. Again, and still in his first year as an M.P., he organised the backbench opposition to the Government's Anti-Dumping Bill which secured from Bonar Law the promise of the "drastic amendments" demanded by Neville. Early in 1920, following on a clash with Carson over Tariff Reform in the Reconstruction Committee, Neville's name was put forward as Chairman, but some opposition developed to this owing to his junior status in the House and a compromise was reached by which Neville became Vice-Chairman (a new post) and an amiable nonentity who could be relied on not to attend the meetings was installed as Chairman. He had used his success in the Ballot for Private Members Bills to introduce a Bastardy Bill (later changed to "Children of Unmarried Persons Bill") to give some protection to the children of unmarried mothers, and carried it on Second Reading against the advice of the Home Secretary, although later he had to accept substantial amendment of the Bill in Committee.

He was, moreover, to his surprise, happy in the House of Commons. Before he had been there a month he was writing to say that "rather reluctantly" he had to confess that the pull of the House was attracting him. He found, again to his surprise, that he was not blamed for the failure of the National Service Department and indeed that the freemasonry of the House which had worked against him while he was not responsible to the House, worked for him now he was part of it. And in his early days in Parliament the friendships were formed—especially with Edward Wood (Halifax), Sam Hoare (Templewood) and Philip Lloyd-Greame (Swinton)—which were to last until his death.

So, then, without a single notable debating triumph to his credit, and envying because he could not emulate the searing phrases of Lloyd George, the polished sentences of Balfour and the carefully fashioned excellence of Winston Churchill's speeches, Neville had arrived. He could reasonably look forward to office. But one thing stood in the way. His own determination, perhaps an obstinate and illogical one but nevertheless founded on deep conviction, never to serve under or, if he could help it, with Lloyd George. The Prime Minister was not himself so conscious of the gulf between them, and authorised Bonar Law to take soundings:

N.C. to Hilda 13.3.1920.

". . . Edmund Talbot met me in the tea-room and said, 'Bonar Law wants to see you in his room.' So I went along and found Bonar

alone. He asked me to sit down and with some diffidence opened up
cautiously, saying that I had been head of a great department and
that he didn't know what I should think of a lower place but it had
been suggested to him by Horne that perhaps I might be willing to
take an Under-Secretaryship. He thought I was worth more but
didn't see how anything more could be offered just now. He suggested Health but said there were a number of places to be filled. He
had spoken to 'George' and he would be very glad if I would take
it."

But Neville was still deeply sensitive because of the treatment
he had received over National Service, and after reciting some of
his grievances to Bonar Law asked for time to consider the offer,
and, having considered it, refused. Perhaps Neville's rejection of
the P.M.'s olive branch—if it was one—was also the reason for
the abrupt conclusion of the next curious advance:

Diary, 8.5.1920.
"Just before the House rose (on 31st March) 'Jerry' McVeagh one of
the Irish Nationalist M.P.'s, sat down beside me in the H. of C.
and after a little talk on Irish Affairs remarked, 'They ought to make
you Irish Secretary instead of Macpherson. If they would make
Granard Lord Lieutenant and you Chief Secretary it would all go
swimmingly.' I did not pay much attention to this remark, but in
the next few days Devlin, Redmond, and T. P. O'Connor all took
occasion to make some friendly remark to me, though I had hardly
ever spoken to them before. I concluded from this that they had
been talking together and that McVeagh's remark was not merely
an *obiter dictum*. After the recess J. M. came to see me again and
said, 'You remember what I said to you some time ago.' I said,
'Yes.' 'Well,' he went on, 'that night I spoke to several Ministers
about it and Fisher and Gordon Hewart (the Attorney General) and
Shortt were all enthusiastic about it, and very keen. And I have
reason to know that soon after it was conveyed to Lloyd George.
But he said, 'Oh, I don't like that fellow' and there the matter
ended."

It was not remotely likely that Lloyd George would make another approach; nor did he. And so while he remained Prime
Minister Neville could not hope for office. It would have been
natural enough in the circumstances if Neville had joined one or
other of the Groups of Unionists (beginning to call themselves

'Conservatives' again) who were muttering against the Coalition and particularly against the Prime Minister. Neville had no affection for the Coalition, but he felt the pull of loyalty towards Austen, particularly when, on Bonar Law's resignation owing to illness in March 1921, Austen succeeded to the leadership of the Party. He played then no part in the manœuvres of the next two years and it was appropriate that he should have been out of the country when the Coalition was finally destroyed at the Carlton Club. But he remained a keen observer of the stresses on the Coalition, and even if he could not see how it was to be brought about, must have longed for Lloyd George's downfall. The Coalition seemed all-powerful. It had all the debating strength in the House, at least until Asquith and Simon were returned at by-elections. Its real leaders were Lloyd George, Churchill, Birkenhead and Beaverbrook, as glittering and effervescent a partnership as English politics has seen. But as Leo Amery shrewdly observes in his book *My Political Life*: "there is an inherent tendency in all coalitions to coalesce more closely at the top than lower down the scale of party organisation". Certainly this was true of the Lloyd George experiment in coalition. At Cabinet level the mutual admiration of the Ministers for each other cloaked their differences. But below the Cabinet the Junior Ministers muttered impotently and the Conservative Party watched Lloyd George, hypnotised by his brilliance and suspicious of his intentions. They did not know where he would lead them. Nor did Lloyd George. Something in due course would have to take the place of the Coalition. Lloyd George at first favoured the creation of a "National Democratic Party" which would embrace all Liberals and all Unionists and which would naturally look to him for leadership. Churchill and Birkenhead were prepared, indeed anxious, to jettison the diehard wing of the Tory Party and the radical wing of the Liberal Party and form a Centre Party, which would naturally look to them for leadership.

Austen, who appears to have worn political blinkers in these months, could see no farther than loyalty to Lloyd George, and that meant Coalition or Fusion, or whatever the Prime Minister called for. Even when the Prime Minister wrote to Austen in February 1922 protesting that he had never sought the Premiership and was ready to retire in Austen's favour, the latter felt himself so bound by loyalty to his chief that he spurned the honeyed chalice.

Beaverbrook's advice to Lloyd George was to put himself at the head of a "Fusion" Party which would follow the pattern of the Centre Party, and in particular exclude the Asquithian Liberals. "Fusion" became the accepted but vague aspiration of the Coalition leaders, and it was generally agreed that an early election would be desirable. There was no opposition at all in the Cabinet except from the taciturn Stanley Baldwin, who had become President of the Board of Trade in the shuffle following on Bonar Law's resignation. But outside the Cabinet powerful forces were mobilising. Sir George Younger, the Chairman of the Conservative Party Organisation, examined carefully a gloomy report from the Principal Agent on the state of morale in the Party, and the growing dissatisfaction with the yoke to the Coalition. The report decided him against an early election, and in a public speech on February 22nd, 1922 he called for an end to the Coalition. Birkenhead's savage immediate rejoinder, in which he called Younger the "cabin boy," strengthened rather than weakened the case against Coalition. To Baldwin's support in Cabinet came Griffith-Boscawen and a hesitant Curzon. No less than seventeen Junior Ministers came to a meeting convened by Leo Amery, then Under-Secretary of State for the Colonies, and attended by Sir Leslie Wilson, the Chief Whip. Here the feeling was all for fighting as a separate Party and for forming a Conservative Government if the election was won. From the Lords, Devonshire, Derby and Salisbury gave weighty support. Most important of all, Bonar Law, now returned to active work in the House, was beginning to bring his formidable guns to bear on the Cabinet. These forces, backed as they were by the party machine, by feeling in the constituencies and by a majority of Conservative Members in the House, were sure to win in the end, however brilliant the leaders against whom they strove. And as 1922 ground on the Tory Party became more and more discontented. Many of them had been deeply uneasy about the Irish Treaty, and came reluctantly (and largely because of Bonar Law's restrained approval) into the Government lobby in December 1921 in its support. There was no peace. The Treaty was denounced in Ireland, and the shootings started again. Field Marshal Sir Henry Wilson was shot dead outside his home in London on June 22nd, and the Government was only saved by the fierce warnings of Winston Churchill to the Irish Government. At home the grubby scandal about the sale of honours hung round the neck of the Government. Abroad the Genoa Conference achieved nothing, and the struggle between Greece and Turkey culminating in the "Chanak" incident stirred deep chords in the Tory Party. Traditionally, with a strong bias towards Turkey, they found Lloyd George's whole-hearted advocacy of the Greek cause at first irritating and then insupportable. And it was Bonar Law's letter to *The Times* on October 6th, with its famous phrase, "We cannot alone act as the policemen of the world," that brought together the fragments of opposition to the Coalition. Lloyd George was determined on an early election. He and Austen Chamberlain decided to confront the rebels. Austen called together the meeting of Conservative M.P.'s and Ministers at the Carlton Club on October 19th. But after long hesitation Bonar Law decided to put himself at the head of the dissidents. By 187 votes to 87 the motion in favour of fighting the General Election as a free independent party was carried. Coalition was dead, and on the same day Lloyd George resigned.

Neville, as has already been noted, was not at this meeting, nor indeed in the country. On September 7th he had left with his wife for a visit to Canada. "Arthur better. Hopes to start earliest possible date" cabled Austen to a mystified Neville on October 4th, explaining in a later letter that "Arthur better" was to be code for a dissolution. However, another telegram announced that "Arthur" had now given up his idea of an early visit, so Neville continued with his tour. And, as usual, an arduous affair it was, packed with public and private meetings, talks with Bennett and Mackenzie King, discussions with everyone he met on every possible subject, all carefully recorded in his letters and his diaries. Canada excited and inspired him, and he loved to hear over and over again the response that his father's name evoked. He would have been well content to stay longer, but another cable from Austen that "Arthur was better again" decided him

86

to make for England. Sailing for home on the *Homeric* Neville tried to record his thoughts as the messages brought the dramatic story of the Carlton Club decision and the subsequent upheaval, Neville was a reluctant Coalitionist, but he had under-estimated the strength of opposition to Lloyd George and was confident that the meeting would uphold Austen. He was "astonished" at the result. Still, on further reflection:

N.C. to Hilda 24.10.1922.

"However, the more I thought of it the more it became clear to me that with no fundamental difference of policy but only of personalities I could not see myself following Ll. G., and that if Austen were out of the question I should have no hesitation in remaining with the Unionists and even, if I were asked, joining the new Government."

Austen was the difficulty, and when, on Neville's arrival at Birmingham, Amery told him that he was commissioned by Bonar Law to offer Neville the office of Postmaster-General it was to Austen that Neville went:

N.C. to Hilda 31.10.1922.

"I went to him as soon as I had the offer and he took the idea very badly, feeling that if I accepted it would be the last drop of bitterness in the cup."

In long talks Neville tried to press the view that if he accepted office he would become a link between Austen and Bonar Law, but Austen would not listen to this argument. Neville then offered to give up the post and with it his political career. This was not advanced either as appeal or as argument, but simply because "I cared more for our personal relations than for politics." But this Austen would not allow and he at once withdrew his opposition, now urging Neville to accept. So it was settled and Neville took up a post of Cabinet rank, although not in the Cabinet, in Bonar Law's administration. He became also a Privy Councillor.

6

IN AND OUT OF OFFICE

(November 1922 – November 1924)

BONAR LAW had little enough talent at his disposal. Under Austen Chamberlain the bulk of the Conservative members of Lloyd George's Coalition Cabinet formed their own cave and waited for the downfall of what they regarded as a Caretaker Government. Curzon, who continued at the Foreign Office, and Baldwin who was put at the Exchequer partly for services rendered in slaying Lloyd George, but principally because there was no other possible candidate, were his chief lieutenants. For the rest he had to make do with an assortment of (mostly diehard) peers and a mixed bag chosen from the Under-Secretaries who had sparked off the revolt. Some of these, Edward Wood and Philip Lloyd-Greame in particular, were men of real ability, but the others were sadly overplaced in a Cabinet. The Prime Minister had, however, outside his Cabinet some men of unproved Parliamentary ability—Neville and the Attorney-General, Douglas Hogg (Hailsham) among them—to whom he looked for reinforcement. Neville was called in to one of the first Cabinets of the new Parliament to discuss a subject that had no possible connection with the Post Office—the refusal of a deputation of hunger marchers to be received by "underlings" in the persons of the Ministers of Health and Labour. Remembering the Lloyd George era, they insisted on being heard by the Prime Minister. Bonar Law felt he should refuse, but his draft letter was obscurely and tentatively worded and the Cabinet decided, with a nervous Minister of Labour, Montagu Barlow, dissenting, that a firmer reply should be sent:

Diary, (undated Dec.) 1922.

"Finally the Lord Chancellor [Cave] and the Attorney-General [Hogg] and I were asked to redraft the letter, which we did (Hogg and I taking the leading part) in such a way as to be perfectly courteous but utterly uncompromising. In the end this firmness had the desired effect."

Bonar Law saw in Neville not only a useful and, perhaps, if he succeeded in his first Ministerial assignment, a formidable colleague, but also the bridge across which Austen and his "Peelites" could march back into the Government. In this he was right although reunion was not to come in his lifetime. From the beginning of his administration he talked privately to Neville, not only about housing but about his anxieties over foreign affairs, and his difficulties with the French over the Ruhr and German Reparations. On foreign affairs this may have been because he hoped to get Austen's views at secondhand, but on housing Bonar Law needed Neville's help. His Minister of Health, Griffith-Boscawen, had been defeated at the General Election and was finding it difficult to secure a seat. He could not be made a peer because the Cabinet, with seven peers out of a membership of sixteen, was already top-heavy. In the end Griffith-Boscawen was adopted for what should have been a safe seat at Mitcham. But the combination of his own unpopular policies of rent de-restriction, and the appearance of an independent "Peelite" candidate unhorsed him. Bonar Law had been considering Neville's position before the by-election took place:

Diary, 26.1.1923.

"The P.M., who was next to me, told me not to go, and after the Cabinet was over he sent for me to his room. Last time I saw him he said he would like to have me in the Cabinet but this was not possible 'unless conditions changed,' which I understood to be an obscure reference to the Min. of Health. He now began by saying G.B. was having much difficulty about his seat and went on to ask what I should think if, supposing G.B. failed, he were to ask Worthington Evans to take the position. He added, 'It would be rough on you because you *ought* to have it.' I said at once that I had already

89

thought over the situation and had fixed on W. E. as the man. I did not want it myself as I wished to 'make good' at the P.O. and I could think of no-one else so suitable. He seemed relieved and said he wished to make sure I should not be hurt. About two days later I had a letter from him asking me to be Paymaster General. . . ."

The addition of this sinecure office to Neville's appointment as P.M.G. was presumably meant as a consolation prize. Neville indeed had good claims on the succession to the Health Ministry; for, apart from his great experience of housing and health, he had been, since the formation of the new Government, a member of the Cabinet Committee on Housing, and was beginning to force his own ideas on the Committee and the Cabinet. But this was Bonar Law's only Cabinet vacancy, and he wished, if he could, to use it to bring back one of the dissident members. After the result at Mitcham was announced, he offered the post not to Worthington Evans but to Sir Robert Horne, who of all Austen's followers had been least critical of the new administration. But this was not a time to attract recruits to man what seemed to be a sinking ship and Horne, after consulting his friends, refused. Bonar Law at once offered the Ministry to Neville. Neville would only take the job on his own terms. Two junior Ministers who had lost their seats at the General Election failed, like Boscawen, and for the same reasons, to win their by-elections at Liverpool and Willesden. Neville asked if he was assured of a free hand over housing and in particular if he could review and, if he so decided, reverse the Government's policy over decontrol. Bonar Law agreed, and the assurance asked for and given was incorporated—most unusually—in the announcement of the appointment.

Neville inherited a thicket of Housing and Rent measures. The two most important were the Housing Bill and the controversial Rent Restriction Bill, about which the Cabinet were completely divided. Something had to be done urgently about rent restriction, for the parent Act was due to expire in a few weeks. Neville bought a little time for the Cabinet to consider its position by pushing through a temporary measure extending the principal Act until July 31st. Some of the Cabinet wanted to damn the consequences of the disastrous by-elections and push ahead with decontrol. Others more prudently wanted to forget their more ambitious plans and have a standstill for a period of two or three years. The Party, shaken by the fierce reaction to Griffith-Boscawen's ideas, was firmly for doing little or nothing. So the "No" Lobby in the Cabinet won, as indeed it nearly always does. Neville's Bill, when he introduced it after Whitsun, was inevitably a compromise. Part I of the Bill continued the present Act more or less intact for a further period of two years. The permitted increases of rent were to remain. But Neville's ideas for Part II of the Bill, dealing with the future of rent restriction, produced strong reactions from his own party. These clauses were to come into effect in two years' time and provided for safeguards during what was planned to be a five-year period of decontrol. Neville's proposals, as outlined in his speech on Second Reading, have a very modern air about them:

N.C. Hansard, 6.6.1923, Col. 2230.

"Before he can get possession of the house he will have to go to Court, and if the Court is of opinion that the proceedings are harsh or oppressive, or even that it would inflict an exceptional hardship upon the tenant . . . then the Court may refuse to make such an order or may suspend the order for a sufficient time to give the tenant reasonable opportunity of looking round for some alternative accommodation."

And again:

N.C. Hansard, 6.6.1923, Col. 2234.

"The tenant, in future, will be able to go to the Sanitary authority and get from them a certificate, if it is justified, that his house is not in a reasonable state of repair. That certificate will state what repairs are required to put the house into reasonable repair, and then the tenant can go to Court and if the Court is satisfied . . . that the house is not in proper repair and that the condition of the house is not due to the fault of the tenant the Court can reduce the rent—and hon. Members will observe that there is no limitation of the amount of reduction that can be made—until the repairs are properly carried out."

These provisions were just acceptable to the Conservative Party then, but Neville went on to propose the establishment of Reference Committees which were to help the County Court and which clearly foreshadowed Rent Tribunals. Sir Kingsley Wood led an attack on this novel idea, but Neville, by an adroit and meaningless concession on the Report Stage, preserved his Bill and saw it on to the Statute Book before the summer recess.

It was easier, if still controversial, to legislate on housing, and Neville was familiar with the Government plans. He had persuaded Bonar Law and the Cabinet before he became Minister that a policy of subsidy was essential. Neville, faithful to his local authority background, would gladly have seen the main burden thrust on to the municipalities, but the Cabinet wanted also a Bill that "made a noise like private enterprise". So the Bill which he introduced on Second Reading on April 24th, 1923 gave what was then the large subsidy of £6 a year for twenty years to private builders, and to local authorities who were able to submit acceptable plans. The houses had to be completed before October 1925 and there was a severe limitation on size.

The subsidy was to be concentrated on what was called the "non-parlour" house and Neville was attacked for trying to lower the standards of the working people by leaving children no room to study in, and sweethearts no place to court. Nor was Neville's defence on Second Reading well judged when he tried to show that a "parlour" (10 feet 6 inches by 9 feet 3 inches) could be provided within the limits of a subsidised house. His real argument was, of course, that only by concentrating the subsidy on the cheaper house would houses for the working class be built at all, especially by private enterprise.

Criticism centred almost wholly on the size of the house, with the Clydeside Members loud in their wrath, and the two days debate ending with the closure having to be moved by Neville in the middle of one of those fierce and often absurd Parliamentary gales that blow up from nowhere—centring this time on who, if anyone, called Mr. Sidney Webb "Nannygoat" when he rose to interrupt. When this had been sorted out the Labour Party and some of the Liberals voted against the Bill, John Simon and his followers abstaining. The Bill had a swift passage to the Statute Book and an unopposed Third Reading in June, although it was, in fact, little altered in Committee. Ramsay MacDonald could find no more convincing argument to justify this than that when the Bill started its journey the subsidy limit was to be "up to £6" and now the amount was fixed at £6. The real point was, of course, that he was not sure if the Bill would or would not produce any large number of houses. Nor was Neville, who only regarded this as a first step in housing legislation, and was well aware of the limitations of his proposal. Yet it was in the end remarkably successful.

By February 1924 Wheatley, the Socialist Minister of Health, announced that some 98,000 approvals had been given under the Act, two-thirds of them to private enterprise. Approvals are often an inflated figure in relation to later actual completions, but there can be no doubt that there was a swift response to Neville's Act, and that Ramsay MacDonald's cagey decision not to record a Third Reading vote against it was wise.

In these months it became clear that Bonar Law was tired and ill, though no one suspected that the lost voice which forced him to take a holiday in April was due to cancer of the throat. From it he returned only to resign. In the drama of Baldwin's succession Neville had no part. Indeed at first he "rather hoped Curzon would be P.M." although he recognised the strength of feeling against him in the House of Commons and the country. Neville had a long interview with the new Prime Minister the day after the appointment was announced. Neville found him "in excellent spirits and very pleased with himself". He confirmed Neville as Minister of Health and, wisely in view of the load of work, offered him Lord Eustace Percy as Parliamentary Secretary in the Commons instead of Lord Onslow in the Lords. He went on to gossip about Austen and the prospects of reunion. His idea was to strengthen the Cabinet by making Horne Chancellor of the Exchequer, Austen Lord Privy Seal and Lord Robert Cecil Chancellor of the Duchy of Lancaster. Neville's Diary finishes on an authentic "Baldwin" note:

Diary, 23.5.1923.

". . . S.B. seemed in good spirits. He declared himself by no means overwhelmed by his responsibilities. He was convinced something must be done to get a move on in Europe—we could not go on drifting. As to domestic politics, we could not think about them till we had got thro' the next nine weeks. We should not have time. He was going to the theatre tonight!"

The plans for Reunion fell through, largely due to Baldwin's clumsy handling of Austen. When Austen refused the Privy Seal Baldwin then offered the Washington Embassy: adding the engaging observation that as he (Baldwin) was a comparatively young man and now blocked the way, Austen might like to take something outside politics. Austen refused angrily and Baldwin then devised a scheme which involved dropping the Duke of Devonshire, who was willing to go out if his place was required, and putting Horne at the Colonial Office and Austen at the Treasury. At this point the opposition from other members of the administration to the ex-Ministers began to crystallise into threats of resignation. Baldwin's interviews with Austen had been exhausting affairs, and he was content to have a good excuse for dropping the negotiations. Devonshire remained at the Colonial Office, Lord Robert Cecil took the Privy Seal, and Reunion had failed again. Neville reproached Baldwin for his clumsiness with Austen and asked the Prime Minister if he would allow him to be of service if he wished to approach Austen again. Baldwin admitted he had been tactless, apologised and changed the subject. But next time he did use Neville. And next time he succeeded.

All this left Baldwin without a Chancellor, and for the time being he carried on himself, bringing his Financial Secretary (Joynson Hicks) into the Cabinet. The Treasury was next offered to McKenna, but his health was indifferent and there arose again the question of finding a safe seat. No Conservative was likely to rush to offer his place to a Liberal free-trader who had in fact left politics, and when the House rose on August 2nd the problem remained unsolved. Neville had spent a short holiday with his family in Wales and then, via Birmingham, had left for Scotland to fish.

N.C. to Ida 20.8.1923.

"On Thursday I received a letter (I need not emphasise the confidential nature of this) from the P.M. saying he wanted me to go to the Exchequer! It was in very complimentary terms saying how reluctant he was to move me but the Treasury was of vital importance and I was the 'one man' to whom he felt he could entrust it safely.

"I suppose he considers that to give it to Jix would be such rapid promotion that other senior members wouldn't like it. On the other hand, I imagine that for some reason he doesn't want to give it to Amery. Worthy has lost caste and who else is there? I have written to decline but can see that he may return to the charge and press so hard as to make it very difficult to hold out. And yet I believe it would be a mistake to accept. I should be a fish out of water. I know nothing of finance; I like spending money much better than saving it; I hate blocking other people's schemes and—I only thought of this after I had written—I shall have to live in Downing St. instead of Eaton Square."

Baldwin, who had had enough of being Chancellor himself and was determined to find a new one before he left at the week-end for his annual holiday at Aix, promptly wired back pressing for reconsideration and asking for a wire in reply. Neville decided that this could hardly be argued at long range, abandoned his holiday and took the sleeper to London.

Diary, 24.8.1923.

"At 10.30 had long interview at Downing Street. The P.M. brushed aside all objections on grounds of inexperience, and we went through all possible alternatives. All were rejected excepted Jix, but S.B. said he wanted a colleague in No. 11 whose judgment he could trust and someone to lead the House in his absence, and he would rather have me than anyone. Jix would be received in the City but I should be welcomed, and McKenna himself has suggested my name. The King had approved it and so had Curzon."

For the third time Neville was offered a post which other men had refused. He was as reluctant to take the Treasury as he had been several years before to become Director of National Service. But—

N.C. to Hilda 26.8.1923.

"I could not consistently with ordinary (not Austen's standard of) loyalty to my chief refuse to stand by him when he appealed in that way. I went back and after consultation with Annie I returned in the afternoon and told the P.M. that I was very miserable but that I was going to accede to his wishes. And he said I had taken a load off his mind."

95

Baldwin then departed cheerfully to Aix for his cure, and Neville less cheerfully to Harrogate for his. The appointment was a popular one.

Neville had had a remarkable year. In twelve months he had travelled from being a Coalition backbencher via the Post Office, Paymaster General's Office and Ministry of Health to the Treasury. It seemed at last that he was to have some security of tenure. The Government had a contented docile majority of about 80 in the House, a new and popular Prime Minister, a fragmented Opposition, and four more years of power. But this serene prospect did not last, and his new appointment proved as temporary as the others. Neville, during this period at the Treasury, hardly had a chance to meet the House of Commons, let alone bring in a Budget. On October 2nd he moved into No. 11. On the 5th he went to Chequers:

N.C. to Hilda 7.10.1923.

"I find the P.M. very seriously considering the party policy and disposed to go a long way in the direction of new duties with preference designed to help the Dominions and to develop Empire sugar, cotton and tobacco, all of which we now have to buy from U.S.A. I need hardly say that I warmly welcome this disposition and believe it will be the salvation of the country and incidentally of the party. We are to some extent hampered by the 'pledge' which in my view debars us from food taxes but not from the extension of the McKenna duties. Look out for B's speech to the Party Conference on October 25th."

The Prime Minister's speech at Plymouth on October 25th declared flatly that he could not fight the growing menace of unemployment unless the home market was protected. The meeting was delighted, but the more the words of the speech were studied the more worried the Conservative Party became. For some the vague phrases did not go far enough, for others they seemed full of menace. Salisbury called together Devonshire, Novar, Lord Robert Cecil and Edward Wood. None of them had been consulted while the Plymouth speech was being planned—Baldwin's confidants were limited in the Cabinet to Amery, Lloyd-Greame and Neville—and they were agreed in advising against an early election. The assurances they received from Baldwin satisfied them,

Neville Chamberlain
as a child . . .

. . . and as a youth, aged
eighteen

A family group at Highbury in 1889. *Back row, left to right*, Ethel, Hilda, Beatrice, Mr. Endicott, Ida. *Front row*, Neville, Mrs. Endicott, Mrs. Joe Chamberlain

Speaking as Lord Mayor to the T.U.C. in 1916

although the words were far from clear. In the end there were no resignations, and in consequence no places for Austen and Birkenhead. But an early election could not be avoided. Bonar Law's pledge had been too specific.

Rt. Hon. Andrew Bonar Law, M.P. 7.11.1922.

"I speak as the leader of the Party which is fighting this Election. What I say must be binding, not only on me but on my successors if I should not be there . . . this Parliament will not make any fundamental change in the fiscal system of this country."

So the House of Commons met on November 13th and the Prime Minister announced that it would be prorogued on the 16th. There was time only to hustle the Workmen's Compensation Bill through all its stages, to hold a rehearsal for the hustings in the shape of a Labour motion of censure on Unemployment, and to bring the Parliament to an end.

Many years later Baldwin used to explain that he had two motives for an action that seemed to almost everyone at the time, in Lloyd George's words in the Censure debate, "ill-considered, precipitate, ill-thought-out and foolish". But in this outburst there may have been an element of sour grapes, for one of the reasons Baldwin later gave was to "dish the Goat"; Lloyd George was on his way back from his tour of North America, and it was believed (and probably correctly) that he was going to advocate a wide extension of protection at home. This is credible, and here Baldwin was wholly successful; at the price, it is true, of reuniting the Liberal party. But the Liberal party, whether united or in disarray, could not long survive unless one of the great parties that flanked it were to be weakened disastrously. His second reason that his speech was part of a carefully laid scheme to reunite the Party and that the election was a "long calculated and not a sudden dissolution" cannot stand up to examination. In the Censure Motion on November 15th Sir John Simon argued convincingly that up till the time the House rose for the summer recess the Prime Minister's speeches and letters showed that he was still following orthodox paths in the search for a lasting cure for unemployment. On August 3rd to the Industrial Group in the House he had written, "The object of the Government is to improve employment by

assisting and facilitating the normal flow of trade." And it passes
belief that even Baldwin's inconsequent mind could have thought
of a Liberal free-trader, McKenna, for his Chancellor of the Exchequer if the idea of a policy based on Tariff Reform had even
begun to occur to him. Nor surely would he have left his new
Chancellor, Neville, who of course would be warmly in his support, completely in the dark about his ideas in the weeks in which
Neville was beginning to settle in to his work at the Treasury.
Yet somewhere on the road to Plymouth Baldwin was converted.
And it was surely the Imperial Conference and its linked Imperial
Economic Conference opening in London on October 1st and
2nd that pushed the idea from the back of the Prime Minister's
mind to the front. The opening speech by Lloyd-Greame to the
Economic Conference contained no hint of a change in policy.
There followed speeches from Smuts and the Australian Prime
Minister Bruce which began to focus attention on the need for
mutual protection. On October 4th Smuts saw the Prime Minister. This seems to have been the moment of decision. Certainly
from that date the Prime Minister moved with unaccustomed
speed. He saw Neville on the 5th and Amery (the High Priest of
Protection) on the 8th. Also on the 8th he warned Stanley Jack-
son, the Chairman of the Party, that an early election on a policy
of general protection might become necessary. Amery and Lloyd-
Greame were called to Chequers to help in the preparation of the
Plymouth speech. It is strange and yet typical of Baldwin that in
spite of this flurry of activity he made little or no effort to carry
the rest of the Cabinet with him. The only other colleague he told
of his plans was Derby, who was loyally in support but gloomy
about the reception the new proposals would get in Lancashire.
In this Derby was right, for at the coming Election much of
Lancashire went Liberal. Not till October 23rd did the Prime
Minister inform the full Cabinet of what he proposed to say.
Curzon and the Salisbury camp objected, and Worthington
Evans and other members came down, not against the policy, but
against the early election which it seemed to make inevitable.
Only Baldwin's three protectionist musketeers were firmly in
support. But Baldwin was determined at last, and of course he had
his way. Neville worked with him on the final drafts of his speech

and they went down to Plymouth together, where Neville spoke to a large overflow meeting. And so the die was cast.

The election produced a fascinating and complex position in the House of Commons. Even though they were still (258) easily the largest party and their total poll fell only by 75,000, the Conservatives had clearly "lost" the Election. But who had won? The Socialists with 191? Or the Liberals with 158? Or a Coalition? And if so between which parties or which men?

Almost everyone had a different solution. Perhaps Balfour, as an elder statesman, should be called on to save the state. Or Baldwin and Asquith. Or Derby and Asquith. Or Austen and Asquith. Anything, any combination to stop the "Reds". For the fear of the Socialist Party was then very real. They were regarded by the establishment as a revolutionary party, and the wilder speeches of their wilder men were taken as proof. But almost all the frenzied schemers for a partnership or understanding with the Liberals assumed that Asquith shared their anxiety. He did not. There were, so it seemed to him, unanswerable arguments for installing Ramsay MacDonald as Prime Minister, as the head of the second largest party in the House of Commons, once a combined Labour-Liberal vote had overthrown Baldwin. And if in due course—as would surely happen—the Socialists in their turn were defeated, there was still no need for a dissolution: the Crown could then turn to the Liberal party. So Asquith reasoned. Baldwin and Neville had come to a subtler conclusion. By all means let the Liberals carry the odium of installing the Socialists in power. Not all the Liberal Party would be able so swiftly to swallow their election speeches. Winston Churchill for one. He had been defeated in Leicester by Pethick-Lawrence, and Asquith's decision caused him to turn his back on the Liberal Party. Writing that "the enthronement in office of a Socialist government will be a serious national misfortune such as has usually befallen states only on the morrow of defeat in war", Churchill began to look to the Conservative Party as the only possible alternative to the Socialists. Churchill was not in the House for the moment, but among the Liberals some were sure to share his views, and support Baldwin in the lobby. So there was everything to be said for meeting Parliament in January, and taking the verdict of the House at the end of the Debate on the

Address. In the Party, and even in the Cabinet, the first rumbles of the "Baldwin must go" campaign, which was to flare intermittently over the next dozen years, were heard. But they soon died away, for there was no-one the malcontents could think of to put in Baldwin's place. The Government turned to the pleasantly irresponsible task of composing a programme of legislation that they knew they would not have to carry through. Not surprisingly, Neville, who took the leading part in its composition, noted:

Diary, 13.1.1924.
"It has been an arduous job keeping some of my colleagues in order, and preventing them turning it into an election manifesto."

The Debate opened on January 15th, and on the third day Clynes moved the Labour motion of No Confidence as an amendment. Asquith, in a speech described (justly) by Neville in his diary as "the speech of his life", at once made it clear that he would support the Socialists. It was indeed a noble speech, but for those with eyes to see and ears to hear it was bound to mean the end of the Liberal Party. No-one saw this more clearly than Austen, who had always hankered after a centre party, and now turned on Asquith with a speech that at once showed his angry dismay, and made possible the reunion of himself and his followers with Baldwin. To great acclaim from the Conservative Party he ended with these savagely prophetic words:

Rt. Hon. Austen Chamberlain, M.P. Hansard 21.1.1924.
"He has taken his choice, and he has by that choice constituted his own immortality. He will go down to history as the last Prime Minister of a Liberal Administration. He has sung the swan song of the Liberal Party. When next the country is called upon for a decision, if it wants a Socialist Government it will vote for a Socialist; if it does not want a Socialist Government it will vote for a Unionist. It will not vote again for those who denatured its mandate and betrayed its trust."

Asquith had decided, and the Socialists were to govern. But his approval was carefully guarded. "We of the Liberal Party," he said, "are deeply and sincerely pledged to give no more countenance to Socialist experiments than to a protectionist experiment." The Socialists were to be allowed to be a Government provided they did not behave like Socialists. Earl Attlee (he became Under-Secretary of State for War) argued in his memoirs that the Socialists were right to take office on these terms on the grounds that the people, if they were to accept that Labour was the alternative to the Conservatives, must see a Labour administration in action.[1] I do not think the argument is sound. As it was, the Labour Government failed quickly and shabbily, and it was over twenty years before the Labour Party was returned with a working majority in the House of Commons. It is hard to believe that it would have been so long if they had refused to exist on Liberal sufferance, and had insisted on, been defeated on, and then appealed to the country on a more robust Socialist programme.

In the end then the Conservatives came best out of the long debate which ended, of course, in their defeat in the lobby. On the last day both Baldwin and Hogg made excellently gay fighting speeches. More important still, ten Liberals came into the Conservative lobby. The decline and fall of the Liberal Party had begun.

Before the election Asquith had gibed that Baldwin's one achievement was to reunite the Liberal Party. But Asquith's speech in the Motion on the Address and Austen's retort to it had created an opportunity at last to cement the Conservatives. Neville set to work. His diary records meetings with Edward Wood, Salisbury, Jix, Hoare and Monsell before he went on to tackle the Prime Minister. The difficulty lay not in accepting Austen, Horne and Balfour, but in joining hands again with Birkenhead. His Rectorial address to Glasgow University offended the moderates and the party managers, his way of life offended the moralists, his brilliance offended the mediocrities. Together they were a formidable lobby. Patiently Neville stuck to his thesis—"better F.E. in than Austen out". He made some progress and when Austen told him that there was a:

Diary, 24.1.1924.

". . . chance of uniting the party but it must be on the condition of all or none. I replied that I was working like a beaver to that end and was hopeful of success."

[1] C. R. Attlee, *As It Happened* (Heinemann, 1954), p. 60.

Neville left for a short holiday with his wife at Wengen, a holiday only made possible by the timely generosity of his sisters, for two General Elections in a year had strained his reserves. As soon as he returned Baldwin summoned him. He had had "a sticky letter" from Salisbury, a fierce one from Lord Robert Cecil, and an uncompromising one from Ormsby-Gore.

Diary, 4.2.1924.

"S.B. said he had not written to A. as he did not wish to do anything without me, but he appeared disposed to go on with reunion and suggested a dinner for the three of us at the Atheneum. I said better dine with me, then no-one will know anything about it and this he agreed to. I then said, 'Will you allow me to suggest how you should go about this? Don't ask A. any questions and don't suggest that there is any doubt about F.E. or that you have to consult anyone. Say *I* have decided to ask you *and your friends* to sit with us on the front bench and to invite you to join our councils on just the same footing as if you had been members of the late Cabinet.' I went on, 'If you deal with A. in this way I think it will be all right, but if you show the slightest hesitation he will say, S.B. doesn't know his own mind and he is only playing with me.' S.B. listened very attentively to my suggestions but as usual only observed that he thought those were the right lines, and I remained not quite certain how far he would adopt them."

But all was to be well:

Diary, 6.2.1924.

". . . and in the evening the famous dinner came off. Annie came for dinner, which passed off with general conversation. When she left I suggested we should get to business and invited S.B. to make his statement. To my great satisfaction he took exactly the line I had suggested. A. looked a little stiff and suspicious, but after a moment's thought frankly said he could do nothing but accept. He had, he said, discussed with F.E. the line they should take in the event of such an offer and F.E. had said he would accept, so that he really could speak for him also, and the conversation then turned with gradually increasing cordiality to the two questions of leadership and policy."

Next day the ex-Ministers attended a meeting of the Shadow Cabinet. Baldwin, making no reference at all to the presence of Austen or his followers, opened a discussion on the line to be taken at the party meeting on the 11th. There was little now to discuss. Baldwin's popularity had grown, not diminished with the unpredictable British public, and all his possible rivals were now his followers. The idea of a General Tariff was to be dropped for the moment, and only Leo Amery protested. The country was to be educated up to the point when Tariff Reform could again be paraded, and the task of education was given to Neville and Amery. The rebellious murmurs were stilled or stillborn and the party meeting proved uneventful. Reunion was complete.

Although Reunion had been primarily Neville's achievement, its immediate effect was to bring into the Shadow Cabinet several colleagues more senior than he. In particular, there were now three ex-Chancellors, Baldwin, Austen and Sir Robert Horne, to share with Neville the leadership in financial debates.

With nearly all the leading members of Baldwin's Cabinet, Curzon, Derby, Salisbury and Devonshire, in the Lords, Neville at the Treasury was bound in time to become the acknowledged Second-in-Command. In fact, neither Neville nor any of his obvious rivals went to the Treasury when Baldwin formed his next Government. Winston Churchill, the unconsidered outsider who eventually won the race, rocked the Conservative Party by running the official candidate to a desperate short-head finish in the Abbey By-Election in March. Churchill stood against Colonel Otho Nicholson in the guise of an Anti-Socialist Constitutionalist candidate and then, honour satisfied, completed his chassé into the Conservative Party by being adopted in the autumn for the safe seat of Epping. But this was in the future. For the moment the Conservatives had to organise their opposition to the new Socialist Government. The fiercest parliamentary battles were sure to be on Housing and Rent Control, especially with John Wheatley, the able militant Clydesider, at the Ministry of Health. Neville played some part in the debates on the Finance Bill, but he was more than content to leave Finance to his more experienced colleagues and concentrate his energies on the Housing debates.

In Wheatley, Neville had a worthy adversary. The Socialist Government could not hope to secure Liberal support for a radical financial policy, but on housing they felt they could be more adventurous. Wheatley was the ablest of their departmental ministers, and planned an ambitious programme of housing reform. He was fierce and formidable in debate, cool and clear in exposition. His programme was for a Rent Restriction Bill (to be introduced as a Private Member's Bill) a Housing Bill, a Rent and Mortgage Bill and a Bill to control the cost and supply of Building Materials. Neville rubbed his hands and sailed into the attack. The Rent Restriction Bill was given a Second Reading in February and was duly strangled in Committee upstairs after a long and sustained filibuster. No time could be found for the Bill on building materials which had to be postponed to the autumn, and so never reached a Second Reading. The real fight was over the Rent and Mortgage Bill, which came up for Second Reading on April 2nd. Clause I proposed that if arrears of rent were due to unemployment the Court could authorise the tenant to withhold the rent unless the landlord could prove that he would thereby suffer the greater hardship. This impossible proposition was torn to pieces by Neville. "A surrender to an ultimatum from the Clyde" he called it, and Maxton and his merry men cheered in agreement. And why, went on Neville, should this admirable principle be confined to housing? If a man was more in need than the butcher, the baker or the candlestick maker, had he not, on the same logic, a pre-emptive right to their goods? If an unemployed man were coatless, had he not a right to the Minister of Health's coat? And if a landlord were also a tenant, could he refuse to pay his rent, if he had been deprived of his income? And who, under these circumstances, would ever willingly let his house again? There was no more to be said. Asquith followed and announced that the Liberals could not support Clause I. The other clauses were unimportant and uncontroversial. So in effect the Socialists could either withdraw the clause or lose the Bill. Clynes intervened to try to save the principle of the clause, promising to bring forward an amendment which would place on public funds the cost of maintaining the tenant in his home. But when the Prime Minister, after a week-end's thought, produced the new amendment, no one could understand it, and Ramsay MacDonald, who clearly couldn't understand it himself, gave up the effort to explain. The division on Second Reading was carried against the Government, and although the Prime Minister, straining to the limit his declaration on taking office that he would not resign unless defeated on a major issue, decided to ignore the decision, the sands were beginning to run out for the Socialist Government.

It was the second defeat within a few days; for on April 2nd, following on the adjourned debate on the Rent and Mortgage Bill, Neville had concluded a good day's work by winding up a short debate condemning the Capital Levy, then the favourite nostrum of the Socialist Party. The words of the Conservative Motion were copied from the Liberal Party Election manifesto, and even Liberal ingenuity could find no way of supporting the Government.

Wheatley's Housing Bill put Neville in something of a dilemma. Instead of scrapping the 1923 Act, Wheatley proposed to extend it for fifteen years. The size of the houses—"rabbit hutches" the Socialists had called them—remained the same as under Neville's Act. Wheatley's main proposal was in the amount of the subsidy. There were to be two schemes. A subsidy, as in the 1923 Act, of £6 a year for forty years on houses built for sale, and a subsidy of £13 10s. a year (£17 in rural areas) for houses built to let. This was Wheatley's attempt to overcome the admitted weakness of the 1923 Act—that it would not produce houses to let, and would make little impact on building in the rural areas and in Scotland (where private enterprise was notoriously unenterprising in the provision of homes). Neville felt that this would lead to a scramble for labour and materials which would force prices up. Because the liability of both the Exchequer and the local authority was fixed under the Wheatley proposals the tenant would have to bear the increase. Neville's instinct was not to oppose the Bill, although he was ready to prophesy disaster for it, but his view did not prevail and the Conservative Party opposed the Bill at all stages.

It was not only in Parliament that 1924 was a busy year for Neville. His constituency, Ladywood, was under fierce concentrated attack from the Socialists, who had adopted Oswald Mosley as their candidate. Even if the Unionist organisation was the better and his own popularity and that of his wife were telling factors, it seemed impossible to him to hold on to Ladywood much longer. He had a chance to move to the safe fortress of Edgbaston, but concluded that he could not leave before he had fought the General

Election, which in the unbalanced state of the parties in the House could not be long delayed. But it meant a good deal of time—given gladly—spent in Birmingham, and he was busy once more with his well-loved interests of the City Orchestra, the Municipal Bank and the local voluntary hospitals. Birmingham he used also as a proving ground for some of his new ideas on social policy, for he was already playing in the Conservative Party a role similar to that of R. A. Butler in the years following 1945. So we find him expounding his theories on a new approach to National Insurance at a P.S.A. meeting in February and at a meeting of the Ancient Order of Foresters. When he was satisfied, he persuaded the Prime Minister to outline his plan:

N.C. to Hilda 22.3.1924.

"S.B. has gone up to Edinburgh with my notes on insurance and means I believe to stick pretty closely to my draft, which lays down four essentials for a satisfactory scheme. (1) It must be contributory. (2) It must be compulsory. (3) It must cover the four main needs for security, unemployment, sickness, old age and death leaving widow and dependants. (4) The provision for old age must offer sufficient to induce the old men to retire. We have now appointed a Committee with myself as Chairman to go into details. . . . I am hopeful that Stanley's words will attract wide attention and peg out our claim to the ground before the others have had time to get in."

Neville and Amery created at this time the first policy secretariat of the Party. Although it was hastily and improvidently abandoned after the General Election victory in the autumn, it was rebuilt under Neville's chairmanship in 1929 and has since, whether the party was in or out of office, been an integral part of its working. In June came "Aims and Principles", a policy statement drafted by Neville, which expounded and expanded the themes of Baldwin's Albert Hall programme. The Conservatives were now the only united party, and the only one with a coherent programme. All they wanted was a General Election. They had not long to wait.

The first Labour Government did not fall because of the Russian Treaty, or because of their failure to deal with unemployment, or even because of the Campbell case. They fell because the Liberals had wearied of giving them support. However constitutionally impeccable Asquith's decision to give the Socialists their opportunity may have been, it was having, as Austen had foreseen, a disastrous effect on Liberal morale. If the Socialists achieved anything—and Ramsay MacDonald had some success in foreign affairs—the Liberals got no credit for it. Where the Socialists failed, the Liberals shared the odium. If it had been necessary to discover an issue on which the Liberals could break away from the Government they would have discovered one. They had no such problem, for the Socialists thoughtfully provided not one but two perfect alibis, and on the same day. For months an Anglo-Russian Conference had plodded on with desultory conversations in London. An undertaking was given by the Prime Minister in June that the British Government would not back a loan to Russia. "Only credulous people," he said, "will believe that." On August 5th the talks broke down and were promptly re-started. On August 7th, the day Parliament rose for the recess, a treaty was signed which pledged the Government to ask Parliament to guarantee a Russian loan. It was also on August 5th that John Ross Campbell, acting Editor of the *Workers' Weekly*, was charged with publishing articles inciting the services to mutiny. He was remanded. When he appeared a week later the charge was withdrawn and the *Workers' Weekly* promptly proclaimed that the Government had been forced to yield to its own backbenchers. Either of these episodes provided excellent grounds for divorce, and the Liberal leaders lost no time in framing their case. The Tories were naturally even more pleased and put down a weighty Motion of Censure (drafted for them, as Neville's diary shows, by Sir John Simon) on the Government's handling of the Campbell case to be debated as soon as the House reassembled on September 30th. For a time it looked as if the Government would still escape. The Liberals, although they longed to be free of the Socialists, had no enthusiasm for the Conservatives, and the Government made clear that on an adverse motion being passed they would resign. So a weak Liberal motion for a Committee of Inquiry was tabled, and Ramsay MacDonald was offered an escape hatch by Asquith. He did not use it. Perhaps he feared the investigation, perhaps he preferred a General Election to a debate on the Russian Treaty. Whatever his motives, the

Prime Minister rejected both motions. Baldwin withdrew his Censure Motion, which would not now attract Liberal support, and led his troops into the Liberal Lobby. The motion, of course, was carried overwhelmingly, and the first Socialist Government fell.

The General Election could scarcely have been fought on ground less favourable to the Socialists and Liberals, nor more favourable to the Conservatives. The Government, for all their high promises, had been unable to cure or to contain unemployment. Already suspect of hankering after extreme policies, they were now accused of surrender to their left wing over the Russian loan and over the Campbell case.

The Conservatives were more popular and the Liberals less popular than they deserved. So a Conservative victory could be safely predicted, but it was much less certain that Neville could hold the poverty-stricken Ladywood constituency against Mosley's flamboyant challenge. Indeed, he would surely have been defeated but for the help of two strange allies—rain and Mr. Zinovieff. On Polling Day Neville had the weather all good Tories pray for: a fine day with rain setting in in the evening, and building up to a downpour in the last two hours before the Poll, when the Socialist vote is always at its heaviest.

Then Neville was helped by the Strange Affair of the Red Letter. Early in October the Foreign Office obtained a copy of a letter purporting to come from Zinovieff, Head of the Comintern. It was addressed to the British Communist Party and contained not very formidable instructions for subversive activities. On Saturday, October 25th, the letter and a Foreign Office note on it was published. The knowledge that the *Daily Mail* had a copy of the letter and intended to publish it forced the Foreign Office's hand, but someone blundered and the Prime Minister, although he had redrafted the note, did not know of the intention to publish until he read the letter and the note in the papers. They created, of course, an immense sensation. "Forgery!" howled the Socialists as soon as they had recovered their breath. Probably the letter was genuine, but the point for the moment was academic since its authenticity or otherwise could not be established before Polling Day on the following Wednesday. What is certain is that it sank the waterlogged Socialist ship. But even if the impact had been marginal it was beyond price to Neville, for at Ladywood four recounts were needed to settle the election. First he was returned by 30. Then by 15, then by 7, then out by 2, and finally in by 77 at 4.30 a.m.

Birmingham had done badly. All the majorities were reduced and Sir Herbert Austin's seat was lost. But the General Election was a Tory triumph. Four hundred and thirteen strong they came back to Westminster. The Socialists, although polling a million more votes, had only 151 seats, and the Liberals were swept away. Only a remnant of forty were returned under the uneasy leadership of Lloyd George and Simon: Asquith, even without a Conservative opponent, was defeated at Paisley. The two-party system had returned.

But Neville wisely saw the dangers of the situation:

N.C. to Ida 1.11.1924.

"What alarms me now is the size of our majority, which is most dangerous . . . unless we leave our mark as Social Reformers the country will take it out of us hereafter, but what we do will depend on how the Cabinet is made up. Poor S.B.!"

It was for this reason that Neville, in the same letter, declared that if given the choice he would prefer to return to the Ministry of Health rather than to the Treasury.

7

MINISTER OF HEALTH

(1924 – 1929)

IF Bonar Law had too few, Baldwin had too many candidates for senior office. The result was a strong but unwieldy Cabinet of twenty-one members. Even to achieve this figure Baldwin had to disappoint a number of those who hoped for high office. Curzon, after a short and tearful interview, was shunted into the Lord Presidency, and the Foreign Office given to Austen Chamberlain. Peers who might well have been included, Balfour, Devonshire, Derby, were not even interviewed. Sir Robert Horne was offered the Ministry of Labour and Baldwin apparently "forgot" to tell him that the Ministry, then of secondary status, was to be upgraded. Horne refused angrily and stayed outside the administration. Baldwin's senior colleagues were very upset about this: Baldwin, one suspects, was not. He may indeed have contrived it.

There remained the Exchequer. Clearly Chamberlain had first refusal of it.

Diary, (undated. ? 5.) 11.1924.

"To-day at S.B.'s request I went to see him at Palace Chambers at 3 p.m. He began by saying, needless to say I want you to go back to the Treasury. I made no comment and he went on to say that he had offered Horne the Ministry of Labour and was awaiting his reply. Horne was not as well thought of in the city as he imagined. At this moment a letter was brought in from Horne and S.B. read it and said, 'He won't take it.' . . . He said he had decided to take Winston in at once—'He would be more under control inside than out'—

and he thought of putting him at Health. He then asked me what I should like and I said I had given the matter full consideration and would like to go back to Health. But who then could be Chancellor, he asked. I enquired whether he had thought of S. Hoare. He said No, and I concluded the idea did not appeal to him. He mentioned Winston but said he supposed there would be a howl from the party. I said I thought there would but that would be so if he came in at all, and I did not know if it would be much louder if he went to the Treasury than to the Admiralty. On the whole I was inclined to say that W. for the Treasury was worth further consideration. We then discussed a good many other posts and I suggested Steel-Maitland for Labour and the Duchess of Atholl as Under-Secretary for Education. Both these suggestions seemed to appeal to him. Presently he said he had another visitor. . . ."

Chamberlain was led out of Palace Chambers by devious means so that he should not meet this next visitor, but the stratagem was spoiled by the sight of Churchill's unmistakeable hat outside the waiting room. Promptly Baldwin offered the Treasury to Churchill, who accepted.

Puzzling over this episode, Chamberlain concluded that the Prime Minister had spoken to Austen who had told him that his brother would prefer to return to Health. Accordingly Baldwin had stage-managed the small drama. But Austen denied this and a later conversation at Chequers with Baldwin convinced Chamberlain that the offer to him of the Treasury had been a genuine one. Chamberlain's reflection in his diary was that the solution "was a much better one than the reversal of our seats". With Chamberlain's incomparable knowledge of all the thousand responsibilities brooded over by the Ministry of Health, the comment seems obvious enough. And yet perhaps the original plan would have been the better. The Treasury was the only one of the many offices that Churchill held that he did not adorn. Indeed his tenure of it was disastrous for the Tory party. "The combination of deflation and free imports which he stubbornly maintained bore its immediate fruit in wage reductions, long-drawn industrial conflict and continuous heavy unemployment; its long-term results in the conviction of the working class that Socialism alone could provide a remedy for unemployment. The chief author of a great Prime Minister's defeat in 1945 was the Chancellor of the Exchequer of twenty years before."[1] Amery, of course, was an ardent protectionist and so a prejudiced judge of Churchill's financial policy. Would Chamberlain have done better?

He also would no doubt have made the return to the Gold Standard a feature of his first Budget as Churchill did, for at the time all parties (including the Socialist) had this as their aim, and very few people except Keynes and, in the House, Horne and the young Boothby spoke against the move. It was in any event less the re-establishment of the Gold Standard than the high rate fixed of $4.86 to the £ that was the mistake. Chamberlain would have been at least as urgent in pressing on with the strong social programme that in fact they evolved between them, but he would perhaps have been more concerned with the state of trade and so of employment that these stagnant years brought to Britain. He had no heritage of free trade to shackle him, and he would surely have turned earlier to Protection and to the Empire. Ottawa might have come in 1928 instead of after the crash in 1932.

And what of Churchill at Health? He would surely have been a success. There was a very strong official team there at the time with Sir Arthur Robinson as Permanent Secretary and Sir George Newman as Chief Medical Officer. In any case, Churchill could master any official brief. The years would have been less fruitful in legislation, the dustier recesses of the work of the Ministry would have been left undisturbed, the Statute Law would have stayed unconsolidated. But Churchill's heart would surely have been struck, as was Chamberlain's, with the tragedy of the slums, and he too would have spear-headed a great and perhaps more dramatic housing drive. And, with Chamberlain at the Treasury, he would have had, to finance and sometimes to recast his plans, a sympathetic and knowledgeable Chancellor. There is some evidence that Churchill would in fact have preferred the Health Ministry:

Diary, 26.11.1924.

"This afternoon I saw Winston Churchill at his room in Treasury about pensions for widows and old age . . . he then expounded to me the picture as he said he had made for himself of his next budget.

[1] L. S. Amery, *My Political Life*, Vol. II (Hutchinson, 1953), p. 300.

At Harrogate, September 1923, when Chancellor of the Exchequer

National Government, 1931. First meeting of the Cabinet at Downing Street. *From bottom to top*, Ramsay MacDonald, J. H. Thomas, Lord Reading, Stanley Baldwin, Philip Snowden, Lord Sankey, Sir Philip Cunliffe-Lister, Sir Samuel Hoare, Neville Chamberlain, Sir Herbert Samuel

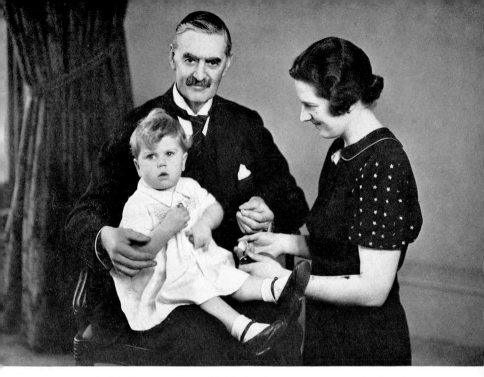

At Westbourne, 1937, with his daughter, Mrs. Stephen Lloyd, and grandson James

With Mrs. Chamberlain and their son at Dalchosnie, Perthshire, 1933

He was anxious to reduce direct taxation in order to relieve industry . . . he might be able to take 6d. off income tax and reduce supertax, possibly making it apply to net instead of gross income, though this might necessitate transferring part of the burden to the medium-sized estates paying death duties. But he would have to balance the benefits by doing something for the working classes and for this he looked to pensions. . . . He wished to treat the subject free from personalities (I gathered that he meant he wasn't going to claim *all* the credit for himself) it would have to be my bill but that he would have to find the money and the question was would I stand in with him, would I enter partnership and work the plan with him *keeping everything secret*. . . . I said I liked his idea and would consider it favourably, that personalities didn't enter into the question so far as I was concerned and I would communicate with him again. . . . it seemed plain to me that he regretted still that he was not Minister of Health . . . a man of tremendous drive and vivid imagination. . . ."

The same pattern persisted throughout the Parliament. As in this case, Chamberlain usually produced the original sketch; Churchill promptly widened the canvas and added his own flourishes; Chamberlain, grumbling that the design was now hopelessly impracticable, set to work to redraw what was now their joint work; and finally Churchill adopted and sometimes adapted the final product. If Churchill was given too much credit for the Widows, Orphans and Old Age Pensions Act which featured in his 1925 Budget, he was given too little for his imaginative contribution to the 1929 Local Government Act. For all their obvious differences in temperament and approach, Churchill and Chamberlain were in fact a surprisingly effective combination.

The Conservatives started the Parliament with a vast majority, and confronted by a divided Labour Party. It was perhaps the happiest moment of Chamberlain's life as he pulled up his chair to the Minister's desk and contemplated four or five secure years at the Ministry of Health to plan and carry out one of the most far-reaching and complicated programmes of legislation any Minister had attempted before or since. He had never less than six, sometimes ten or more, Bills to pilot through the House each session. But his achievement in these years—Sir Keith Feiling[1] calls

[1] *The Life of Neville Chamberlain* (Macmillan, 1946), p. 127.

it, justly, "massive and unquestioned, the chapter of his public life least controverted"—is not to be measured by his prodigious legislative output alone. His work is the link between the Liberal programme of social reform in 1906 and the Labour programme in 1945. Reading the Hansards of those days there are times when it seems as if there was only one Minister in the Government, and it seems incredible that anyone could take the hideous strain. "It is just striking midnight as I start this letter" is a regular opening to his weekly letters in 1925, but they are still full of exact and sometimes lyrical descriptions of his garden and patient meticulous replies to the endless queries his sisters raised on obscure points in the Bills he was pushing through the House. On the Rating and Valuation Bill: "I slaved away at it every night till one and two in the morning so that when the time came I really felt I had mastered the beastly thing." The climax came when he had both his major Bills in Committee at the same time:

N.C. to Ida 5.7.1925

"On Tuesday I started on R. & V. Committee at 11 and on Pensions Bill at 4 and then sat right on till 7 a.m. At 9 a.m. I got out of bed again and went to the office, where I arrived soon after 10. At 11.30 we had Cabinet till 1.30. At 2.30 I addressed the International Congress of Radiologists and at 3.45 I began Pensions again and sat on till 6 a.m. on Thursday. At 11 I got out of bed, having breakfasted, and went to the office; I lunched at the House and answered my questions as a demonstration and then went on Pensions again till 8.15."

The Pensions Bill was the highlight of the session, but to Chamberlain the Rating and Valuation Bill was the key to his future work. Without this measure there could be no true reform of local government, and it was also an essential part of his housing plans. The opening stages of the Bill were deceptively calm:

N.C. Hansard. 13.5.1925.

"This Bill provides for the final disappearance of the overseers from the Statute of 1601. . . . The duties of the overseers are to be transferred, under the Bill, to the real living bodies of today, that is to say the local authorities, the borough councils, the urban district councils and the rural district councils. They will form the new rating authorities and the main rates . . . will be consolidated into a single general rate."

So he explained the Bill's purpose on Second Reading. But the Bill had few real friends and the Committee stage was long and acrimonious. Indeed, there were times when Attlee and Wedgwood, leading for the Socialists, were his allies against the stubborn rearguard actions of his own country members. The Whips were gloomy about the Bill's chances of survival and gloomier still about its effects on the Government's popularity in the country and in due course on their electoral chances. And although Chamberlain managed with Baldwin's spasmodic aid to thwart them, and keep the Bill in the programme, the Whips were right. To reduce the number of rating authorities from 15,546 to 1,767 as the Act finally did was necessary, but many corns were trodden on. To introduce uniformity into rating was wholly desirable— and extremely unpopular. Finally, to bring most of the valuation lists into force on April 1st, 1929, when the assessments were bound to show a large general increase just about the time of the General Election, left Conservative candidates with a very difficult task of explanation, and their opponents a fruitful field to exploit. When the House rose for the summer recess he had carried the whole of his programme except Rating and Valuation and that "contrary to universal expectation" was at least through Committee. In the end, with the help of an Autumn session and a sad series of reluctant concessions he brought the Bill safely home just before Prorogation. The Socialists put up only token resistance on Third Reading and were joined in their thin lobby by the Marquess of Hartington who voted against the Bill because it "nationalised local government and seriously affected the liberties of our English country people". And so in a way it did.

By contrast the Widows', Orphans and Old Age Pensions Bill had a reasonably peaceful passage. Industry grumbled at the load of contributions, and the Labour Party that the scheme was contributory at all, but neither made a formidable case. The Bill had been launched by Churchill in his Budget, but Chamberlain was of course in charge of its passage. His sympathetic and efficient handling of it brought praise from the King and from the

House of Commons, and a puzzled comment from the *Sunday Times*:

"A Student of Politics." Sunday Times, 24.5.1925.

"Politics last week entered on a new and extremely interesting development with the introduction of the new Pensions Bill. Mr. Neville Chamberlain, who was in charge of the Bill, has the family gift of lucid exposition, and he showed, too, that he can strike a genuine note of human sympathy. After all, he comes of an old Radical family . . . a plain man might be excused a feeling of dizziness last week in seeing the Conservative party under Mr. Baldwin taking up the social reform work of the 1906 Government."

It was indeed a great advance. The 1908 and subsequent Acts had made the payment of pensions dependent on a means test, as well as tests of nationality and residence. The new Act was compulsory and contributory. Linking with the National Health Insurance, with Workmen's Compensation and Unemployment Insurance, it provided a fairly complete scheme of protection against the major risks that might affect the working classes. As the Rating and Valuation Bill pointed the way to the abolition of the guardians and, in time, of the Poor Law, so the 1925 Act points the way to Beveridge. For Chamberlain it was the end of the task with which he had been entrusted by Baldwin in opposition, and of his own earlier study of the problem. And it was proof on the Statute Book of his own philosophy.

N.C. Hansard. 22.7.1925, 3rd Reading.

"We have introduced this Bill in fulfilment of our Election pledges. . . . Personally I do not think there is anything to be ashamed of in a desire for office, provided that that desire is founded, not on personal aggrandisement, or even party aggrandisement, but on the consciousness that office is the only instrument by which you can carry into operation Measures which you believe to be right. It is because we believe that a Measure of this kind, a contributory scheme of pensions, was right and was good, because we believe it would have a great effect in strengthening the moral character of the nation, that we have advocated it at Election times and that we are now carrying it into effect."

In spite of a useful legislative programme the Conservative Government lost a lot of support in its first session. The Budget—

as is the way with most popular Budgets—did not hold its first appeal. The Pensions Bill had not had time to be popular, and the Rating Bill was unpopular. Beaverbrook and Rothermere pounded away at Baldwin. The trade depression deepened, and a coal crisis in July threatened to lead to a General Strike. This only a subsidy and an inquiry could avert, and a strong minority in the Cabinet were not prepared to pay this price. But Baldwin, Churchill and Neville Chamberlain (the three 'Prime Ministers' of the Cabinet) led and won the argument for peace and went together to meet the coal owners. As in 1938, time but not peace was bought.

From this marsh of unpopularity the Government was largely rescued by Austen Chamberlain's brilliant triumph at Locarno. For a change the Press was united in its praise, and to Neville and his sisters the success was particularly sweet after the many disappointments of Austen's career. But the offer of the Garter to Austen (which he accepted) caused much heart-searching at first, for the acceptance of honours was not in the Chamberlain tradition of independent nonconformity. In the end, however, even Neville, "once he had got over the shock", came round and in fact suggested that Austen should take a peerage on the ground that if one was to have a title "one might as well go the whole hog and have a good one".

Another family conference resulted in a decision to leave Ladywood. It was unlikely that the constituency could be held in a normal election, except perhaps by more intensive nursing before the campaign than the busiest of Ministers could manage. The new seat had of course to be a Birmingham one and, after consultation with Austen, Neville allowed his name to go forward for Edgbaston. His place as prospective candidate at Ladywood went to Geoffrey Lloyd.

The next year, 1926, was a bad one for the country, for the Conservative Party and for Chamberlain. There was as always a large number of useful bills for the Minister of Health to conduct through the House. But two other measures, the Economy Act and the Guardians (Default) Act, brought him into open and fierce conflict with the Labour Party. The Economy Act—really, of course, Churchill's rather than Chamberlain's—brought from

Lloyd George a strong attack designed to show that the proposal to reduce the State contribution to National Health Insurance was a breach of faith with the approved societies; it was, he proclaimed, "plucking feathers out of the pillows of a sick man". But Chamberlain's memory was too good for that shaft to pierce his armour. Gently, in reply, he reminded Lloyd George of the Act of 1920 when Lloyd George had been Prime Minister and the State contribution under the Act for women had been reduced. Does this mean, he enquired, that one is "at liberty to pluck the feathers from the pillows of the women, but you must not pluck them from the pillows of the men?"

He got no other enjoyment out of the Act, of which he had to carry the burden in the House and for which he incurred the wrath of Socialists and Liberals alike. For himself, he cursed the measure and the amount of Parliamentary time that obstructive tactics meant had to be taken for it. He was only really concerned to save his own Estimates from Churchill's axe and in this he succeeded.

In July 1926, shortly before the summer recess and with the passions of the General Strike still smouldering in the House, Chamberlain introduced the Board of Guardians (Default) Bill. By this measure "where it appears to the Minister of Health that the Board of Guardians for any Poor Law Union have ceased . . . to discharge all or any of the functions exercisable by the Board, the Minister may . . . appoint Commissioners to supersede the Board of Guardians". The period of the order was for twelve months but the orders were renewable. In the event three orders were made—West Ham, Chester-le-Street and Bedwellty—and were renewed while the Baldwin Government was in power. The real issue of "Poplarism" as proclaimed by George Lansbury was whether it was proper to use monies collected from the rates not just for the urgent relief of poverty but as an instrument of social reform. Could Boards of Guardians set their own standards of relief far higher sometimes than mere necessity would demand and expect to recoup themselves from the public purse? "Yes" said the Socialist Party—or rather most of them, for their front bench spokesmen, especially of course Sidney Webb, were more cautious. "No" said Chamberlain, and with this and two other measures directed against Poplarism set himself to struggle for efficient and economical local authority administration.

In the same week that the Second Reading was taken the Labour Party launched a more personal attack on Chamberlain. He had, in accordance with the rules then governing directorships, resigned his directorships in public companies on taking up office but had remained in theory a director of the private company of Hoskins', although since the election he had taken no part in their affairs and knew nothing of their contracts. It turned out that some 2 per cent of these were for Government contracts. This was the peg for the censure motion, an echo of the one pressed against Joe a generation earlier. Baldwin and Hogg spoke in the debate and had no difficulty in dealing with the charge—indeed, it was not seriously pressed. But Arthur Henderson's last words showed that the Censure Motion was in fact a reprisal. Referring to the Second Reading of the Guardians (Default) Bill, he said:

"The author of such legislation should remember that those who live in glass houses should never throw stones."

George Lansbury, who had perhaps more reason than anyone else for attacking Chamberlain, preferred to attack Baldwin and the Coal Mines Bill instead, ending ferociously with—

"I charge those who passed the Bill with having passed it and with having risked the murder and maiming and bruising of miners in order to feather their own nests."

This aroused no comment in those more robust days either from the Speaker or from the House. But for Chamberlain's relations with the Labour Party this week was of decisive importance. From now on their suspicion deepened, and his bitterness grew. His letters and his diaries begin to fill first with expressions of his exasperation and then of his contempt for them. For their part no chance was let slip to torment him. And so a gulf opened and widened between the most progressive social reformer in the Government and the official Opposition. Once more, as with Lloyd George, almost by accident a disastrous personal relationship was begun which was to leave its mark on the history of the next dozen years. Lloyd George and Chamberlain could see no good in each other, and they were both wrong. Nor from this week could the Labour Party and Chamberlain, and again they were both wrong.

Perhaps if they had known more of what he was trying to achieve during the General Strike and during the drafting of the Trade Disputes Act 1927, the Labour Party might have judged him more charitably. But it is on the whole unlikely, for logic plays small part in these Parliamentary antipathies. Nevertheless, the story is important. He believed firmly, and he was surely right, that the General Strike, once started, must be opposed and defeated. But even though the combination of the anger (on both sides, of course) aroused by the strike and the existence of a large Conservative majority in Parliament made some sort of Trade Union legislation inevitable, Chamberlain from the first tried to ensure that it was also constructive. His proposal was for something very like the Industrial Disputes Tribunal set up in 1940 and finally abolished by the author against half-hearted and brief opposition by the Labour Party and the T.U.C. in 1959. Chamberlain's ideas for this form of compulsory arbitration were that no strike should start unless there had been a hearing by a tribunal and committee on which employers and employees would sit. There was and is much to be said for such a proposal although in peace time perhaps the arguments against are stronger. But in the aftermath of a General Strike these constructive proposals might have had some chance of general acquiescence, if not agreement. Certainly they would have changed the whole nature of the Trade Disputes Act 1927. But:

Diary, 16.3.1927.

"Trade Union Bill. The P.M. called a special meeting of the Cabinet last night at 6 to consider the Bill, my proposals having been circulated in a separate memo. He himself opened the proceedings by saying he was strongly impressed with the desirability of two proposals, the declaration of illegality of the General Strike and the amendment of the law regarding 'peaceful' picketing. On political levy he was undecided but inclined to include it on grounds of political expediency. He thought it very desirable to make the Bill as short as possible. Every Member was then invited to express his views on the Bill. The main points were the two first mentioned by the P.M., on which there was unanimity, the political levy on which there was much difference (Hogg and I against) but on the whole a disposition to include it—while admitting that it would have very little result.[1]

. . . and finally my proposals which the P.M. had not mentioned at all. On this to my surprise there was almost universal agreement, the only dissenter being F. E. (who has been thoroughly unsound on the bill throughout), S[teel] M[aitland] whose opposition was determined but rather muddled and obscure, and the H[ome] S[ecretary]. . . . The final conclusion was that the Bill was to be redrafted and sent back to the Cttee. but it looks as though my proposals would be adopted, in which case I anticipate they will form the principal feature of the Bill and the one which will attract most attention."

Chamberlain was too optimistic. When the Committee met, the Lord Chancellor was ill and F.E. took the chair. The Minister of Labour continued his laborious (and, one suspects, departmental) opposition, and in the end, although narrowly, and after a further reference to the Cabinet, the "noes" had it. A similar sort of clause was put forward by backbenchers in the debate, but this was remitted to a Committee and of course stifled. So the clause was lost. The Chamberlain clause, if adopted, could have made the establishment of the Industrial Disputes Tribunal unnecessary, and might have survived the Socialist repeal in 1946 of the 1927 Act; for the prohibition of a strike, if reference to the Tribunal had been made by either side, lasted until 1951.

Although there was an impressive output of social legislation in these years, comparatively little of it was directly concerned with housing, perhaps the most important of the numerous functions of the Ministry of Health. The twin pillars of housing policy continued to be the "Chamberlain" Act of 1923 and the "Wheatley" Act of 1924. There was also the sad legacy of the Housing and Town Planning Act of 1919. "Homes for Heroes" had been the popular pledge, but the promise proved as empty as the windy words spoken by Socialist leaders in the General Election of 1945. In his last speech on housing to the House of Commons Chamberlain had a fine story to tell. 800,000 houses

[1] Not, incidentally, an accurate judgment. 55–60 per cent was the average number "contracting in" and the finances of the Labour Party suffered accordingly.

built during the lifetime of the Baldwin Government, with a peak of 273,000 in the year September 1926 – September 1927, both of them records unequalled by any previous administration. On the public cost of these houses the figures were also impressive. 378,000 had been completed under the "Chamberlain" Act, each of which cost £4 p.a. for twenty years, 229,000 under the "Wheatley" Act at an annual cost of £7 10s. for forty years. Non-subsidy houses accounted for the remainder. Chamberlain added mischievously that every "Lloyd George" house (and there had been only 175,000 of them since 1919) cost the nation £38 10s. for sixty years. "Addison" houses would have been a more accurate title, but the chuckle at his old opponent was too good to miss.

Chamberlain's experience in Birmingham and a lifetime of study of housing and local government problems were of course tremendous assets to him. The one gap in his practical knowledge was of housing in a rural area, and here Ida, one of the two sisters with whom Chamberlain maintained his long correspondence, was of immense help to him. Ida had become a Hampshire County Councillor and took a leading part on the Housing Committee. Chamberlain, especially during the passage of the Housing (Rural Workers) Act 1926, frequently consulted her in his letters and often took her advice.

The slum clearance record of the Government was less impressive, but slum clearance is bound to follow and not precede a housing drive. So the Conservatives for their General Election manifesto in 1929 switched the emphasis to slum clearance, just as did the Conservative Government in 1955 and 1959. Even so, fifty-eight slum clearance schemes were confirmed and 31,000 people actually re-housed in those years. Chamberlain's policy of subsidy reduction in March and September 1927 brought another blast of fury from the Labour Party, even though in the event prices fell a good deal, the average cost of a non-parlour house dropping by more than £100 before the Election. Actually in December 1928, a few months before the Election, Parliamentary authority was obtained for reducing from October 1929 the subsidy on "Wheatley" houses and abolishing it on "Chamberlain" houses. No one could accuse this Government of being adroit in their political timing of events!

Yet when the Election came Housing was certainly one of the strongest planks in the Conservative platform, and much of the great shortage of housing accommodation had been overtaken. Chamberlain himself had lost nothing and perhaps politically had gained much, as did Harold Macmillan in 1951, by taking on the endless tough challenging work of the Ministry.

Endless the tasks were. For the Ministry was then responsible not only for housing, but for civil pensions and National Health Insurance, for the administration of the Poor Law and for the Public Health Services. Much of the legislation has an important place in the development of the Welfare State. For example, the National Health Insurance Act of 1928, which greatly extended and improved health insurance benefits; giving new additional benefits of specialist advice and surgical treatment to members of Approved Societies, softening the requirements to help the unemployed, married women and the old, and, in all, bringing added help to some sixteen and a half million men and women workers. In four years 440 more Infant Welfare Centres were opened and 300 more ante-natal clinics, while the number of practising midwives increased by 860. The infant mortality rate, 132 per 1000 live births in 1906, 75 in 1924, was 65 in 1928, and has dropped fairly steadily ever since to the latest available figure of 21·7 for 1960. But the maternal mortality rate which had been virtually stationary for twenty years stayed obstinately high and Chamberlain, mainly through the Midwives and Maternity Homes Act 1926, by supervising Nursing Homes through Local Authorities by the Act of 1927, and by greatly increased expenditure on the Maternity and Child Welfare Services, worked tirelessly to reduce it. On his final review to the House of Commons, Chamberlain turned once more to this problem:

N.C. Hansard. 1.5.1929.

"I set on foot an investigation with the help of the general practitioners of the B.M.A. and the local authorities with a view to getting a report on every case of maternal death right through the country. . . . I say with some confidence that from the mere fact of this attention being given without any special steps having been taken, we shall see a large reduction in this figure which has persisted for so many years."

In the domain of Public Health there was legislation on clean food, clean water and clean air as well as the important Public Health Act of 1925. The "policy of sewage" inspired by Disraeli was in good hands.

Chamberlain too was an insatiable traveller as all Ministers of Health have to be. And perhaps only another Minister of Health can really appreciate the meticulous careful diary entries which covered every day of his journeyings. There were the gargantuan luncheons and dinners which are a necessary part of each excursion. Necessary because only so can one meet and thank a fraction of the men and women who work in the health services or local government. There were the miles of stone passageways to be tramped in old hospitals, and the smell of polish and ether and linen that went with them. And in the evening often there was a political speech somewhere to be made or a town reception to be attended, and wherever one went the red ministerial boxes followed one with a malignant fidelity and the homework for the next day had often to be done late at night in bed. But again one can appreciate with him the humour, intentional or otherwise, of some of the speeches and occasions: the fine evidence of new growth and better conditions: the exciting study of new methods in hospitals and clinics and the pleasure of meeting the men and women at work there: above all, of meeting the patients.

Chamberlain, as he went round the country on his tours, was concerned above all things to test the adequacy of local administration. Birmingham, of course, was large and efficient, but many of the District Councils he studied were neither. Larger authorities with greater executive and supervisory powers were needed, and throughout the Parliament Chamberlain argued tenaciously for the measure that became the Local Government Act 1929.

It is in the long and complicated journey that the Local Government Act had to reach the Statute Book that the Churchill-Chamberlain relationship in that Parliament is seen most clearly. The two men started from very different points. At the Exchequer Churchill watched anxiously the mounting figures of unemployment and the slow decline in trade. There had been a steady fall of unemployment during the first year of office of Baldwin's Government and this was continued into 1926; the figure of registered unemployed falling below the million mark, for the first time since 1920, in April 1926. In May came the General Strike and the succeeding coal strike kept the figures high. This time they stayed high and there were nearly one and a quarter million unemployed in Great Britain in June 1928, almost half of them in four or five "heavy" industries. Churchill could not stomach a protectionist solution and devised the idea of subsidising the rates out of taxation so that relief could be given to industry and agriculture. Chamberlain meanwhile burrowed away at his scheme of Poor Law Reform, of replacing percentage grants by weighted block grants and of strengthening the powers of the County Councils and County Boroughs in relation to the smaller Districts.

N.C. to Hilda 27.11.1926.

"I had a not unsatisfactory reception at the Cabinet for my Poor Law proposals. I did not ask for any decision but was allowed to talk for about 40 minutes. . . . There were some murmurings about the effect on the rates, but in Walter Guinness' absence (Minister of Agriculture) they did not go very far. Winston, of course, was eloquent upon his grand scheme, but it seemed to me that it met a rather chilly atmosphere. On the whole I thought it was not a bad beginning."

But there was a long way to go. For two whole years the argument went on. Churchill and Chamberlain advanced towards each other and retreated. The end was inevitable. Neither could do without the other and in the end their ideas began to fuse. Chamberlain's side of this lengthy saga is best told from his diary:

Diary, 12. 2. 1927.

"With regard to Poor Law, the Cabinet decided on Wednesday the 2nd that it should go into the King's Speech minus block grants which were to be discussed during the summer and introduced next year. But on Friday B. Monsell, the Chief Whip, appeared with a timetable based on a proposal to conclude the session by the 4th August and in this table there was insufficient time for P.L. The P.M. then asked whether, if a new session was begun in November, I saw any objection to postponing P.L. till then and dealing with block grants simultaneously. I do not really know how I was so successful on Wednesday seeing that the great majority of the Cabinet was obviously hostile to P.L. Reform, not on merits, but because they think it will be unpopular. When the Chief Whip produced his timetable I could see at once how joyfully they welcomed an excuse for putting it off and I therefore jumped at the P.M.'s proposal as the only chance. But of course I was desperately disappointed. . . ."

9.12.1927.

"The plan was accepted by the Committee on Thursday and submitted to the Cabinet on Wednesday. Winston was extraordinarily tiresome working himself up into the most violent and persistent opposition . . . however, Winston was utterly and finally defeated, his only supporters being A. J. B[alfour] who does not seem to hear what is going on and is generally far away from realities, and F.E. who now seems determined to support his friend Winston irrespective of merits. The plan was outlined by Sir P. C-L. [Cunliffe-Lister, formerly Lloyd-Greame, President of the Board of Trade] in his speech on the Vote of Censure Debate on Wednesday afternoon, but in such a way as to excite the least possible interest and attention. . . ."

22.12.1927.

"On the 17th I received a letter from Winston enclosing a print of his draft scheme in outline. It was very vague indeed. . . . I replied to W. on the 20th with a serious warning that I saw grave difficulties though I did not commit myself to a final opinion. The same day (Tuesday) he spoke to me in the lobby saying he was much disappointed at my chilly reception and in the course of conversation he observed that he would not circulate the print he had sent me to the Cabinet. Unless the P.M. and I agreed he would drop the scheme. He was not going to have another Gallipoli and find himself all alone when the wind of criticism began to blow. . . ."

4.4.1928.

"The Plan has at last been settled. I drafted and Gilmour signed the Minority Report and on Monday the 2nd inst. it came before a special Cabinet which sat both morning and afternoon to consider it (the papers said we were discussing Egypt). . . . Further discussion continued yesterday morning and it presently became apparent, first that no-one had a good word to say for the railway derating scheme, second that I had a very considerable amount of support, and Winston began to trim his sails to the wind. He declared it obvious that we must be united; clearly the consent of the Minister of

Health who had shown himself such a perfect master of the subject was absolutely vital: there was no-one who could compete with him there. Presently he passed a note asking if I would be prepared to discuss with him a fractional rate. I sent an affirmative—but not too enthusiastic—answer; this was shown to the P.M. and finally the latter suggested a conference between us before any further action was taken, expressing his view that we had gone too far to draw back and that unity was essential. . . ."

A policy committee was set up to decide between Churchill's suggestion of 1/5th and Chamberlain's of 1/3rd. Not surprisingly they settled on 1/4th. Churchill's allies wanted to hold out against this obvious compromise but:

Diary, 4.4.1928 (contd.).
". . . Winston said he wouldn't stand on such a small difference and accepted. Whereon we shook hands and vowed eternal friendship. No doubt he always intended to settle on the 1/4th, as I did."

So it was agreed that industry was to be relieved of the burden of three-quarters of the local rates in respect of factories and workshops but not in relation to offices. Agricultural land and buildings were to be completely freed from all rates except those on the farmhouse. But the railways issue was not yet finally decided. Winston, now supported by Baldwin, returned to the attack. The Central Office complained to the P.M. that the most attractive part of the scheme was the derating of railways. Macmillan and Boothby formed a deputation to protest to Chamberlain and:

Diary, 19.4.1928.
". . . feeling embarrassed at discussing the propriety of Cabinet discussions with these young men I only argued shortly with them and then said I must talk to the P.M."

In the end, after much discussion with Baldwin, Chamberlain surrendered the point, insisting, however, that if there was to be rate relief (again to the extent of three-quarters of local rates) to railways, canals, harbours and docks, that equivalent reductions wherever possible should be made in their transport charges. So in the end the two schemes became one. Churchill announced his share (the derating proposals) in the Budget of 1928 and finally Chamberlain brought his work to fruition in December.

"Last Monday I moved the 2nd Reading of the Local Government Bill in a speech which lasted 2½ hours. I had taken an immense amount of trouble in preparing it, sitting up till one o'clock every morning and devoting practically the whole of Saturday and Sunday to the same purpose. D. Hogg asked me on Friday if I was going to lay down any principles as he had done in the Trades Dispute Bill. I had not at that time got the speech much beyond disjointed sections, the arrangement being still undecided, and I thanked him for his suggestion which I embodied afterwards in the five main defects of Local Govt. Annie also urged me to put in something human lest the speech should appear to be devoted too exclusively to the coldly mechanical efficiency of administration. This led to a sketch of Local Government as it appeared to the people of Birmingham and was one of the most effective passages.

"When I sat down the House cheered continuously for several minutes (Worthy said longer than he had ever known it in all his 18 years' experience) and what particularly struck and touched me was that Liberals and Labour men—even bitter opponents like Mackinder—joined with the greatest heartiness in paying their acknowledgments."

Before the General Election in the spring of 1929 this great Act of more than one hundred clauses was on the Statute Book. It was a noble ending to Chamberlain's work at the Ministry of Health. *Finis Coronat* was the title of *The Times'* leading article on the day that the Royal Assent was given:

"The great scheme of rating reform which has been the principal Government measure during the present Session is thus finally completed. It is a measure of which its authors may justly be proud . . . it may safely be predicted that when the history of the present age is written the Local Government Act of 1929 will take its place as one of the outstanding legislative achievements of the twentieth century. Hardly ever in the whole course of our Parliamentary history has a Government in its last year of office ventured to initiate a measure which, while containing so little to attract the popular favours so eagerly pursued by the party tactician, appeals so profoundly to all that is solid and statesmanlike in the judgment of the country. The credit for this remarkable achievement must be accorded in the first place to Mr. Neville Chamberlain. . . . Nor should it be forgotten how much these great reforms owe to the imagination and courage of Mr. Churchill. . . ."

Equal honour may fairly be given to them. They were also at the time the only two possible contenders for the succession. Douglas Hogg would certainly have been a third if the Lord Chancellorship had not been thrust upon him on the resignation of Lord Cave.

N.C. to Hilda 31.3.1928.

"You are right about Douglas Hogg. I regard his promotion as rather a calamity and it was all rushed through in a very unfortunate way. He had always told me that he would want my advice before he decided, but on Friday the 23rd the P.M. sent for him and after telling him that F. E. had refused when it was put that way and though he didn't think he had quite committed himself he admitted when he came to see me on Tuesday that he had not been very definite in saying no. I strongly urged him to delay and said I would ask the P.M. to press F.E. again, but on Wednesday morning I found it was too late as S.B. had already given the Attorney-Generalship to Inskip and made Merriman Solicitor. Poor Douglas was very unhappy for he had realised that when it came to the point he wanted to continue his political career and of course the tragedy is that he is now barred from the chance of becoming P.M. when S.B. retires. To my mind this is a great misfortune for I believe he would have had a very good chance and I am sure he is the best man we have for such a position. . . . He and I have been very close together on nearly every point that has arisen and I have a very high opinion of his character and judgement. I would gladly serve under him as I believe he would under me, but I have never regarded him as a rival, having no ambition to become P.M. myself. . . ."

So, as Lord Hailsham, Douglas Hogg took the Woolsack and disappeared from the House of Commons. Chamberlain was left as the natural heir of the orthodox Conservatives. He had been in Parliament only ten years.

8

PARTY CHAIRMAN

(March 1929 – April 1931)

IN the months immediately preceding the 1929 General
Election, the reconstruction of the Cabinet was seriously considered. Baldwin was full of ideas for drastic changes, which he
discussed in detail with Chamberlain. The older men, particularly
Salisbury and Joynson-Hicks, were to be dropped and "youth
was to have its chance". He had thoughts, delightfully ironic in
retrospect, of putting Churchill at the India Office. This would
leave the Treasury vacant: if Chamberlain would consent to go
there, it would be very popular in the Party who "liked to have
the next man to the P.M. in that office". Chamberlain said he
would not refuse to consider this, but would much prefer the
Colonies. By early May it was clear that the Prime Minister had
characteristically decided to temporise, but equally clear that if
and when the changes came Chamberlain would get his wish.

N.C. to Hilda 5.5.1929.

"I think it's pretty well settled in S.B.'s mind now that I shall go to
the C.O. and retain the D.O. He spoke to Winston about it and he
expressed great pleasure at the idea; perhaps he didn't want me at
No. 11! It was rather curious that in a Committee engaged in drawing up the P.M.'s election address . . . I was asked to draft the paragraph on Colonial Development. It is true that Leo [Amery] was not
present at the moment, but the request came quite naturally and
arose out of some remark I made on the subject."

This election address, indeed, opened with a fanfare for the
Empire; but the trumpets gave an uncertain sound. The Party, it

said, wished to promote all forms of helpful co-operation with the Dominions. Among these was Imperial Preference. But this had to be promoted subject to Baldwin's pledge "not to impose any protective taxation on food". On Colonial development, Chamberlain's draft piously quoted his father. Not even in Birmingham did this cut much ice: Edgbaston proved safe enough for Neville, but Austen escaped defeat only by 43 votes, and the city, hitherto an impregnable stronghold, yielded six seats to Labour. Elsewhere there was a similar story to tell. Baldwin's lack of initiative, the uninspiring policy of "safety first", the continuing unemployment and trade depression, inept timing of the introduction of rating and other reforms, above all, perhaps, the general sense that it was time for a change—all were reflected in the final figures which gave Labour 287 seats and the Conservatives 261, with 59 Liberals holding the balance. Rejecting Chamberlain's advice to "ride for a fall" and put the onus of installing a Labour Government on the Liberals, Baldwin resigned on June 4th and MacDonald took over.

If the new Prime Minister played his cards badly, reflected Chamberlain, the Conservatives might be back before two years were up; if he played them cleverly they might be out for seven —and what then, at the age of 67, would be his own prospects? "Gladstone and Disraeli," he jested to Ida on June 2nd, "were both Prime Ministers in their old age. But they didn't altogether make a success of it!" It was, however, the immediate rather than the ultimate prospect that he found most depressing. Administration always interested him far more than the mere game of politics, he felt his physical vigour unimpaired and his mental powers at their zenith, and he was immensely looking forward to following in his father's footsteps. A long entry in his diary on June 8th ends on this note of frustration: "I should have liked to have had a go at the Colonies *now*!"

In the event, some of his period in Opposition was spent in informing himself on Colonial matters at first hand, and more in working out behind the scenes a practical Imperial policy. In July, he secured Baldwin's ready assent to his visiting East Africa in the coming winter. But on matters of policy he found his Leader's moods and methods utterly exasperating. Baldwin had led his Party to defeat twice in a decade, and was subjected to a steady rain of criticism thereafter. He did not shine in Opposition. Chamberlain noted that his conditional agreement to the re-announcement of eventual Dominion status for India, without any consultation with his colleagues, showed lack of touch; and that when Baldwin was asked to see leading industrialists and financiers on tariff questions, the meeting ended without his knowing what they had said and without their knowing why they had been sent for.

N.C. to Hilda 26.10.1929

"I told him of the criticisms that were reaching me from all quarters about his want of leadership and told him that he must give a lead and be a bit more aggressive if the Party was to be held together. . . . It is all very depressing and particularly embarrassing for me because everyone I meet tells me of S.B.'s failings and many suggest that I should do better in his place. Heaven knows I don't want the job. It is a thankless one at any time and never more so than now when the Party is all to pieces. Moreover S.B. is my friend as well as my leader and I would not on any account play L.G. to his Asquith. . . .

"The situation is enormously complicated by Beaverbrook's campaign which you are probably unaware of as you don't see the *Express*. He is pushing it very hard and very cleverly so as to catch thoughtless and disgruntled Conservatives and everyone who knows him tells me his dominating motive is detestation of S.B. It is difficult to see how we can have any accommodation with him if that be so."

Nevertheless, an attempt at accommodation was made. On November 4th Chamberlain and Beaverbrook, dining with Hoare, met for the first time and appear to have been rather impressed with one another. Beaverbrook's particular policy, thought Chamberlain, was "obsolete, impracticable and mischievous"; but he saw no reason why, for the purpose of negotiating treaties for mutual advantage with Dominions and Colonies, the Party should not hold itself free of limiting pledges, provided the treaties were subject to Parliamentary ratification. Beaverbrook raised objections, said the issue of food taxes should be faced fairly and squarely, and proposed to run Crusader candidates at by-elections. But next day he told Hoare on the telephone that if they came to him meaning business he would be prepared to "do a deal"; and Chamberlain's diary for November 5th adds: "his personal feelings about S.B. would not stand in the way as he cared more about Empire Free Trade than he did about his vendetta". This was the prelude to an inconclusive but not unfriendly interview between Beaverbrook, Baldwin and Chamberlain—held on Armistice Day, as Baldwin gaily observed—and "an overture to understanding" in Baldwin's speech at the 1929 Party Conference.

Thus Chamberlain departed for East Africa in relatively good heart. He had taken little part in House of Commons work since the Election, except to lead the opposition to the Pensions Bill (an occasion when he had proclaimed himself attracted to the idea of an "all-in" or comprehensive insurance scheme). But in the making of Imperial policy thought was on the move.

He was away with his wife and daughter from December 11th to March 8th, seven weeks of which were spent in Kenya, Uganda and Tanganyika. Occasionally he relaxed—an afternoon's fishing for rainbow trout at Nyeri and an expedition by steamer to the Murchison Falls were especially appreciated—and there was at least one "adventure", when their car got stuck in a donga on the plains of Athi and they were stranded for hours in pitch darkness surrounded by the snorting and roaring of wild animals. For the rest, it was the strenuous but orthodox tour of an ex-Cabinet Minister—inspecting schools and hospitals, railway workshops and agricultural research laboratories; talking with and winning respect from settlers, officials and native notables; and gradually familiarising himself with the economic and political problems of the territories. Speaking at Dar-es-Salaam he took as his text "father's two lines of conduct, trusteeship for the backward races and development of undeveloped estates" and noted how many settlers had come out "with a little capital and no experience and now had a little experience and no capital"; and on his return home he stressed how some closer union of the territories would help development plans to go forward.

Letters, particularly from Hoare and Cunliffe-Lister, his two closest associates, had kept him abreast of political news at home, including Beaverbrook's launching of a new United Empire Party. A few days before his return the situation had been momentarily transformed by Baldwin's speech to the Central Council of the National Union. In this, at Beaverbrook's suggestion, he announced that there would be a referendum on food taxes if these should be proposed as part of a mutually beneficial Empire trade agreement. Beaverbrook thereupon dissolved his new Party; but he was still far from satisfied when Chamberlain saw him on March 11th.

Diary, 12.3.1930.

"He said he had proposed the referendum as the only way of saving the Conservative party from destruction but he didn't like it and hoped that presently we should drop it. I begged him to say nothing of the kind to anyone else as it would scare the party blue but agreed that if the country really showed signs of its willingness to adopt food taxes it might be possible to get rid of a referendum and if it were possible it would be desirable . . .

"This afternoon we screwed up S.B. to agree to weekly meetings of a 'committee of business' a sort of inner Cabinet to discuss questions of policy generally, and also to form a Committee of which Beaverbrook should be invited to be a member to discuss ways and means of promoting 'Empire Free Trade'."

Chamberlain's central position in this work of policy making was now strengthened and formalised by his taking over the chairmanship of the Research Department, which he described as "an Information Bureau providing data and briefs for leaders, and a long range Research body". A not very successful start had been made with this under Eustace Percy's direction whilst Chamberlain had been in Africa. In April 1930, the new Department moved into premises in Old Queen Street and overlooking Birdcage Walk, and an atmosphere of excitement and bustle was at once evident. Small policy committees, serviced by the Department and consisting of Members of Parliament and others, were set up with precise terms of reference. Of these, the most important perhaps were the committee on agricultural policy (under the chairmanship of Lord Wolmer), whose influence was soon to be seen in Chamberlain's own speeches, and Cunliffe-Lister's committee on tariff policy, whose secretary was Henry Brooke, and whose report was later made much use of in the tariff legislation of the National Government.

Any hope that Beaverbrook's energy might somehow be harnessed to this official chariot soon faded. Chamberlain did his best; but observed ruefully that little assistance was forthcoming from some of his colleagues. His letters and diaries record how Churchill was fulminating against food taxes; how Salisbury in a letter to *The Times* had implied that the re-equipment and re-organisation of domestic industry took precedence over the tariff question; how Davidson, the Chairman of the Party, had prepared in Central Office some badly worded leaflets in connection with the Party's propaganda campaign in May; and how Baldwin's speeches during this campaign dwelt too much on the safeguards against food taxes and too little on the positive advantages to be derived from a constructive Empire policy. Beaverbrook became impatient, resentful and suspicious of the Party leadership. Allied with Rothermere, he declared war on Baldwin. The *Daily Express* and the *Daily Mail* went into action. Baldwin, however, counter-attacked masterfully at a Party meeting in the Caxton Hall on June 24th, which gave him an overwhelming vote of confidence. The ill-humour of the Party, which was certainly not confined to the Press Barons, vented itself instead on the head of Davidson whose resignation as Chairman had to be announced before Whitsun.

Diary, 22.6.1930.

"I had made up my mind that Geoffrey Ellis would be the best man to succeed him and had ascertained that he would be prepared to undertake the job which should entail the clearing out of some of the old gang at Palace Chambers. But the long delay, the consequent canvassing of other names and the hostility of the Central Office itself have combined to make it pretty certain that the party would not now accept him alone. Almost every other conceivable name has been considered but at last everyone seems to have come to the conclusion that I am the one man whose name would command general confidence and rather reluctantly S.B. asked me to take the place on Friday. I have made up my mind to accept though realising the risks, but I believe it is true that I can render a service which is possible to no-one else and in the circumstances I cannot hesitate."

Through all this difficult period he counted on the friendship and advice of Hoare and Cunliffe-Lister. Arguing with Central Office about the May campaign literature, "I have taken the precaution of ensuring Sam's and Philip's support." "Sam and Philip both want me to do it,' he informed his sisters before accepting the chairmanship of the Party. Now as Chairman he attempted once more a *rapprochement* with Beaverbrook, inviting him to dine at Eaton Square on July 18th, "and Sam Hoare and Philip Cunliffe-Lister came too".

According to Chamberlain's version, Beaverbrook was in a very friendly mood which was never once ruffled despite much frank talk. He seemed especially anxious to discuss what would happen at Bromley where there would soon be a vacancy. Chamberlain replied that they could not have different plans in different constituencies; there must be a general agreement or nothing. He then produced his terms. Beaverbrook must call off his attacks on Baldwin and the Party, cease to include offensive cartoons and paragraphs in the *Evening Standard*, and stop inviting Conservatives to direct subscriptions to him in order that they might be used to run candidates against official Conservatives. In return, Central Office would support any Conservative who accepted the official policy, even though he expressed personal agreement with Beaverbrook, and tried to persuade his local association to adopt these views. Beaverbrook, in a phrase reminiscent of the Spenlow and Jorkins incident in *David Copperfield*, said he personally would jump at these terms if it were not for his "partner" Rothermere, whom he at once promised to consult. The outcome was failure; for Chamberlain could not agree to act on Rothermere's "straight tip" that the Party could count on their "100 per cent" support provided Chamberlain was substituted for Baldwin as Leader of the Party.

N.C. to Ida 26.7.1930.

"The commonest loyalty makes it impossible to listen to such a suggestion and yet the tragedy is that—most reluctantly—I have come to the conclusion that if S.B. would go the whole party would heave a sigh of relief. Everywhere I hear that there is no confidence in his leadership or belief in his determination to carry any policy through. Yet it looks as if I might have to go down fighting for S.B.

when my own desire is, as it always has been, to go for the free hand."

Within three months of this, however, Chamberlain's skill had achieved both "the free hand" for the Party and a new vote of confidence for its leader. In two important speeches, in Midlothian on August 2nd and at the Crystal Palace on September 20th, he flew several policy kites. "My unauthorised programme" as he described it with a nice sense of history, included drastic economy, the reduction of direct taxation and the thorough reform of the unemployment insurance system; the introduction of an emergency tariff to protect manufacturing industries; a quota system for wheat and, "if the people are prepared to give the Conservative Party a free hand in negotiating with the Dominions to make the best bargain they can, whether it includes food taxes or not, I shall be very glad to see the end of the referendum". All this was well received, and when Baldwin returned from his holiday in Aix at the end of September, Chamberlain advised him to make an official statement of policy along these lines. Baldwin agreed and called a meeting of the Business Committee for October 7th. The Committee did not seriously object to the programme, but some doubts were expressed particularly about the quota and particularly by Churchill; so they adjourned for a week. On the following day, October 8th, the second meeting of the Imperial Conference took place in London, and Bennett, the Prime Minister of Canada, unfolded a plan for reciprocal Imperial Preferences which was supported by other delegations but coldly received by Britain's Labour Government. Chamberlain at once realised the opportunity that had been given the Conservative Party, and drafted a statement which Baldwin agreed should be issued to the Press that night in his name: "whatever the Socialist Government may do, the Conservative Party accepts the principle put forward with such weight and unanimity. Further, the Conservative Party, guided by the views expressed at this Conference, will formulate its own proposals for carrying that principle into effect, and will submit them to the people at the next election for their *final and definite assent.*" Thus the referendum was dead and buried; and a few days later Chamberlain's "unauthorised programme" became official policy, amplified in a letter from the Leader to the Chairman of the Party which Chamberlain himself wrote, but which Baldwin read out to the Business Committee as the "result of our meditations". So it came about that at a Party meeting at the Caxton Hall called at the instance of the die-hards, Baldwin could declare: "Our fiscal policy is the policy of the free hand, and I ask you to endorse it." It was endorsed with only one dissentient—Lord Beaverbrook; and the meeting went on to vote its confidence in the Leader by 462 votes to 116.

This was on October 30th; by the following February the crisis had broken out anew.

Diary, 23.2.1931.

"The question of leadership is again growing acute . . . I am getting letters and communications from all over the country . . . Sam Hoare . . . reports that the feeling in the House could not be worse. I cannot see any way out. I am the one person who might bring about S.B.'s retirement but I cannot act when my action might put me in his place."

The discomfort of Chamberlain's position was aggravated by private irritations and resentments which his businesslike yet sensitive mind found it difficult to discount. "Imagine my fury" he had written to Ida in the summer when Baldwin had suddenly cancelled a Business Committee without letting anybody know. "It is curiously characteristic of him that he hasn't said a word of thanks to me," he wrote in October after the successful publication of the new policy. In November when Baldwin cried off appearing in a Disraeli film because he had apparently strained a ligament in his foot during his sleep, he observed sardonically, "Any ordinary mortal would have telephoned to save my going round to his house, but the poetic temperament does not work that way." And after a Party Luncheon for the Australian delegation to the Imperial Conference he angrily wrote to Hilda, "S.B. would only make jokes about his leg and couldn't be got into general conversation".

Baldwin's eccentricities and limitations as a negotiator threw a particularly heavy burden on Chamberlain during these winter months, when there were yet further attempts to heal the breach with Beaverbrook and inconclusive soundings were taken of some of Lloyd George's followers. Even regarding India, the great question on which Churchill finally broke from his colleagues in January, Chamberlain thought that Baldwin had fumbled badly from the Party's point of view.

N.C. to Hilda 31.1.1931.

"Sam Hoare dined with S.B. on the night of Winston's India speech in the House in order to coach him in his reply. Afterwards he told me that S.B. had conducted himself so clumsily that he had stirred up all our die-hards who had been satisfied with his own account of our official position but felt that S.B. had departed from it as much on the one side as Winston had on the other. I am afraid the explanation is that S.B. has never taken the trouble to master the situation and that in his anxiety to dissociate himself from reaction he laid all the emphasis on the advance he would like to make and slurred over the safeguards without which no advance ought to be made. . . . The longer an election is delayed, the more difficult it is going to be to keep the party behind the leader."

This was equally the view of Topping, the General Director of Central Office, who had already expressed his apprehensions to Chamberlain in the previous autumn. Now in February he deposited a time-bomb on the Chairman's desk.

Sir Robert Topping to N.C. 25.2.1931.

"It has been evident to me during the last few weeks that there is a growing concern in the ranks of the Party with regard to the position of the Leader. I have given very careful thought to the matter during the past few days and have come to the conclusion that I would be guilty of a neglect of duty were I to conceal from you the views which have been expressed to me by various representative members of the Party Organisation.

"After the Caxton Hall Meeting I watched the effect on the Party in the country and came to the conclusion that for the time being the Leader had re-established his position, and although there were still some discontented people in the ranks, the majority were prepared to support him. There was at that time an overwhelming desire for unity in the Party, which caused considerable resentment against Beaverbrook and Rothermere, and resulted in a large volume of support for Mr. Baldwin. Not much time elapsed, however, before a gradual drift away from him became noticed. Looking back on the events of the last few months, it appears to me that up to the date of

the Caxton Hall Meeting there was a movement towards Beaverbrook in the Party, the Leader still retaining the support of a very
large section, but since the Caxton Hall Meeting there has not been
so much support for Beaverbrook, but there has been a very definite
feeling that the Leader is not strong enough to carry the Party to
victory, and that feeling appears to have grown stronger every day.

"This is clearly apparent not only to me, but to my colleagues in
the office who have the opportunity of coming in touch with the
officials of the Party throughout the country, and although I have
made no attempt to collect views on the subject from these people,
no day now passes without anxiety being expressed to us about the
present situation.

"I have gathered recently that our officials in other parts of the
country have the same experience and although the feeling of apprehension is greater in some districts than in others, from practically
all quarters one hears the view that it would be in the interests of the
Party that the Leader should reconsider his position.

"We are, of course, receiving daily resolutions from associations
throughout the country pledging support to Mr. Baldwin, and so
long as he is the Leader those resolutions will continue to be passed.
It would be a mistake, however, to assume that there is no feeling of
disquiet in the organisations which express the support of the Leader
of the Party in this way. The Party spirit is very strong, and the
great body of our members are loyal. There are few who have not
great regard, which in many cases amounts to affection, for Mr.
Baldwin as an individual, and the only criticism one ever hears is with
regard to his leadership and my strong impression is that if it were
possible to obtain the collective opinion of those very people who
hold him in such high esteem, they would advise him that he does
not hold a strong position in the Party at the present moment.

"There has, of course, been dissatisfaction with the leadership of
the Party ever since the Beaverbrook and Rothermere campaign
started, but for a long time it was confined to a comparatively small
section. To-day, however, the feeling that he is not a strong Leader
is widely felt and cannot, in my opinion, be ignored.

"During the last week or so, and particularly during the last few
days, I have felt that there is a grave apprehension in the minds of
some of our supporters lest a sudden development might bring about
a change which would not eventually prove an advantage to the
Party. Many of our supporters are worried about the question of
India. They lean much more towards the views of Mr. Churchill

than to those expressed by Mr. Baldwin in the House of Commons, but they would be very perturbed at the possibility of any change of leadership taking place as a result of the differences between those two statesmen. They would prefer, I believe, that if a new Leader is to be chosen, he should be elected on broad policy and not on any one single issue. The feeling in the Party at the present moment is such that I gather some of the more experienced politicians in the country are apprehensive of the possibilities in the present situation.

"The position appears to me to be so serious that I feel compelled to place my impression of it before you, and while I would not at all relish the task, if it is considered my duty to place these impressions before the Leader himself, I am prepared to do so."

On receipt of this memorandum, never before published, Chamberlain consulted separately his brother Austen, Cunliffe-Lister, Hoare, Eyres-Monsell the Chief Whip, Hailsham and Bridgeman. They agreed about the strength of the anti-Baldwin feeling, and though everyone except Bridgeman felt that Baldwin would have to resign, no-one disputed the necessity of showing him the memorandum. Hailsham, however, suggested a short delay. Baldwin was due to make a major speech the following week and it would be hard lines to give him such a shock just when he was preparing for a great effort. Chamberlain did not relish the prospect of having it said that he had hustled Baldwin off the throne, and agreed to hold up the memorandum. Austen then telephoned Neville to say he was unhappy about this decision, feeling that the imminence of a big speech was a reason for letting Baldwin know his real position, not for hiding it from him. What finally made Chamberlain's mind up were two announcements in the papers on February 28th about the St. George's by-election; first that Sir Ernest Petter would stand as an anti-Baldwin candidate, with the support of Beaverbrook and Rothermere, and second that Moore-Brabazon had withdrawn rather than champion Baldwin.

On the morning of Sunday March 1st, Topping's memorandum, with the omission of a couple of wounding phrases (not included in the quotation above), was sent round to Baldwin by hand. Chamberlain did not now expect Baldwin to resign immediately: indeed, he noted it as an irony of politics that Beaverbrook's intervention at St. George's would cause Baldwin to dig his toes in and rally the disaffected round him. Baldwin's first reaction, however, was quite different. He and his wife, he told Chamberlain the same afternoon, both felt he should go. "I did not seek in any way to combat this resolution," Chamberlain wrote in his diary. But late that night Bridgeman combated it hard, and even suggested that Baldwin should counter-attack, resign his own seat, and fight St. George's himself. Such a melodramatic gesture was frowned upon by Chamberlain and Topping, who considered it preposterous to submit the leadership of the Party to a single constituency; and similar advice came from Geoffrey Dawson, the editor of *The Times*, and from Camrose who warned that if Baldwin stood the *Daily Telegraph* would not support him. Accordingly the diary for March 3rd records, "I saw S.B. who told me that Duff Cooper would stand for St. George's, but he said nothing about resignation".

Resignation before the by-election would in any case be disastrous, reported the Whips; but in the minds of most of Baldwin's colleagues the question had been postponed, not settled.

N.C. to Ida 7.3.1931.

"Personally I do not believe anything but a very early General Election can save him and evidently other people think so too as my friends tell me that there is any amount of lobbying going on for Winston and Horne as successors. So far as I am concerned I am doing nothing except that I dined with Hailsham privately on Thursday night and discussed the whole situation with him . . . we were in complete agreement that either of us would serve under the other and that either of us would accept the party's decision as to who should lead. Geoffrey Ellis who came to see me says that the Hailsham-N.C. combination is what the City would like and that if it were known that we would act together no other alternative would have a chance."

A few days later he was informed by Joseph Ball, the Director of the Research Department, who had had a long conversation with Davidson, that Baldwin had "definitely made up his mind not to go unless he was kicked out", that he was very angry with some of his colleagues, particularly Hailsham, who, he believed, had been plotting against him, and that he was sore against

Chamberlain for not having supported him more stoutly. Austen now added fat to this fire. Without consulting his brother, he bluntly asked Baldwin at a meeting of the Business Committee to release Neville from the Central Office in order to strengthen their front-bench debating talent. Both men were now smarting with resentment, and seeing insults where perhaps none was intended. Chamberlain decided he must escape from an acutely difficult position which had already shadowed their relationship. A series of unsatisfactory interviews took place in which the question of his successor at Central Office was discussed but in which Baldwin expressed "no single word of surprise, regret or satisfaction at my decision". Matters came to a head on March 24th when a basic misunderstanding was brought to light. It concerned their conversation on the afternoon of March 1st when Baldwin had decided to resign. According to Chamberlain, Baldwin had told him immediately he arrived that he had resolved to go, and only later on asked him whether he thought his colleagues would agree with the course he was taking. According to Baldwin, he came to his decision only when Chamberlain told him his colleagues wished him to go; it was therefore his colleagues whom he blamed. Both held to their own versions, but at least the air had been cleared; grievances were buried, apologies were made and, in the words of the diary, "we parted shaking hands and with the clouds removed". Next day, peace was made with the colleagues, though not without some brutal talk, particularly from Austen.

Whilst reflection convinced him that he was right to leave the Central Office, Chamberlain found the decision painful. He had been reluctant to go there in the first place and had stipulated in his letter of acceptance to Baldwin "that I may be released from the office as soon as I can report to you that I have carried out such measures of reorganisation as I may find to be desirable, and that the work can be expected to proceed smoothly without me". In fact, despite the personal embarrassments involved, he had found the work of administration congenial and perhaps some consolation for being out of office.

A number of notable reforms stem from his nine months' tenure. Remembering a very stormy debate on the subject at the

1929 Party Conference, he decided that the long-standing and undemocratic arrangement whereby the Chairman of the Party was also Chairman of the Executive Committee of the National Union should cease; and in October 1930, Kingsley Wood was elected Chairman of the Executive. By February 1931, Chamberlain's committee of investigation of which Hoare and Geoffrey Ellis were members, had devised a practical scheme which he thought would add considerably to the efficiency of the Party machine and lead to great economy also. The present structure of the Central Office derives in almost every particular from this document. The title of "Principal Agent" was absorbed in that of the "General Director" who would be in control of every branch of the Central Office. Lower down in the hierarchy the new broom swept clean; and though the Opposition Press declared that Central Office was "seething with discontent", he wrote to Hilda that "the only unhappy ones are those who to their astonishment and dismay are being asked to do something to earn their salaries" and those who had received notice to quit—"the tallest poppies but...not all that will be felled by the mowing machine!". Perhaps most revealing of his enthusiasm for the work and his desire to continue it, he empowered the Chairman of the Party to create "the new office of Deputy Chairman to be filled *if I enter a Government*".

Fate decreed otherwise, and Stonehaven succeeded him in April 1931; but not before he had brought off one final coup. At Hoare's suggestion, he got in touch with Beaverbrook a few days after Duff Cooper's victory at St. George's, and found him ready to come to terms. An agreed correspondence was released to the Press on March 30th in which Beaverbrook promised to help the Conservative Party at the next Election if he were assured, as Chamberlain did assure him, that its policy would aim at increasing not only manufacturing but also agricultural production by the most efficient and practicable method. Beaverbrook himself held that duties on foreign foodstuffs were best, but recognised that quotas and prohibitions had advantages in relation to some foodstuffs. "The cause," he added, "is infinitely greater than the quarrel." Thus a temporary truce was called, though only after protracted haggling over vocabulary.

N.C. to Ida 5.4.1931.

"I have been overwhelmed with congratulations which have come from all quarters (except S.B. who can't bear the thought of making it up with the Press Lords and doesn't see how it has helped his own position). . . . I am not quite sure what will happen to negotiations of this kind when I am no longer Chairman. But I daresay I shall still be wanted to take part in them, just as I don't expect to part entirely from the Office. The staff who seemed most genuinely grieved and upset over my departure are anxious to maintain contact after I go and my retention of the Research Department will make it easier to ensure this."

9

CRISIS AND PROTECTION

(April 1931 – December 1932)

BY the early months of 1931, the imminence of a major economic crisis had become apparent. The springs of international trade were fast drying up, and the unemployment figures in Britain under the Labour Government had more than doubled in less than two years. A strong movement of opinion, now no longer confined to the Conservative Party, manifested itself in favour of a tariff. Not only the Federation of British Industries but also the economic committee of the Trades Union Congress, not only Oswald Mosley, recently severed from Labour, but also Maynard Keynes and John Simon, the brains of Liberalism, were saying the same thing in different ways. But to all these voices the Government and its obstinate Chancellor, Philip Snowden, shut their ears. "The reflection which came to me," said Chamberlain in the Budget debate on April 28th, "was that here is the last Chancellor of the Exchequer who will ever again introduce a Free Trade Budget in this House . . . it will remain a mark to show the end of an obsolete and worn-out system and the beginning of something more adaptable to the needs of modern industrial civilization."

His words were probably just and certainly prophetic. The delicate system of international trade, based on the gold standard, had been dislocated by the war. This dislocation had been aggravated by war debts and reparations. The tariff policies of the two chief creditor countries, the United States and France, rendered impossible the discharge of debt by payment in goods and services. Hence vast quantities of gold, amounting by 1931 to three-fifths of the world's supply, accumulated in New York and Paris. As long as American loans poured into Europe, and particularly into Germany, this dangerous lack of balance was concealed; but in the autumn of 1929 Wall Street crashed, the loans dried up, trade contracted and ruin crept on Europe. In May 1931, the principal Austrian bank failed; financial panic spread to Germany; and by July there was a serious run on sterling which two increases in Bank Rate in successive weeks did nothing to stem.

"The problem, once it became centred in London," writes Harold Nicolson in his *Life of George V*, "ceased to be a purely monetary or banking problem and became political. The following harsh syllogism was imposed. The Bank of England could not save the pound sterling unless it could obtain large credits in New York and Paris: it would fail to obtain those credits unless the British Government produced a balanced budget: it would be impossible to balance that budget unless drastic economies were made: and if the world were to be convinced of the sincerity and efficacy of our policy of retrenchment, it was essential that among our economies should figure prominently some reduction of the benefits paid to the unemployed."[1]

To no-one was this logic clearer than to Chamberlain. On July 30th, the eve of Parliament's rising for the summer recess, he opened a debate in the Commons on the financial situation. Various things had happened since the Budget, he said, to confirm and strengthen the views he had then expressed. The most important was the relationship between the Exchequer and the unemployment insurance fund, upon which debt was then being incurred at the rate of about £1,000,000 a week. The return of prosperity ultimately depended on tariffs and a close trade combination within the Empire; but this would take time, whereas the situation was urgent and critical. What was immediately needed, therefore, was economy, involving sacrifices in which all must share.

N.C. Hansard 30.7.1931.

"The people of this country have got to realise that foreign confidence in the credit of this country has been shaken, because they have

[1] *King George V* (Constable, 1952) .p .450.

watched the expenditure of this country growing faster than its income, and the restoration of that confidence can only be brought about when the foreigner is convinced, first, that the people of this country realise the situation, and, secondly, that they are going to have the courage to take the necessary steps to deal with it. At bottom, I believe there is no foundation whatever for this want of confidence in British stability.''

The last sentence, and much else in the same vein, redeemed a promise that Chamberlain had given the Chancellor privately the day before. He had intended to make a strong attack on the Government, but found the City nervous that provocative speeches on both sides might accelerate the flight from the pound. So he went to see Snowden and told him that if he would give an assurance that he would use the recess to study ways and means of economy, he would tone down his own speech, say nothing offensive, express confidence in the soundness of the position, and end with an appeal instead of an attack. Snowden at once accepted the offer, and in his autobiography was later to record: "Mr. Chamberlain's speech next day was singularly free from the slightest spirit of partisanship. It was couched in language which showed that his desire was not to secure a Party triumph, but how best to serve the interests of the country."[1]

Chamberlain's analysis was much more than borne out by the Report of the Committee on National Expenditure, under the chairmanship of Sir George May, which was published immediately after Parliament rose. The Committee estimated that to balance the Budget in 1932 a deficiency of about £120 million would have to be made good by fresh taxation or by economy. In one of the most draconian State papers of modern times, they recommended economies of at least £96½ million, to be made by reducing official salaries and pay and by cutting unemployment expenditures to the tune of £66½ million, including a 20 per cent reduction in rates of benefit. The Report administered a salutary shock to the British public, but at the same time adversely affected the confidence of the foreign investor. The heavy drain on gold was resumed. The Prime Minister was warned by Ernest Harvey, Deputy Governor of the Bank, that "we were on the edge of the

[1] *An Autobiography* (Ivor Nicholson & Watson, 1934), Vol. 2, p. 929.

precipice" and assented to the facts being put before the other Parties.

In response to a message from Harvey, Chamberlain broke his holiday in Perthshire and returned to London.

N.C. to Hilda 16.8.1931.

"I had to take the night train on the 12th and next morning met S.B. who had also been summoned from France. We saw the P.M. and Snowden that afternoon. They said they had decided that the Budget must be balanced and that economies must be made to the extent, though not necessarily in the precise ways, suggested by the Economy Committee. They felt however that the occasion demanded sacrifices all round and they were considering in what way these could be obtained. . . . If they could be assured of our general support they proposed to summon Parliament in the first fortnight in September to pass a supplementary Budget and an Economy Bill. . . .

"To secure such a measure of relief and to do it through a Socialist Government seems to me so important in the national interest that we must give it our support provided the proposals for 'equal sacrifice' do not imperil British credit or too brazenly affront ordinary rules of justice and fair play. And I don't think they will do either. . . .

"Anyway the decisions are left to me as S.B. is not coming back. I think he would agree that crises of this kind are not his forte. He had apparently given no thought to the situation, asked no intelligent question, made no helpful suggestion and indeed was chiefly anxious to be gone before he was 'drawn into something'. He left a final message for me that he was most grateful to me for sparing him the necessity of returning and he would 'back me to the end!' So I go back tomorrow night. I have asked Sam Hoare to come and attend the conference with me."

Four days that changed the alignments of British politics were now at hand—a "time of great mental tension" Chamberlain wrote to his wife, and some physical discomfort too, according to Hoare; for it was a cold, wet August and both Chamberlain's house and Hoare's were shut, as was the main building of the Carlton Club. The attitude of the Conservative Party in this great crisis was therefore determined by the two friends in their bedrooms in the Club's annexe and over lunch and dinner at a small restaurant in Sloane Square.

On August 20th, with the Liberals Herbert Samuel and Donald Maclean, they went to No. 10 where Snowden told them that the Budget deficit would be larger than the May Committee's estimate, namely £170 million, but that the economies tentatively proposed were less than the May recommendations, only amounting to £78½ million. Chamberlain argued strongly the inadequacy of this cut and the need to deal with unemployment benefit. So when they returned to Downing Street next day they were astounded to hear that the biggest cut the Cabinet would agree to was £56 million, only £5 million of which represented a real saving on unemployment insurance. Asked what would happen if this failed to restore foreign confidence, Snowden replied "the deluge". This provoked a strong protest from Hoare, upon which the Prime Minister asked, in what Chamberlain's diary calls a jocular way, "Well, are you prepared to join the Board of Directors?" Hoare said that "if seriously meant, that was a proposition which would demand serious consideration". Then, at Herbert Samuel's suggestion, the Conservatives and Liberals withdrew to consult among themselves and afterwards among their colleagues. At 9.30 that night they returned to find MacDonald alone.

Diary, 22.8.1931.

"I opened first and intimated (1) that if these were the final proposals . . . we should turn them out immediately the House met, (2) that before then we anticipated that the financial crash must come, (3) that we considered that it was his, the P.M.'s bounden duty to avoid that crash, and (4) that we were ready to give him any support in our power for that purpose either with his present or in a reconstructed Government. Samuel followed on exactly the same lines, not a word being said about a National Government though I think it was fairly clear that we were not excluding such an eventuality. In reply the P.M. began by drawing a touching picture of his own position (a thing he loves to do). He had founded, nursed, cherished, built up the Socialist Party. It was painful enough to leave an old Party: what must it be for him to contemplate killing his own child. He did not think resignation would help. He would remain P.M., assert his own views, invite his colleagues to support him and tell those who would not that they might go 'where they liked'."

Events now moved swiftly towards the formation of a National Government. Chamberlain's papers suggest that from early in July MacDonald had been confiding in "leaky vessels" his taste for such a Government in which he might serve as Foreign Secretary under Baldwin. On July 29th, Chamberlain had discussed the question with his brother Austen, Hailsham, Cunliffe-Lister and Hoare, none of whom wanted a coalition, but all of whom thought it might be unavoidable, "though only on condition that tariffs were accepted". From the conversations of August 21st, he drew the correct conclusions that all-Party agreement was essential, and that the Labour Party might easily be split and MacDonald detached from it. On August 22nd the Cabinet empowered the Prime Minister to enquire of the Opposition Parties if they would support the Government on the basis of economies amounting to £68½ million. "Now," wrote Chamberlain to Ida that day, "the only way in which the economy figures could be raised was by cutting the dole and if once we could fasten that on the Labour Party they would be irrevocably split. R.M.'s proposal therefore suited me down to the ground." So it proved. On the evening of August 23rd the Prime Minister reported to Baldwin, Chamberlain and Samuel that his Cabinet was indeed irrevocably split and that he had advised the King to see the three Party leaders next morning.

Diary, 23.8.1931.

"For himself, he would help us to get these proposals through though it means his death warrant, but it would be of no use for him to join a Government. He would be a ridiculous figure unable to command support and would bring odium on us as well as himself . . . I then intervened . . . had he considered that, though not commanding many votes in the House he might command much support in the country. And would not a Government including members of all Parties hold a much stronger position than a two-Party combination. R.M. said his mind was not finally made up but that was his present mood. I then suggested that many people would not understand why if he supported the new Government he refused to enter it and would criticise him on that ground. He replied that that was a worrying point, but people would say he had stuck to his office for the sake of the salary, to which I replied that if several of his colleagues accompanied him the odium would at least be spread. Finally I asked him if he had considered the effect on foreign opinion which was all important. . . . This argument took him in a weak place. He said without egotism he thought his name did carry weight in America. . . . Samuel supported me strongly though S.B. maintained silence and we did not pursue the matter further then."

Thus Chamberlain went home that night, as he told an audience at Dumfries on September 12th, believing that Baldwin would be sent for to form a Government next day and, as he did not tell them, unsure if it would be a National Government or if MacDonald would join it. In fact he had argued his case perhaps too well, and next day MacDonald was not only in but at the head of the National Government—not, announced the Downing Street statement, a Coalition Government in the usual sense of the term, but a Government of co-operation for the one purpose of dealing with the national emergency.

Behind the scenes, both the composition and the policy of the new Government became subjects of instant acrimony and dispute. Though MacDonald could count on a mere handful of Labour supporters, he gave Baldwin only four places to dispose of in a Cabinet of ten[1] and vetoed the inclusion of Hailsham as "particularly obnoxious to the Labour Party". Chamberlain accepted the Ministry of Health and secured Cabinet posts for Hoare and Cunliffe-Lister, but "to my very great distress" found Austen deeply humiliated to be fobbed off with the Admiralty. On policy, Samuel privately pressed on the Conservatives a scheme of Lothian's for a capital levy. "The more I think of it, the less I like it," wrote Chamberlain in his diary on August 27th, and it was dropped, due to the opposition of the Bank. Beaverbrook, on the other hand, who dined alone with Chamberlain on September 3rd, was for jettisoning Samuel and unpopular policies alike and going to the country at once on the full tariff programme. To this Chamberlain demurred. The tariff must come, he was sure, but they could not go into an Election with the necessary economies still to be made and candidates all over the country pledging themselves not to cut this or that.

[1] MacDonald, Sankey, Snowden and Thomas (Labour), Baldwin, Chamberlain, Hoare and Cunliffe-Lister (Conservative), Samuel and Reading (Liberal).

Accordingly the economies were made. A second Snowden Budget imposed new taxation and an Economy Bill prescribed unpopular cuts—so unpopular that teachers resorted to street processions, sporadic clashes took place between unemployed and police, and naval ratings of the Atlantic Fleet at Invergordon demonstrated an unrest that was interpreted as "mutiny". "The world is completely out of joint," comments the diary for September 19th, and two days later Britain was obliged to go off the gold standard. Chamberlain's reaction was quick and clear: the crisis had not been surmounted by emergency measures, new measures would only be effective if the Government taking them had a clear expression of public approval behind it, and, provided he was willing to accept the tariff, MacDonald's continued leadership was a price worth paying since it would make that approval easier to secure. In this sense Chamberlain briefed the friendly Press, and on September 24th the Conservative Business Committee unanimously took the same line and further agreed that "if we went to election with R.M. as P.M. we must accept him as P.M. when we came back, though we might well have an understanding as to the filling of the posts in a new Government".

The objective now was threefold: to secure a prompt dissolution on a manifesto drafted by Chamberlain "which should ask for a free hand while indicating that tariffs would be considered by the new Government"; to retain MacDonald as Prime Minister; and to oust Samuel if he would not swallow Chamberlain's formula. After more than a week of disputatious and inconclusive Cabinets, of private meetings and of noises off from Lloyd George's sick-bed at Churt, a rather different conclusion emerged. An early appeal under MacDonald's leadership was indeed decided upon on October 5th, but only after the Liberal leaders had agreed to Snowden's suggestion that the Prime Minister should issue his own manifesto asking for a free hand whilst the Party leaders issued their own appeals to their own Parties.

N.C. to Hilda 10.10.1931.

"We are now committed to this extraordinary proceeding under which we go to the country as a united Government, one section of which is to advocate tariffs while the other declares it has an open

mind but is unalterably convinced of the virtues of Free Trade. . . .
I never fought an election under such a difficulty. . . . I hope we may
win the victory which we anticipate but if we do I foresee a peck
of troubles as soon as the election is over, first in the formation of the
Government and then in the formulation of policy."

The victory came in unprecedented measure—a Parliamentary
majority exceeding 500, more than 200 Conservative gains from
Labour, and, with the single exception of Lansbury, a clean sweep
of the Opposition front bench. But the "peck of troubles" came
too, just as Chamberlain had foreseen. The King's Private Secretary recorded on November 2nd Baldwin's impatience at Mac-
Donald's hesitant Cabinet-making, and added, "The King thought
that Neville Chamberlain was so good as Minister of Health that
it would be a pity to make him Chancellor of the Exchequer,
where he would be suspected of ultra-protectionist views. His
Majesty said that he thought he, Mr. Baldwin, should go as
Chancellor of the Exchequer, but the latter said he had asked for
no portfolio . . . Mr. Baldwin advocated Mr. Neville Chamberlain being at the Foreign Office."[1] In the end, and only after an
uncomfortable half-hour when the *Evening News* had telephoned
him that John Simon had been appointed, he was duly installed
at the Treasury. He had hoped that Cunliffe-Lister would stay at
the Board of Trade to work with him, but protectionists in both
key economic positions was more than Snowden and the Samuelites could be expected to stomach, and Runciman got the job
instead.

Chamberlain's determination now was to effect the fiscal revolution his father had dreamt of and his Party was bent upon. By
February he had achieved the first part of the policy, the protection of the home market. First came the emergency tariffs provided by the Abnormal Importations Act, which safeguarded the
position while the Government was working out its permanent
policy and gave immediate protection against dumping. In a letter
of November 15th we have Chamberlain's own account of the
inception of this Act. At a Cabinet earlier that week he had given
warning of the adverse balance of trade and the marked increase
in imports. Samuel took alarm at once, but could not refuse Mac-

[1] Nicolson, *op. cit.*, p. 494.

Donald's proposal to refer the matter to the Chancellor and the President of the Board of Trade to investigate facts and report. When the two met later in the day, Runciman himself proposed an enabling Bill giving power to impose a 10 per cent duty on excessive imports. Chamberlain told him he must not tie his own hands more than necessary. He should therefore name not an invariable but a maximum rate with power to vary downwards at his discretion, and for this purpose 10 per cent was not high enough. Runciman then suggested 20 per cent but Chamberlain preferred to leave the figure blank. Let them accept the outline of the Bill, he advised, and then we will settle the rate. Immediately the Cabinet had agreed the principle, after strenuous objection from Samuel and Maclean, Chamberlain asked Snowden what rate he would suggest. Chamberlain's account proceeds, "As I had hoped, he said 'What about 100 per cent?' Runciman at once agreed . . . So there it is. Comic, isn't it, to think of the Free Traders giving power to two Ministers to put a 100 per cent duty on any mortal manufactured article they like!" Equally comic he found their acceptance of a tariff on certain vegetables, fruit and flowers—possibly the thin end of a food taxes wedge—contained in the Horticultural Tariffs Act. "Snowden growled but almost inaudibly" he wrote on November 29th, "and the Samuelites offered no objection . . . But as for me, I laff and laff".

The final policy hurdle, the *permanent* tariff, was, however, no laughing matter. As the winter months went by, the battle waxed furious in Cabinet Committee. Chamberlain was in the chair, and Snowden and Samuel fought stubbornly against him. Runciman, on the other hand, was now so much converted that by January he was speaking of resigning if a general 10 per cent tariff was not agreed. Matters came to a head at a Cabinet on January 21st, when the Prime Minister declared in favour of the proposals and Samuel, Maclean, Sinclair and Snowden threatened resignation. When they met again next day, MacDonald drew attention to the disastrous effect abroad of a break-up, and then dwelt on his own embarrassment, forced as he would be to fill all the vacancies with Conservatives. Chamberlain intervened at once, refusing to compromise and declaring that the resignations would not affect Conservative loyalty to the Prime Minister. At this point, however, Hailsham came forward with the proposal that all the dissentients should be allowed to express their objections to the tariff while remaining members of the Government. Chamberlain had earlier suggested to the Prime Minister that Snowden, since he was now in the Lords, might take this course, but had not thought it possible for members of the House of Commons. To his astonishment the dissentients accepted the proposal, and the "agreement to differ" on this one point became one of the curiosities of constitutional history. But the battle was won.

On February 4th, 1932, "the great day of my life" as he wrote to his sister, the House and galleries were full. He took the notes for his speech from the red dispatch box which had been his father's as Colonial Secretary. But for more than an hour of lucid exposition he avoided any personal reference or emotion. A general tariff, he claimed, would help to correct the balance of payments, raise fresh revenue, prevent an unchecked depreciation of the pound, and decrease unemployment by transferring "to our own factories and fields work which is now done elsewhere". He therefore moved that with effect from March 1st there should be charged on all goods imported into the United Kingdom, save those specifically exempted, a duty of 10 per cent of their value. On the basis of this general flat rate would be built a superstructure of additional duties, but only upon the advice of an independent Committee removed from political pressures. By the use of this "system of moderate Protection" the Government hoped to encourage greater efficiency in home industry and to secure a bargaining factor in tariff negotiations with other countries. None of the new duties, however, would apply to goods from the Dominions, at least until after the Ottawa Conference, "since we desire to mark at every stage our wish to approach this conference in the true spirit of Imperial unity and harmony".

Then, fearful as he later admitted that he might not be able to control his voice, he came to the peroration.

N.C. Hansard 4.2.1932.

"There can have been few occasions in all our long political history when to the son of a man who counted for something in his day and generation has been vouchsafed the privilege of setting the seal on the work which the father began but had perforce to leave unfinished. Nearly 29 years have passed since Joseph Chamberlain entered upon his great campaign in favour of Imperial Preference and Tariff Reform. More than 17 years have gone by since he died, without having seen the fulfilment of his aims and yet convinced that, if not exactly in his way, yet in some modified form his vision would eventually take shape. His work was not in vain. Time and the misfortunes of the country have brought conviction to many who did not feel that they could agree with him then. I believe he would have found consolation for the bitterness of his disappointment if he could have foreseen that these proposals, which are the direct and legitimate descendants of his own conception, would be laid before the House of Commons, which he loved, in the presence of one and by the lips of the other of the two immediate successors to his name and blood."

Austen came down to the Treasury Bench and silently shook hands with his brother while the House cheered and cheered again; next day shoals of letters and telegrams brought congratulations from a cross-section of the nation "ranging from the King to my tailor".

He had written in his New Year letter to Hilda that he felt 1932 was going to be a very momentous year for him, probably a turning point in his political career, and it proved no less. In February had come the tariff, in August the Ottawa Conference was to establish firmly the complementary system of Imperial Preference. Between these two dates his first Budget, his great conversion scheme and his work at the Lausanne Conference on reparations added to the new Chancellor's reputation. The one big shadow this year was his personal health; for a severe recurrence of gout put him out of action for the Finance Bill, hampered him at Lausanne, and caused ideas of retirement to come briefly into his mind.

The Budget, which he opened on April 19th, was certainly not popular, but its austerity commanded respect. "The path of financial stability is not only hard and stony but long and weary," he warned. He had been driven to the conclusion that if we were to avoid violent and perilous fluctuations in our currency, especially those due to speculative operations, it was essential to hold adequate reserves of gold and foreign exchange. For this purpose he proposed, in a decision of great future importance, to borrow up to £150 millions to establish a new Exchequer Equalisation Account. As far as revenue was concerned, the previous year's depression would mean a heavy fall in the coming year's yield of income tax and surtax. The prospective deficit of £35 million would be largely made good by his tariff, though partly by a tax on tea; but there could be no remissions. "Nothing could be more harmful to the ultimate material recovery of this country or to its present moral fibre, than that we should indulge ourselves with hopes possibly ill-founded, certainly premature, which might tempt us to relax the efforts which have already produced a wonderful revival of public confidence."

This revival was the strongest of Chamberlain's arguments for the timing of the conversion scheme which he announced to the Commons on June 30th. Talk of conversion had been in the air for a long while; for it had become increasingly obvious that War Loan at 5 per cent was out of relation to other Government securities, and since it attached to so large a body of stock it was "hanging like a cloud over the capital market", a source of depression and a hindrance to the expansion of trade. To reduce the rate of interest, as he now proposed, to $3\frac{1}{2}$ per cent (with a cash bonus to those who continued in the Loan) would also mean a net saving to the Exchequer in interest charges of about £23 million a year. The more than 90 per cent success of the operation exceeded the most optimistic forecasts, and further conversions in the course of the year brought the total annual saving in interest up to £40 million. They had a tonic effect on the economy and strengthened the position of the Government.

The Conference at Lausanne, from which Chamberlain had briefly returned to announce the conversion, accomplished something less than he had hoped. At the opening session on June 17th he had come out flatly for cancellation all round of both war debts and reparations. This proved unacceptable to the French, and what had to be accepted instead was a German lump sum in lieu of reparations, accompanied by a declaration that a new order was going to begin, "since financial confidence depended on a sense that political relations were really improved". For this Chamberlain was obliged to work extremely hard.

"The P.M. is I think getting to rely on my help very much. He has a good deal of difficulty in following the more technical side and he doesn't understand French, so he likes to have me about and in fact he won't now conduct any conversations with the other delegations without having me there too. I get on very well with the French— the Wigrams declare that Herriot 'adores 'me, and also with the Germans, though I must say the latter, especially von Papen, are incredibly stupid."

The trust and affection that Chamberlain had inspired in Herriot was indeed what saved the day, and both the final sum to be paid and the final formula to be used in the political declaration were settled between the two at three o'clock on the morning of July 8th, the day the agreement was signed.

Within a week of Lausanne he had set sail for Ottawa, one of a delegation which included Baldwin, Hailsham, Runciman, Thomas, Gilmour and Cunliffe-Lister. Crossing on the *Empress of Britain*, he was soon driving himself, and the others, hard; insisting on continual conferences, re-drafting Baldwin's opening speech, and drawing up "a series of general propositions for the approval of the Conference, both in order to give the lead to the Dominions and the outside public and to form a test to which every proposition afterwards put forward could be submitted". This set of resolutions, by which he set great store, was brushed aside by the Canadian Prime Minister, Bennett. All that emerged, buried in the final report, was a declaration that the lowering or removal of Empire tariff barriers would facilitate the flow of trade, and that the agreements made in Ottawa were "a step forward which should in future lead to further progress in the same direction".

That they were a step forward could not, however, be denied. Agreements were severally negotiated between the United Kingdom and the Dominions and India, in which the principle of reciprocal preference was enshrined. In these agreements both of the practical ideas which Chamberlain himself developed at Ottawa found their place. He had explained to Bennett on August 9th that even if the Dominions gave Britain everything she asked for, the immediate effect of these concessions would not be comparable with what Britain gave them. If they were to carry the British people with them, future policy should hold out the hope of a gradually descending scale of duties giving to British exporters the ultimate position of a domestic competitor. Accordingly in the final agreements Canada and Australia gave an undertaking that they would not in future protect uneconomic industries and that their Tariff Boards, before which British manufacturers would be free to appear, would, within a reasonable period, reduce protective duties to a "level which should give United Kingdom producers full opportunity of reasonable competition in the Dominion markets".

Chamberlain's second idea concerned agricultural products, and particularly meat in whose wholesale price there had been a disastrous fall. The Dominions considered that Britain should restrict foreign imports until the price rose to a level which would enable their farmers to earn a living. But, as Chamberlain pointed out, it was in fact the Dominions themselves who had broken the price by increasing their production. His solution was that, instead of our simply restricting imports, they should, over five or ten years, voluntarily restrict production, thus enabling us to guarantee stability and progressively increase the Dominion share in our market. It was not possible at Ottawa to carry to a conclusion so large an arrangement, but pending a more permanent scheme an eighteen-months' temporary programme was agreed with Australia and New Zealand.

Both the meat agreement and the agreement with Canada were arrived at only at the eleventh hour, and in circumstances in which the breakdown of the Conference and the break-up of the British Government were alike contemplated.

N.C. to Ida 21.8.1932.

"I hope I may never have to go through such an experience again. I don't think I ever worked so hard in my life, for the heaviest of the strain fell on me. Hailsham who had the next most strenuous time nearly collapsed on Friday night. . . .

"As the Duke said to Creevey of Waterloo, It was a d——d close-run thing. So close, indeed, that I only initialled the Canadian agreement at 1.30 on Saturday morning after a prolonged and desperate battle with Bennett. I had begun my day's work on Friday at 9.0 a.m. and had been fighting all day with almost every delegation in turn. It was only by the exercise of almost incredible patience, self-restraint in face of outrageous provocation, ingenuity in finding new ways round unexpected obstacles, and complete confidence in one another that we achieved success. . . . Bruce [Australia] and Coates [New Zealand] refused to make an agreement unless we gave them the duty on meat. . . . J. H. Thomas said he would not embarrass his colleagues but if a duty were given he would just fade quietly out of the picture when we got home. Runciman said the same. . . . After the others had gone I stopped behind with S.B. I told him that I had felt that it would be unfair as well as distasteful to bandy resignations about with my colleagues, but that I could not retain my position if the Conference failed because we had refused a duty on meat. . . . S.B. at once sent for Thomas to come back . . . it ended by Thomas saying that he had never had such splendid colleagues, that he thought anything was preferable to a breakdown of the Conference, and that he would sacrifice his own opinions. . . . In our turn we played the game and keeping a bold and un-flinching front we got an agreement without the duty after all.

"In spite of the anxieties they caused us I have no complaint to make of the Australians or the New Zealanders. They had to think of their difficulties with their own people . . . they were quite straightforward about it.

"Bennett was a different proposition . . . he alternately blustered, bullied, sobbed, prevaricated, delayed and obstructed to the very last moment. . . .

"I ought to add after giving such an account of Bennett that it was he who asked that I might sign the Canadian Treaty and that when he said goodbye at Quebec he begged me not to bear malice against him and finished with, Love to Annie and God bless you."

At home, the reception was mixed. His audience of the King at Balmoral scarcely touched on Ottawa, and he was "rather disappointed that Majesty did not take a more serious view". Snowden, Samuel and Sinclair, together with a handful of junior Ministers, came to the parting of the ways and resigned on September 28th; Snowden characteristically denouncing Ottawa as involving a policy of national humiliation and bondage in which Free Traders could not be expected to acquiesce even passively. Since they would now be a more homogeneous team, Chamberlain reflected, they might "move towards that fused Party under a National name which I regard as certain to come"—a phrase which recalls a letter twelve months earlier, hoping "that we may presently develop into a National Party and get rid of that odious title of Conservative which has kept so many from joining us in the past". Meanwhile it was in this, his own Party, that he received most honour. One mark of this he found particularly gratifying. In December his fellow Birmingham members presented him with a massive silver salver engraved with the Chamberlain crest and the inscription, *Quos pater incepit post bis tria lustra labores Optatum ad finem filius expediit.*

10

CHANCELLOR OF THE EXCHEQUER

(End–1932 – Mid–1935)

THOSE who have written the story of the early 1930s have acknowledged Chamberlain as the dynamic element in MacDonald's last Government. In part, no doubt, this reflected the failings of his leaders and the lack of competition. The Prime Minister's health proved weaker than his courage and he proceeded to "outlive himself not in retirement but in office". Baldwin's distaste for detail grew with the years. Hailsham was unhappy leading the Lords, Simon utterly misplaced at the Foreign Office, and Hoare so immersed in Indian affairs that for weeks on end he would absent himself even from Cabinet. In part also, Chamberlain's strength derived from his dual role as Chancellor of the Exchequer and Chairman of the Conservative Research Department. No aspect of politics could lie quite outside the purview of a man who controlled both the nation's purse-strings and the Party's thinking machine. Early in 1934, he persuaded Baldwin to set up what came to be known in high Party circles as the C.C.C. (Cabinet Conservative Committee). This met regularly at 24 Old Queen Street and thrashed out a forward programme ranging from the extension of Ottawa to centralised slaughtering, and from Parliamentary reform to the improvement of the national physique. "At Mr. Baldwin's request, Mr. Chamberlain opened the proceedings *as usual,*" note the minutes of the tenth meeting with perhaps unintentional humour.

But even more than his colleagues or his offices, it was his temperament which determined Chamberlain's constructive part. "The amount of work you have to do," he wrote philosophically, "largely depends on what you make for yourself. Unhappily it is part of my nature that I cannot contemplate any problem without trying to find a solution for it." A letter to Hilda, dated October 15th, 1932, declares: "I have conceived a bold plan which I have imparted to the Minister of Labour and upon which the permanent officials are now working. It is nothing less than taking the whole relief of the able-bodied away from local authorities and Ministers and putting it outside Party politics." The Unemployment Assistance Board was thus the product of Chamberlain's thought—and when the Board, and the Government, ran into trouble over the operation of the means test at the beginning of 1935, he was Chairman of the Cabinet Committee which mitigated the severity of the regulations; at the same time persuading Oliver Stanley not to resign. As an ex-Minister of Health he pressed his ideas for slum clearance and the elimination of overcrowding on Hilton Young and rightly claimed in his private letters that all the main features of the 1934 housing proposals "came straight from me". He worked very closely, though not always uncritically, with Walter Elliot in the development of agricultural policy and the regulation of the market. His activities became so various that even his personal diary began to have sub-headings to mark the many irons he had in the fire. His conscientiousness was such that he was prepared, for example, to break off in the middle of preparing his Budget speech to draft for the Minister of Labour new instructions to the Commissioners for special areas.

At first he enjoyed this process unashamedly. To Hilda in October 1932 he admitted: "It amuses me to find a new policy for each of my colleagues in turn." By the spring of 1935, however, the tone had become a little querulous: "I am more and more carrying this Government on my back. . . . It is certainly time there was a change." MacDonald frequently, and Baldwin sometimes, hinted at retirement, but neither retired; and to be number three in a Government in which he was doing a wider range of constructive work than anyone else was, perhaps, bound to lead to some sense of frustration.

N.C. to Hilda 23.3.1935.

"As you will see I have become a sort of Acting P.M.—only without the actual power of the P.M. I have to say 'Have you thought' or 'What would you say' when it would be quicker to say 'This is what you must do'."

Moreover, as his powers grew with the full stretch of responsibility, his self-confidence became more often and more clearly tinged with a certain impatience. There were public reprimands to the Archbishop of York for suggesting how the Budget surplus of 1934 might best be allocated, confidential fears expressed to Kingsley Wood lest the Prime Minister should muscle in on his regular briefing of lobby correspondents, private complaints about opposition from "fellows who think they ought to have had office and want to show the Government what a mistake was made in leaving them out", and Cabinet scuffles with those he sardonically christened "the Boys' Brigade", led by Elliot and Ormsby-Gore. He did not like not getting his own way.

Yet even in domestic matters, several of his pet schemes fell by the wayside. One of these was for the reform of the House of Lords. As early as 1931 he had set up a strong Party committee under Linlithgow which had produced, with the aid of the Research Department, a plan for cutting down the hereditary peers to one hundred and adding one hundred life peers. Only Duff Cooper had dissented, but the scheme was pigeonholed because, as Joseph Ball wrote to Baldwin in October 1933, "we felt that the subject was too thorny to touch unless and until we were absolutely obliged to deal with it". At the beginning of 1934, Chamberlain again strongly pressed the case for reform, partly on merits and partly because it might distract the right wing of the Conservative Party from excessive concentration on India. He even saw Hadley, the editor of the *Sunday Times*, and suggested to him that he might do some propaganda on the subject. Ministers, however, could not agree. When Salisbury introduced a Bill in May, a temporising reply had to be made on behalf of the Government, and in November, to the annoyance of Chamberlain and Hailsham, Baldwin dealt early reform a public death blow.

Scarcely less irritating was the fate of the "Department of

Housing" which had been suggested to Chamberlain by Ball in February 1934. The object was to convince the public that the Government were in earnest about slum clearance, and also to get the exposition of housing policy away from the rather uninspired Hilton Young. Geoffrey Lloyd, "a young man with enthusiasm who has made a special study of the subject and sits for a slum constituency" (Chamberlain's old seat, Ladywood) was suggested for the job by Chamberlain. But a leak to the press caused the idea to go off at half-cock. Chamberlain's alternative suggestion was a Cabinet shuffle in which Kingsley Wood would go to Health, Hilton Young to the War Office, Hailsham to the Woolsack, and Sankey into retirement. But Sankey made a terrible fuss ("I gather he wept!") and MacDonald decided to do nothing.

Neither of these incidents affected Chamberlain so deeply as the defeat of the "limited liability plan", one of his earliest incursions into the field of foreign affairs which henceforth increasingly occupied his mind. The plan originated during a defence debate on March 21st, 1934, in a series of written exchanges between Chamberlain and Simon who were sitting next to one another on the Government front bench. Simon passed to Chamberlain a short memorandum on the subject of economic and financial sanctions as a guarantee of security. Chamberlain replied with a counter-memorandum advocating what amounted to an international police force. In outline, the plan consisted of "a mutual guarantee by, say, Germany, France, Italy, U.K., Poland and Czechoslovakia, under which on breach of the convention each of the other signatories undertakes to put a limited specified force at the disposal of the joint body to be used to support the aggrieved party". For weeks he urged this initiative on his colleagues, and though Vansittart agreed that "further progress could only be made by exploring guarantees of security", the idea was finally killed by the stonewalling of the Chiefs of Staff and a formidable memorandum from Hankey, the Secretary of the Cabinet.

In matters of finance, however, he reigned supreme. At the beginning of 1933 there was considerable agitation in favour of deliberately unbalancing the Budget in order to cut income tax and give a psychological stimulus to the economy. "That proposal," as he noted in his Budget speech, "has been supported by eminent economists, powerful journalists, and, if my information is correct, by some hon. Members of this House." The eminent economists included Keynes, the powerful journalists belonged not only to *The Times* but also the *Daily Mail* and the *Daily Express*, and in the House the leading spokesman was Harold Macmillan. But Chamberlain would have nothing to do with what was to him unorthodox finance.

N.C. Hansard 25.4.1933.

"What would happen supposing that the reaction to the reduction of direct taxation did not actually materialise, as is so confidently expected? Do not let us forget that we are not immune, that we cannot be immune, from those grim forces that hold the world in their grip. With world trade shrinking, with world prices falling, can we really persuade ourselves that by unbalancing our Budget we are going to reverse these world movements, and that so rapidly that confidence would not wilt and falter while we were waiting for the upward turn? . . .

"Look round the world to-day and you see that badly unbalanced Budgets are the rule rather than the exception. Everywhere there appear Budget deficits piling up, yet they do not produce those favourable results which it is claimed would happen to us. On the contrary, I find that Budget deficits repeated year after year may be accompanied by deepening depression and by a constantly falling price level. . . . Of all countries passing through these difficult times the one that has stood the test with the greatest measure of success is the United Kingdom. Without under-rating the hardships of our situation—the long tragedy of the unemployed, the grievous burden of taxation, the arduous and painful struggle of those engaged in trade and industry—at any rate we are free from that fear, which besets so many less fortunately placed, the fear that things are going to get worse. We owe our freedom from that fear largely to the fact that we have balanced our Budget. By following a sound financial policy we have been enabled to secure low interest rates for industry, and it would be the height of folly to throw away that advantage."

A strictly balanced Budget, in which current expenditure was completely covered by current revenue, was therefore introduced. It was received with apathy and rated "dull". Momentarily this depressed the Chancellor, who saw endless struggles ahead with a disgruntled public opinion and even wondered if it would seem worth while for him to go on after the next Election.

Long before then, however, the economic tide had begun to turn. In 1934 Chamberlain could report a small but distinct rise in wholesale prices, new low records in the rate of short-term interest, Consols standing higher that they had before the war, an increase in the volume of industrial production, and something like equilibrium in the balance of payments. We had finished the story of *Bleak House*, he observed, and could now sit down to enjoy the first chapter of *Great Expectations*. The Budget surplus was £29 million, and his first priority was to restore the cuts imposed in the crisis of 1931. The whole of the cut in unemployment benefit and half the reduction in the pay of State and local government employees were restored, and the 6d. increase in the standard rate of income tax was removed. In 1935 he completed the process. The pay cuts were then restored in full and the smaller income-tax payers were relieved by changes in allowances. Only the method of achieving his 1935 surplus was seriously criticised: for £4½ million out of the £11 million had come from a "raid" on the Road Fund. Of the Minister of Transport's attitude to this he wrote in his diary: "Hore-Belisha is of course furious and has sent in a written protest accompanied by requests for assurances to which I shall pay no attention"; and in the House he argued: "Really it is ridiculous for anybody ... to pretend that any Minister can commit succeeding Parliaments for all time to carry out a pledge which he might give as to the destination of particular taxes."

The 1935 statement had begun with an encouraging, and in some respects a light-hearted, review of the year. Not only had industrial and manufacturing production risen and our export trade increased by £30 million, but in the ordinary household budget the improvement in the standard and enjoyment of living had been marked. The British people, he observed, had "sweetened their lives", with 80,000 tons more sugar than in the previous year, smoked the equivalent of 2,600,000,000 extra cigarettes, spent £2¾ million more on entertainments, and "washed away their troubles" with 270,000,000 more pints of beer—a statistic which was naturally greeted with loud "Hear, Hear's". Closing this fourth Budget he allowed himself also to give what amounted to his own summary of his own achievement.

N.C. Hansard 15.4.1935.

"Taking the country as a whole, looking back over these three-and-a-half years, we can see the improvement has been solid, continuous and steady. To that result many things have made their contribution —tariffs, conversion operations, cheap money, balanced Budgets, remissions of taxation. They have done it largely by creating a spirit of confidence. Confidence is the mother of enterprise, and, when it operates upon many individuals and through many channels, it is far and away the most effective form of promoting a general and rapid expansion of economic activities. Broadly speaking, we may say that we have recovered in this country 80 per cent of our prosperity."

The figure Chamberlain gave was no doubt impressionistic, but certainly the key indices of economic health had all begun to point in the same direction. In 1931 there had been an unfavourable trade balance of £104 million, in 1935 there was a surplus of £32 million. In 1931 the annual index of production of the London and Cambridge Economic Service (1929 = 100) stood at 84, by 1935 it had recovered to 110. In 1931 the total unemployed almost touched three millions, in 1935 it at last fell below two millions. "Recovery, despaired of in 1931, was in the air by 1933, obvious by 1935," writes C. L. Mowat, a recent historian of the inter-war years; but he adds: "The National Government got little thanks for it, partly because it did not deserve it—its policies, as will be seen, neither helped nor hindered very much— partly because recovery, like the depression, was uneven, so that the misery of the depressed areas drew attention away from the return of prosperity elsewhere."[1] The view that Chamberlain's policies did not help recovery very much is slenderly based, and is quite effectively contradicted by the same authority who later notes: "The National Government's financial policies made the best of both worlds: they seemed sufficiently deflationary to restore confidence; they were in fact sufficiently inflationary to assist recovery by maintaining the purchasing power of the people."[2]

[1] *Britain between the Wars* (Methuen, 1955), p. 432.   [2] *Op. cit.*, p. 455.

Nor can the observation on the depressed areas pass without en-
largement; and here the best source is a speech by Chamberlain
to the Commons in November 1934.

N.C. Hansard 14.11.1934.

"Since the commencement of the great industrial depression successive
Governments have been well aware that certain particular parts of
the country were specially hard hit. They were parts which were
particularly associated with one or two industries, and when those
industries fell upon bad times the inhabitants in those districts had no
alternative employment to fall back upon. For a period, which
lasted into the time when the present Government took office, there
was no prospect of any general recovery, and these particular areas
were merely the blackest spots in a picture of a generally gloomy
character. . . .

"Happily during the last two years a welcome change has taken
place in the general situation . . . this improvement in the national
position has only served to throw into higher relief the contrast with
the particular areas of which I speak, for they have not shared in the
general recovery. Those great industries with which they are concerned—coal mining, engineering, iron and steel, and shipbuilding
—are among those which have suffered most from the contraction of
their markets. . . .

"At the time when the Unemployment Act was being drafted
. . . we had it in mind that the Unemployment Assistance Board,
when it was constituted, would in all probability make a special
study of the conditions of the unemployed in the areas which had
been most affected by the depression, but before very long . . . we
could not help feeling that to ask people of these areas who are still
in the shadow when others are coming into the sunshine to go on
waiting for many more months . . . would be to put an unreasonable strain upon their patience and endurance.

"Therefore, we made up our minds not to wait any longer but
at once to send into those areas which appeared to us to be the worst
affected [West Cumberland, Durham and Tyneside, South Wales
and Scotland] investigators who might look into the whole situation
on the spot and after an examination of conditions as they then
existed might give us the benefit of any ideas which might occur to
them as to the best way of improving those conditions. . . .

"The reports of the investigators which are the result of that
action are now before the House . . . while they have very properly

pointed out the limitations upon what it is possible to do to help, they have nevertheless made a large number of extremely interesting and valuable suggestions which have been of great assistance to the Government. . . .

"But, when all is said and done, when all these individual recommendations have been considered, we cannot help feeling that in this case the ordinary procedure, which consists, of course, in referring each recommendation to the appropriate Government Department for examination, subjecting it to the ordinary checks—the consideration of whether it infringes old precedents or creates undesirable new ones— . . . is a procedure which is neither appropriate nor adequate to the special conditions of these areas. . . . What we want here, as it seems to us, is something more rapid, more direct, less orthodox if you like. . . .

"We have decided to appoint two Commissioners, one dealing with England and Wales and the other with Scotland, who will devote their whole time and attention to the initiation, organisation and prosecution of schemes designed to facilitate economic development and social improvement in the four areas surveyed by the investigators. . . .

"They will have to be furnished with funds [£2 million initially with further sums in each successive year as required]. . . . We are going to give the Commissioners a very wide discretion. They must not be afraid of trying experiments, even if these experiments fail. . . . We do not anticipate spectacular results. But we are sure that they will bring to their task the qualities of imagination, of courage, and of sympathy which we regard as essential for success, and we trust that with their help the long-suffering people in these depressed areas may be able to help themselves back again to a happier and a more hopeful existence."

With this announcement began the "special areas" policy—since developed by more than a quarter of a century's experience—and behind it at every stage had been Chamberlain's thought and initiative.

The Third Reading debate on the Bill to give effect to these proposals was enlivened by a vigorous attack from Lloyd George, who contrasted it unfavourably with the programmes of Roosevelt's New Deal. A few weeks later, at Bangor, he launched his own "New Deal"—including a vast programme of public works,

the floating of a "prosperity loan", a double Budget, a development council and a non-departmental Cabinet. "The poorest
stuff imaginable," sniffed Chamberlain, "vague, rhetorical and
containing not a single new idea." But others in the Party, and
some in the Cabinet, thought differently, and even toyed with the
possibility of bringing Lloyd George into the National Government to give it a "new look". To Baldwin and other colleagues,
Chamberlain made it plain that he would in no circumstances sit
in a Cabinet with Lloyd George; and Lloyd George's feelings
about Chamberlain were probably equally strong. Eventually, in
March, it was decided to ask Lloyd George to submit his plans,
and a series of inconclusive interviews took place with the Cabinet's general purposes committee. "Our meetings were studiously
pleasant," said Lloyd George, "but they knew in their hearts that
they were going to knife me"[1]; and all our evidence shows that
he was correct. "My motives," explained Neville to Austen,
"were not personal dislike, but profound conviction that our ideas
were incompatible"; an incompatibility which was at last spelt
out in the Government's destructive analysis of the "New Deal"
published in July.

Months before that, replying to a censure debate, Chamberlain
had high-lighted the doctrinal difference.

N.C. Hansard 14.2.1935.

"The continually repeated cry that the Government have no policy
on employment always has behind it the implication that there can
be no policy which does not involve a large expenditure of public
money, whether directly in public works carried out by the Government, or in subventions to other bodies doing similar things. I
believe that to contain a complete fallacy. There may be circumstances when it is right and sound to follow a policy of that kind,
but not for the purpose of providing employment, because the whole
experience of the past shows that, for the purpose of providing
employment, this policy of public works is always disappointing. In
that respect the experience of this country is no different from that
of other countries which have tried the same thing.

"It should be remembered that the amount that can really, actually be spent by a Government in work of this kind in a year is small

[1] Frank Owen, *Tempestuous Journey* (Hutchinson, 1954), p. 729.

in comparison with the amount which is normally spent on capital works through the ordinary channels of trade and by local authorities. . . . The conclusion I draw from that is that the quickest and most effective contribution which any Government can make towards an increase of employment is to create conditions which will encourage and facilitate improvement in ordinary trade."

The objection, it will be seen, was not to public works and subventions as such. In that very February telephone developments costing £34 million had been approved; the following June there was an Exchequer guarantee of £35 million for London Transport. In the previous year, the completion of the *Queen Mary* had been financed by the Government, "mainly as a lever for bringing about a merger between the Cunard and White Star lines, thus establishing a strong British firm in the North Atlantic trade". These were examples he gave himself when charged with being against all kinds of public works. The Government were ready "to seize all opportunities of promoting public works which fulfilled certain conditions". What he was not prepared to consider was a programme for the creation of jobs, conceived on the lines of the American "New Deal", when experience in this country had shown that in the seven years ending in 1931 a £700 million expenditure on public works had at no time found employment for above 100,000 men. "I imagine," he had written to Ida early in 1935, "that Roosevelt's spectacular pronouncements will give great encouragement to L.G. and the Conservative 'planners' group, headed by Macmillan and Eustace Percy, and that the *Daily Mail* and the *Express*, will use them vigorously as a stick to beat the Government with. I shall do my best to hold the fort. . . ." In public his language was more diplomatic. In other countries, he remarked in his 1935 Budget statement, statesmen were striving to bring back prosperity "by such means as seem to them appropriate to their own conditions"; he did not claim that his methods were better than theirs, "but in view of our incorrigible habit of self-depreciation, it does not seem unpardonable to point out that nowhere else can you find a parallel to the results which have been achieved here". This was a modest statement of the truth; and certainly the sharp recession in America in 1937 was later to show the vulnerability of the New Deal.

Nor was it only in this respect that he found himself in opposition to Roosevelt's policies. More directly than in their effect upon opinion they clashed with his aims. The theme which dictated Chamberlain's own approach to the World Economic Conference in the summer of 1933 had been "that the chief troubles from which the world is suffering today are international in their origin, and that they can only be solved by international action and agreement". This apparently had been Roosevelt's view too; for he made a statement on May 16th specifically calling on the Conference to "establish order in place of the present chaos, by the stabilisation of currencies" and in other co-operative ways. Yet on July 3rd, in a message to the American delegation singularly abrupt and infelicitous in its phrasing, he rejected a provisional agreement, which was supposed to exhibit some desire to avoid competitive depreciation of currencies.

Diary, 4.7.1933.

"The whole situation was changed . . . by the issue of the President's most offensive message to his Secretary of State. This effusion so completely declared his intention to go his own way . . . dismissing the effect of dollar depreciation as a trifling incident of no importance, as to cause the gold countries to declare that it was useless to go on with the Conference."

A Dominions' declaration, he felt, had salvaged something from the wreck; but this was little comfort to Chamberlain and less to MacDonald who had presided at the Conference.

There was also the failure to reach a satisfactory agreement on the question of the American debt, in the two years after Lausanne. Long before the British default in 1934 it had become clear that "the present settlement imposes upon the people of this country a burden which is both unreasonable in itself and inequitable in relation to the treatment accorded to other countries."[1] At the end of 1932, when the last full payment was made, it was accompanied by a Note which, in Chamberlain's words, "warned the Americans pretty plainly that there are limits to our squeezeability". In 1933, two half-yearly "token payments" were

---

[1] Quoted from the British Note to the United States Government, "over which", wrote Chamberlain to Ida on June 9th, 1934, "I took a lot of trouble".

made, pending a mutually acceptable settlement of the problem and statements were extracted from Roosevelt expressing his personal view that Britain was not in default. Such a procedure was, however, barred in 1934 by the Johnson Act, and since negotiations for a final settlement proved impossible, Chamberlain was faced with the alternative of either paying in full the sum of 262 million dollars or defaulting. There could be no doubt which was the right course; and upon four grounds it was taken. First, that the burden was preposterous; in respect of war advances totalling 4,277 million dollars we had paid some 2,000 million dollars to date, and yet still had a nominal debt of over 4,700 million dollars. Second, that other countries had got off far more lightly; we had paid three times as much as America's other European debtors, though in sum they owed 25 per cent more than we did. Third, that the basic difficulty had been brought about by United States' tariff policy; the Americans insisted on payment of debts whilst refusing to allow them to be paid for in goods and services. Fourth, that we had suspended claims on our own debtors: if we resumed full payments to America we should need to make corresponding demands on them, and this "would re-create the conditions which existed prior to the world crisis and were in large measure responsible for it. Such a procedure would throw a bombshell into the European arena which would have financial and economic repercussions over all the five continents and would postpone indefinitely the chances of world recovery."[1]

This default occurred almost simultaneously with the Reichsbank's suspension of interest payments on Germany's long-term foreign loans. Chamberlain lost no time in passing legislation through the House of Commons providing for an Anglo-German clearing house to protect British bond-holders. He could not help reflecting, however, that whilst there was in fact no comparison between the two cases, their coincidence might "encourage people to say that we refuse to pay our debts while we get very angry because others refuse to pay us". German envoys soon arrived in London to negotiate, and a letter to Ida in July 1934 records:

[1] *Ibid.*, see *Documents on British Foreign Policy 1919–1939* (H.M.S.O., 1957), Second Series, Vol. 6, pp. 931–935.

"It was hard for them to believe that we really meant business. But finally we gave them an ultimatum and they collapsed."

That same month, the murder of the Austrian Chancellor, Dollfuss, evoked from Chamberlain a letter deeply expressive of his hatred of Nazism, his zeal for British rearmament against the German menace, and his anxiety about the conduct of our foreign policy.

N.C. to Hilda 28.7.1934.

"That those beasts should have got him at last and that they should have treated him with such callous brutality makes me hate Nazi-ism and all its works with a greater loathing than ever. . . . I was glad to hear of Mussolini's movements of troops. It's the only thing Germans understand. . . . So far as home affairs are concerned I reckon the effect of the German and now the Austrian murders and shootings will be further to discredit Mosley and all political 'armies' and moreover to convince the country as a whole that the Government is right in restoring our defences. . . . I anticipate that the vote of censure debate will show a stronger feeling for the suggestion that we are doing too little than Attlee or Herbert Samuel can bring to their exclamations of horror that we should be doing so much. . . . But what does not satisfy me is that we do not shape our foreign policy accordingly."

It is important not to forget the political climate in which these thoughts had grown. In January 1933 Hitler had come to power; in October Germany withdrew from the League of Nations. "By the autumn of 1933," writes Churchill in *The Gathering Storm*, "it was plain that neither by precept nor still less by example would the British effort for disarmament succeed."[1] Yet this was precisely the moment when the most forceful demonstrations were given of "the passionate desire for peace which animated the uninformed, misinformed majority of the British people, and seemed to threaten with political extinction any party or politician who dared to take any other line". This was the autumn in which the Labour Party Conference threatened a general strike in the event of war or the threat of war, and its leader, George Lansbury, declared: "I would close every recruiting station, disband the Army and dismiss the Air Force. I would abolish the whole dreadful

[1] *The Second World War* (Cassell, 1948), Vol. I, p. 88.

equipment of war and say to the world 'Do your worst'." It was also the autumn in which the Samuelite Liberals went into formal opposition partly on the grounds that we were not getting on with disarmament, and in which Lloyd George was indicating France rather than Germany. The notorious vote of the Oxford Union earlier in the year against "fighting for King and Country" reflected the same mood. But its most dramatic expression by far came in October at the by-election in East Fulham where a Conservative majority of 14,521 was replaced by a Labour majority of 4,840 apparently on the issue of armaments. "I always felt," writes Baldwin's biographer, "that the nerve, injured in October 1933, the East Fulham nerve, never quite healed: he was afraid of the pacifists: he could not bring himself quite to say, perhaps not quite to think, 'Germany is arming and we must arm too'."[1] This was certainly not true of Chamberlain. On East Fulham, his judgement was casual, almost slapdash.

N.C. to Ida 28.10.1933.

"Fulham made the P.M. very miserable but I confess I did not lose a minute's sleep over it. The press put it all down to Housing and lies about War. Both no doubt were factors but I heard yesterday from a friend who had been talking to a speaker (street corner) in Fulham what I had all along suspected, that the real attack was on the means test."

As for rearmament, he wrote to Hilda a week earlier that caution was needed in foreign policy, "But common prudence would seem to indicate some strengthening of our defences and happily we are no longer expecting a deficit at the end of the financial year".

As Chancellor, it is true, he regarded the possibility of spending, say, £85 million on rearmament as a "staggering prospect". But in Cabinet in March 1934, he utterly rejected the view of those who were for avoiding European entanglements. Either they must explore his "limited liability plan" for an international police force, or they must resign themselves to filling up our defence deficiencies at once. "For the old aphorism 'Force is no remedy'," he wrote, "I would substitute 'The Fear of Force is the only

---

[1] G. M. Young, *Stanley Baldwin* (Rupert Hart-Davis, 1952), p. 200.

remedy'." Limited liability having been shot down, as we have seen, he set to work on the Defence Requirements Committee. In June he scaled down their estimated expenditure, which eventually worked out at £76 million, to £50 million, "in the light of politics and finance". Politics meant a clear recognition that Germany was the potential enemy: he therefore raised by 50 per cent the proposed strength of the home Air Force. Finance meant that we could not at that stage afford to take on Japan as well: he therefore postponed the replacement of capital ships, and spent much of his summer vacation composing a memorandum that advocated "making eyes at Japan"—an unfruitful process, as the autumn proved.

With each succeeding month the strength of his convictions about rearmament grew, and so did his preoccupation with foreign policy. His speeches hammered home the truth that, "We shall not make peace certain by leaving ourselves so weak that we become a temptation to other powers to bully us." His letters were full of a grim realism: "In the absence of security other nations won't give up aircraft or bombing and we shall be more likely to deter Germany from mad dogging if we have an air force which in case of need could bomb the Ruhr from Belgium." In June 1934, he urged, without success, "a unilateral declaration that the integrity of the Low Countries is a vital interest to us and we should have to resist its violation by all the means in our power". In December, backed up by strong representations from Eden in Geneva, he successfully pressed upon a nervous Cabinet the initiative in proposing an international force to police the Saar during the plebiscite. In March 1935, he justified the passages in the Defence White Paper which had given most offence in Germany and which he had himself toned down: "Hitler's Germany is the bully of Europe . . . it will be necessary for Simon to talk plainly in Berlin." Of the Japanese talks in November 1934, he wrote: "I wish I were in at the conversations but of course I have no status"; and when Eden's health prevented him from accompanying Simon to Stresa in April 1935, Chamberlain observed wistfully, "I believe the best person to go would be myself but that of course is impossible."

If he had wanted the Foreign Office, he could have had it.

Vansittart's retrospective denigration—"An earnest and opinion-ated provincial was bound to err if he plunged into diplomacy"[1]—was an easy jibe to make thirty years on, but it did not reflect the opinion of the best judges of the day. In 1928 Churchill had suggested Neville Chamberlain as Foreign Secretary in a conver-sation with Baldwin. Baldwin had remembered in 1931, and sug-gested it to the King. In 1933 MacDonald and Thomas discussing the shortcomings of Simon, could think of no-one to succeed him but Chamberlain who was, however, still indispensable at the Exchequer. In the spring of 1934 Halifax had expressed himself in the same sense. At the end of the year the Chief Whip, David Margesson, backed by a strong group of Ministers, warned Mac-Donald that Simon at the Foreign Office was the Government's biggest liability; adding "what the House and the country would like would be the Chancellor of the Exchequer", who might best be succeeded by Cunliffe-Lister. Chamberlain's diary takes up the story.

4.12.1934.

"I pointed out the difficulty of my position. He [Margesson] had proposed that Simon should be ejected and that I should take his place. The change would not be welcome to me. The F.O. was expensive and I could not afford it; moreover I should hate the journeys to Geneva and above all I should loathe and detest the social ceremonies. . . . But in addition to all that to expose myself to the suggestion that I had worked for this change, perhaps because I saw Budgetary difficulties ahead and wanted to avoid them and get a new place where I might have the chance to make myself interest-ing, this was too much to ask."

11.12.1934.

"The more I think of the suggestion that I should transfer to the F.O. the less I like it."

13.12.1934.

"I spoke to S.B. this morning at No. 11. . . . I said I had decided that I would not change to the F.O. if I were asked during this Parliament. . . . I walked down to the House with Sam Hoare who asked me how the talks on Cabinet reconstruction were proceeding. I gave him a

[1] *The Mist Procession* (Hutchinson, 1958), p. 430.

faithful account to date—when he burst out saying he resented these discussions about the Cabinet by junior Ministers and especially the Chief Whip. It was no business of theirs and if there were any changes it would make a lot of bad blood. He added: I shall not stand at the next election unless I see something to interest me. I concluded that he wants the F.O. himself."

When Baldwin and MacDonald swopped offices on June 7th, 1935, and Cabinet reconstruction came at long last, Hoare went to the Foreign Office at Chamberlain's suggestion, and Simon to the Home Office, to which was added ("to soften his fall") the deputy leadership of the House. Eden would be disappointed, reflected Chamberlain, but "he will certainly be Foreign Secretary some day".

11

PRIME MINISTER DESIGNATE
(Mid-1935 – May 1937)

"GOVERNMENTS are strong," observed that acute political analyst Walter Bagehot, "only when public opinion is definite and decided." In the summer of 1935 public opinion in Britain still appeared, on the contrary, to be hesitant and confused. The Peace Ballot, fathered by the League of Nations Union, discovered over 10 million people willing to carry collective security to the point of economic sanctions, but only two-thirds of this total prepared to contemplate the ultimate sanction of force. Since it is impossible to impose an effective economic blockade with any certainty that it will not lead to war this was in itself muddled thinking—soon to be reflected, only too faithfully, in the handling of the Abyssinian crisis. Beneath this muddle, however, lay an even more disastrous fallacy. This was the notion, implicit in the criticisms of the Labour Opposition, that collective security was something that could exist independently of the policies and the armaments of the great powers who were members of the League. "Terribly mischievous," Chamberlain called the Ballot when it was first announced, and later he wrote contemptuously of "the League of Nations Union cranks" who had been "infuriated" by the White Paper on rearmament published in March 1935.

This White Paper, so cautious and even nebulous as it seems in retrospect, stung the Opposition into a paroxysm of censure. "We reject the use of force as an instrument of policy," declared Attlee in the House of Commons, whilst the *Daily Herald* after describing the White Paper as "an insult to Germany" and "the rejection of the entire system of collective security", added darkly: "But let the world understand—it is important that the world understands—that this is not the voice of the British people." To Chamberlain it seemed important that the world should understand the exact reverse, and that British public opinion should now be led to pronounce unmistakably in favour of re-armament. "What I shall work for," he wrote to Ida in August, "is a Britain strong enough to make it impossible for her wishes to be flouted as Mussolini has flouted them now," and to his colleagues he propounded the bold course of appealing to the country, first and foremost, on a defence programme. Party advantage as well as national interest, he thought, dictated this.

Diary, 2.8.1935.

"I have been revolving in my mind the election issue. S.B. and the C[entral] O[ffice] have been talking on the assumption that it would turn on unemployment and especially the depressed areas. . . . We shall in fact have, I hope, in the autumn a number of plans which will help in this direction . . . [but] we can never win an election on them. What we want is some issue that will put them in the background and if possible substitute for the hope of fresh benefits a fear in the public mind—always the strongest motive to induce people to vote. Now the Labour Party obviously intend to fasten upon our backs the accusation of being warmongers and they are suggesting that we have 'hush-hush' plans for rearmament which we are concealing from the people. As a matter of fact we are working on plans for rearmament at an early date, for the situation in Europe is most alarming. Germany is said to be borrowing over £1,000 millions a year to get herself rearmed and she has perfected a wonderful industrial organisation capable of rapid expansion for the production of the materials of war. With Mussolini hopelessly tied up with Abyssinia and Great Britain disarmed, the temptation in a few years' time to demand territory etc., might be too great for Goering, Goebbels, and their like to resist. Therefore we must hurry our own rearmament and in the course of the next 4 or 5 years we shall probably have to spend an extra £120 m. or more in doing so. We are not yet sufficiently advanced to reveal our ideas to the public but of course we cannot deny the general charge of rearmament, and no doubt if we tried to keep our ideas secret till after the election we should either fail or if we succeeded lay ourselves open to the far more damaging accusation that we had deliberately deceived the people."

This accusation that the National Government won the General Election of 1935 by deliberate deceit, has in fact long had a place in political mythology.[1] It is based on a passage in a speech which Baldwin made to Parliament on November 12th, 1936 ("I put before the whole House my own views with an appalling frankness"). Chamberlain's letters reveal that it was the only passage Baldwin did not read from manuscript, and the improvisation certainly resulted in some ambiguity. What he was actually explaining was why he had chosen 1935 in preference to 1933 or 1934, to seek a mandate for rearmament ("a democracy is always two years behind the dictator"); but his words have been interpreted as a confession that the Government shirked the rearmament issue in 1935 itself.

Now it is perfectly true that, after weeks of hesitation by his leader, Chamberlain wrote in his diary that he had "got a hint from Horace Wilson [the Government's chief industrial adviser] that S.B. was frightened of making defence the *prime* issue and at the same time the idea was put forward (whether it emanated from Wilson or from S.B. himself I don't know) that we could give as good reason for going to the country the probability that we were in for a long and anxious period in foreign affairs in which it was essential that we should have a stable Government with the authority of the nation behind it". Chamberlain loyally grasped at this idea, putting it forward as the primary reason in a speech in St. Andrew's Hall on October 14th; but "I gave defence as a secondary reason for requiring to know the country's mind". The same emphasis was to be seen in the Government's Election Manifesto of which Chamberlain was the chief draftsman ("We have made it clear that we must in the course of the next few years do what is necessary to repair the gaps in our defences"). This vagueness was less than Chamberlain himself had advocated but it was scarcely deceiving the electors and, so far from being shirked, rearmament became during the campaign the subject of

[1] See R. Bassett, "Telling the truth to the people: the myth of the Baldwin 'confession'," *Cambridge Journal*, II, pp. 84–95 (November 1948).

the hottest and crudest exchanges. A baby in a gas-mask featured in Labour's election posters, and Chamberlain in particular was pilloried as a warmonger, just as Churchill was to be fifteen years later.

Attlee, acting as Labour Party leader on Lansbury's resignation, ridiculed the Chancellor's belief that "a tremendous and costly rearmament programme" was any solution of our difficulties. Arthur Greenwood declared that it was "the merest scaremongering, disgraceful in a statesman in Mr. Chamberlain's responsible position, to suggest that more millions of money needed to be spent on armaments". Herbert Morrison bracketed together Chamberlain, Churchill and Leo Amery as "fire-eaters" and "militarists", and described the Chancellor as having the appearance of a death's head. "The Government leaders," ran the report of a typical Morrison speech on November 3rd, "were all urging a policy of rearmament, and Mr. Chamberlain was ready and anxious to spend millions of pounds on machines of destruction. He had no money, however, for the unemployed, the depressed areas and social services. He would spend on the means of death, but not on the means of life, and that was the sort of fellow he looked too." Next day, at Cardiff, the Chancellor replied good-humouredly that he would not attempt to compete in looks with "such a magnificent specimen of humanity" as Morrison. The "means of life", however, were certainly not to be neglected. He underlined the constructive proposals in the Manifesto for a further drive in housing, for educational reform including the raising of the school-leaving age, for voluntary extension of the pensions scheme to black-coated workers, for raising the standards of national health and physique and, above all, for bringing new industries into the Special Areas. As for the "means of death", Chamberlain stuck to his guns. He held out the hope of a munitions factory for South Wales; he stressed the age of our ships, the dangerous meagreness of our Air Force; and finally he put this Election issue into an epigrammatic nutshell: "Our policy is defence without defiance; their policy is defiance without defence."

On these issues the country spoke emphatically on November 14th. The Conservative Central Office had estimated their likely majority at about 100; Chamberlain's diary records that he had heard 200 mentioned; in the event, despite recovery of ground by Labour in London, Yorkshire and Scotland, the Government romped back with 247 seats more than the combined Opposition. In Birmingham, for the second time running, they won all twelve seats, and Chamberlain increased his own majority at Edgbaston from 14,000 to nearly 22,000. "I am bound to recognise," he wrote to Hilda at the close of the campaign, "that if I supply the policy and the drive, S.B. does also supply something that is perhaps even more valuable in retaining the floating vote."[1] The previous month, Thomas Jones had written of Baldwin's speech at the Party Conference that he "reconciled the Party to the League by supporting rearmament, and reconciled the pacifists to rearmament by supporting the Covenant"; adding: "All with an eye to the election."[2] Electorally the formula was serviceable; brought up against the immediate realities of Italian power politics, it could not suffice.

Mussolini's Abyssinian aggression was branded by Chamberlain as "barbarous". But it arose, as he subsequently acknowledged, not only from motives of prestige, but from Italy's economic need for essential raw materials as well as an outlet for her prolific population. Abyssinia had long been recognised as within the Italian sphere of influence, and in 1935, as Churchill saw and said, no-one could pretend that she was "a fit, worthy, and equal member of a league of civilized nations". Nevertheless, a member of the League of Nations she had been since 1923—at Italian insistence—and an attack by one member of the League upon another must put this instrument of collective security to the crucial test. If in the end, Chamberlain pointed out to his colleagues on July 2nd, "the League were demonstrated to be incapable of effective intervention to stop this war it would be practically impossible to maintain the fiction that its existence was justified at all".

In British official circles there was small faith left in the League. Of the seven great powers, only three remained in it: Italy, France and ourselves. To act with the French to put pressure on

[1] Baldwin wrote to Chamberlain on November 5th: "The fact is you and I are complementary: each puts into the pool his own contribution and we make a jolly effective unit!"
[2] *A Diary with Letters* (O.U.P., 1954), p. 155.

Mussolini that would dissuade him from the use of force was Chamberlain's first thought. But by July 6th he was writing to his sisters that "it seems more than ever unlikely that Laval will consent to anything that might embroil him with Mussolini". The French Government was indeed obsessed, as well it might be, by the need to preserve Italian friendship and prevent Mussolini from being driven into the German camp. This fear of estranging Italy and altering the balance of power in Europe was also present in the minds of Hoare and Vansittart. But, as Chamberlain had foreseen as early as May, it was scarcely echoed by their country-men who suddenly became, in Vansittart's phrase, "eager to kill Musso with their mouths". They were certainly not eager to kill him with anything else, and since the brunt of doing so would have fallen on out-of-date battleships inadequately protected by air cover, the cost could have been fearful.

Out of this tangled predicament emerged a policy of bluff. Hoare determined to make what he called "a revivalist appeal to the Assembly. At best, it might start a new chapter of League re-covery, at worst, it might deter Mussolini by a display of League fervour. If there was any element of bluff in it, it was a moment when bluff was not only legitimate but inescapable."[1] Now, as so often before, Chamberlain found himself in accord and sympathy with Hoare.

N.C. to Hilda 7.9.1935.

"We discussed at considerable length what he should say at Geneva and as usual found ourselves in agreement. He first asked me my opinion and then, when I had given it, he produced bits of his draft which showed that he had been on the same idea. He then modified the emphasis or elaborated the argument in accordance with my suggestions."

The speech was delivered on September 11th. "In conformity with its precise and explicit obligations, the League stands, and my country stands with it, for the collective maintenance of the Covenant in its entirety, and particularly for steady and collective resistance to all acts of unprovoked aggression"—this was the sen-tence that rallied the Assembly and reverberated throughout the

[1] *Nine Troubled Years* (Collins, 1954), p. 166.

world. But elation is no substitute for action. Would the League be willing to intimidate the aggressor? "If risks for peace are to be run, they must be run by all," warned Hoare as British warships moved into the Mediterranean; but no other country, and decidedly not France, moved a ship, a plane or a man. Could the aggressor be deterred if the controversy were shifted from political to economic ground? "Better means must be found to make it possible for all countries to obtain the raw materials that they require for their existence," Hoare promised; but the end of the rainy season was all that Mussolini was waiting for now. Italy invaded Abyssinia on October 3rd. The bluff had been called.

The League members now determined to apply certain financial and economic sanctions to Italy. In August, Chamberlain had written that since Germany and America were not members of the League such sanctions would be "utterly futile", and according to Leo Amery he continued to adopt a "frankly cynical" attitude to them.[1] This is not borne out by his papers; for in September he wrote to his wife that sanctions might force Italy to halt, which in turn might make Hitler waver, and in discussions with his Ministerial colleagues in November he was a leading advocate for trying to extend sanctions to oil, which Mussolini had warned would be taken as an "act of war".

Diary, 29.11.1935.

"The decision really turned on the possibility of making an embargo effective ... U.S.A. has already gone a good deal further than usual. The President's discretionary powers do not cover oil but he and Cordell Hull have made it very clear that in their opinion oil should not be supplied to Italy. Consequently the question is being taken seriously. Mussolini is making violent threats and Laval once again has been wriggling. ... S[am] H[oare] said he thought if others were prepared to enforce them he could not refuse to do so but we need not take the initiative. I replied that if anyone else would give the lead, well and good, but in the last resort if necessary we ought to give the lead ourselves rather than let the question go by default. I pointed out that this was really a critical point in the League's history. If we weakened now because of Mussolini's threats we should leave the Americans in the air and they would be unable to

[1] *My Political Life* (Hutchinson, 1955), Vol. III, p. 174.

resist the argument of their oil producers. . . . It was inevitable that in such circumstances U.S.A. should decline in future to help us in any way, sanctions would crumble, the League would lose its coherence and our whole policy would be destroyed. I said however that I thought we should press Laval to tell Mussolini that if he attacked us France would at once come to our assistance and if he evaded this request we should make it clear at Geneva that France, and not we, were blocking oil sanctions. . . .

"I saw Sam again after his talk with the P.M. on Wednesday [27th.] He said the latter had been very difficult to corner, only saying that we mustn't have war, but finally he said that if Laval gave the desired assurances and the League agreed he thought we could not refuse to accept our share. . . . Finally, on Friday [29th] S.H., Simon, Eden, W. Runciman and I met in my room and discussed the situation. W.R. showed great reluctance to agree to our joining in oil sanctions but would not face the alternatives. S.H., rather against Eden's inclinations, was inclined to hold up the embargo long enough to allow further conversations in Paris to test out the possibility of a general settlement. I was prepared to agree to this."

In Paris, on his way to Switzerland for a badly needed holiday, Hoare was persuaded by Laval to agree to peace proposals under which Italy would have absorbed the greater part of Abyssinia. These proposals were "leaked" to the French press, and the Cabinet on December 9th found it could not reject them without, as Chamberlain later put it in Parliament, "everybody knowing that we had thrown over our Foreign Secretary". Hoare's precipitate conduct bewildered Chamberlain: perhaps "he was too tired and bothered to struggle any longer", perhaps "he thought we should be at liberty to pull the proposals about." At all events, the Government's stock fell dramatically ("If we had to fight the election over again we should probably be beaten") and public clamour demanded the Foreign Secretary's resignation ("This of course is absurd").

His loyalty to his friend burned brightly as the shadows fell. On the 17th, Duff Cooper, who had until lately been Chamberlain's Financial Secretary to the Treasury and was now Secretary for War, came to report "that there was a strong and growing feeling in the Cabinet that Sam should be asked to resign".

He mentioned Oliver Stanley, Ormsby-Gore and Walter Elliot as taking this view. With some *hauteur*, Chamberlain replied that to demand a colleague's resignation in his absence would be unprecedented and improper and that, since the whole Cabinet had accepted responsibility for the Hoare-Laval pact, the House would condemn it for now making a scapegoat of the Foreign Secretary. That evening he received from Hoare, who was confined to bed under doctor's orders, a copy of the speech he proposed to deliver in the House. Chamberlain sat up late making an abstract of it, which he communicated to the Cabinet next day. It had a very bad reception. "Generally," the diary records, "it was felt that we must own up to a mistake and Halifax carried most weight when he said that, unless Sam went, the whole moral force of the Government would be gone." Battling on in the last ditch, Chamberlain wrote a note to Halifax: might not Hoare say he had *offered* his resignation, leaving it to be accepted or not according to the result of the debate? This, of course, would not do; Hoare resigned that night, and Eden succeeded him.

Diary, 21.12.1935.

"I went to see Sam to say goodbye on Friday and found him more emotional than usual and, as I thought, a little inclined to bitterness. . . . He was rather comforted by an enormous and sympathetic correspondence (200 letters that day) but, when I said something about returning presently to the Cabinet, he said 'It's all right between you and me, but I am not so sure about some of my colleagues.'"

Historically, the Abyssinian crisis has often been presented as a side-show compared with the main drama of Germany's advance to world conquest. In fact, it was the turning-point of the 'thirties. Hitler was not slow to act upon this evidence of our weakness—and, of course, our lately soured relationship with France and our newly earned enmity with Italy. On March 7th, 1936, German troops marched into the Rhineland, which had been declared permanently demilitarised by the Treaty of Versailles. Diplomatic debate found itself now on only-too-well-trodden ground. Our obligations under the Treaty of Locarno were plain; so too was the disinclination to fulfil them. "Everyone agreed," records Chamberlain's diary, when the Cabinet met on March 11th, "that we could not contemplate war, but we must make every effort to avoid repudiation of Locarno." Negotiations proved protracted but fruitless, and whilst Mussolini was completing the conquest of Abyssinia, Hitler got safely away with his own swag.

In one important respect, the episodes differed. British public opinion was deeply moved by the Italo-Abyssinian war; to the remilitarisation of the Rhineland, on the other hand, it remained lethargically indifferent. The distinction was well represented by Hugh Dalton, the Opposition's spokesman: "It is only right to say bluntly and frankly that public opinion in this country would not support, and certainly the Labour Party would not support, the taking of military sanctions or even economic sanctions against Germany at this time . . . Public opinion here does, I think, draw a clear distinction between the action of Signor Mussolini in resorting to aggressive war and waging it beyond his frontiers and the actions, up-to-date at any rate, of Herr Hitler which, much as we may regard them as reprehensible, have taken place within the frontiers of the German Reich."[1] Chamberlain had said as much to the French Foreign Minister a fortnight earlier:

Diary, 12.3.1936.
"Lunched at French Embassy after Cabinet and talked to Flandin, emphasising that public opinion here would not support us in sanctions of any kind. His view is that if a firm front is maintained by France and England, Germany will yield without war. We cannot accept this as a reliable estimate of a mad dictator's reactions."

To this it is necessary to add that French "firmness" in the Rhineland crisis has been absurdly exaggerated. General Gamelin's attitude was negative, Sarraut's Cabinet was split. Flandin failed to give it a determined lead, and the British became a convenient excuse for inertia.[2]

If Hitler had correctly interpreted the lesson of Abyssinia, so too had Chamberlain. In a fine debating speech after Hoare's resignation he had castigated the Labour "intellectuals" who urged

[1] March 26th, 1936, *Hansard*, Vol. 310, c. 1454.
[2] See L. B. Namier, *Europe in Decay* (Macmillan, 1950), pp. 22–25.

"sanctions whatever the cost" and who at the same time said, "Above all do not let us have any armaments." And now, though grumbling privately that four years of fruitful finance were to be undone, he became the chief architect of the Defence White Papers of 1936 and 1937. This was a strange role for a Chancellor of the Exchequer to fill, but in fact he was acting more as Prime Minister designate. Taken together, these two White Papers envisaged for the Navy, the laying down of five new capital ships, an increase of twenty cruisers and four aircraft carriers and a steady replacement programme for destroyers and submarines; for the Army the raising of four new battalions of infantry, the modernization of equipment and the expansion of the T.A. for anti-aircraft defences; and for the Air Force, a front line strength of 1,750 aircraft, exclusive of the Fleet Air Arm. In addition, the 1937 White Paper told of the steps being taken to build up war potential by the construction of "shadow" aircraft factories and the extension of munitions plant, and also of the first local schemes of air raid precautions. In 1935–36, defence expenditure had totalled £137 million, and we have recorded that in August 1935, when Chamberlain advocated going to the country primarily on the defence issue, he was thinking in terms of an extra £120 million or so in the following four or five years. How sharply he revised his estimate of the emergency after Abyssinia and the Rhineland may be gauged from the 1937 White Paper which spoke of £1,500 million during the next five years.

These programmes continued to be challenged and resisted by the official Opposition. Attlee accused the Chancellor of introducing "a sequence of war Budgets"; to which his homely but striking defence was that "no man hesitates to set his fire-fighting appliances in readiness when already he can feel the heat of the flames on his face". In 1936, as well as initiating a series of measures to deal with tax avoidance, he appropriated the sum of £5¼ million which stood to the credit of the Road Fund, increased the standard rate of income tax from 4s. 6d. to 4s. 9d. in the £, and added 2d. a pound to the duty on tea. At the same time, he expressed the view that it was inequitable that the whole cost of the defence programme should fall upon the revenue "which has to be extracted from the people in the course of a single five-year period". Accordingly, in February 1937, he introduced legislation authorising the Government to meet up to £400 million of the emergency expenditure out of loan. Two months later, trusting that the taxpayer would "find some consolation in the thought that his additional contributions represent an ever quickening approach to the goal of safety", he put income tax up to 5s. in the £ and proposed a graduated tax upon the growth of business profits which he styled the National Defence Contribution. The Government's Election Manifesto in 1935 had promised that the defence programme would be carried out without "unreasonable profit to contractors"; and the N.D.C. was designed, not only to raise revenue, but also to forestall serious labour unrest in the event of profiteering and rising prices. It was greeted with a Stock Exchange slump, a torrent of protest from City and Party, and a devastating criticism by Keynes who dubbed it "a tax on enterprise, growth and youth". A major political crisis was not to be averted by minor concessions, and in the end a straight tax on profits ("a simpler tax with a larger yield") had to be imposed instead. "What a frightful bill we do owe to Master Hitler, d—n him!" he wrote to his sisters shortly before this last Budget. "If only it wasn't for Germany we should be having such a wonderful time just now."

A new post of Minister for the Co-ordination of Defence was created in 1936. Inevitably it was offered to Chamberlain. He had himself suggested better co-ordinating machinery the previous year, and had later argued strongly for the new Ministry in Cabinet. His first instinct, he told Baldwin, was not to leave the Exchequer, and in this resolve he was strengthened by the advice of his private secretary, his brother and the friend to whom he would now increasingly turn, Kingsley Wood. For the best part of a month, alternative names were canvassed. Austen declined to be considered; Swinton was ruled out because of constitutional difficulties over Ministers in the Lords, Runciman because the Party would resent a Liberal. The return of Hoare to the Government was anxiously debated, the inclusion of Churchill not entirely ruled out. The climax and conclusion are explained in Chamberlain's diary.

8.3.1936.

"S.B. had gone off to Chequers but wrote to say he had been shaken
for the first time (!) by a conversation with A. Eden who said Sam's
appointment would make things very difficult for him."[1]

11.3.1936.

"Sam spoke on Monday. He began well but shocked the House at
the end of his speech by an elaborate tribute to S.B. which sounded
like an obvious and clumsy bid for power and created a thoroughly
bad impression. Winston on the other hand suppressed the attack
he had intended and made a constructive and helpful speech. . . .
J. R. M[acDonald] reacted violently against Sam. . . . Simon was
less definite. . . . We discussed various other names including
Morrison, the F.S.T., and Inskip [the Attorney-General]. It was
generally agreed that the latter would be safe but not inspiring . . . .
Margesson [the Chief Whip] pressed for Inskip as the safest man.
. . . I summed up my opinion as follows. Every name involved risks
and I should play for safety. The events of the weekend (occupation
of the Rhineland by Hitler) afforded an excellent reason for dis-
carding both Winston and Sam since both had European reputations
which might make it dangerous to add them to the Cabinet at a
critical moment. Inskip would create no jealousies. He would excite
no enthusiasm but he would involve us in no fresh perplexities."

And so the sad decision was taken and Inskip (later Lord Calde-
cote) was appointed.

In the scope and in the strategy of our defence effort Chamberlain's continued to be the decisive voice. If attack from Germany
was imminent, he argued in November 1936, there was nothing
we could do which would make us ready to meet it. But we
might have a few years more, and indeed, by careful diplomacy,
might stave off war indefinitely. Meanwhile, it would be rash
and panicky to follow Churchill's advice that "we must lay aside
every impediment in raising our own strength"; for the sacrifices demanded would injure trade for generations, destroy confidence and cripple the revenue. At the same time, he did not consider that the next war, if it came, would be like the last, "and I

[1] Baldwin's letter, dated March 6th, says: "He thinks the appointment would
make his work much more difficult during the next few months. He would
welcome his return and believes no ill effect could follow by the Admiralty
appointment later." Hoare became First Lord of the Admiralty in June.

believe our resources will be more profitably employed in the air and on the sea than in building up great armies". On this subject— not resolved until February 1937, when the War Office "renounced all idea of a Continental army on the scale of 1914–18"— his papers speak of interview after interview with Inskip. "This is, of course," says a letter of November 14th, 1936, "another case of my doing the P.M.'s work, but as he won't or can't do it himself, someone must do it for him."

As Baldwin's health deteriorated during 1936 and a date was put to his retirement, the Chancellor's grip upon the whole range of policy perceptibly tightened. His Exchequer responsibilities included a currency agreement with France and the United States and a new Special Areas Bill ("pretty thin", he admitted). On the domestic front, he was deeply engaged in the revision of the Unemployment Assistance Board regulations, in the preparation of a Bill to extinguish tithes, in the development of meat policy, and in the framing of new proposals for Ministerial salaries and a White Paper on physical training. His initiatives also strayed more than once into the field of foreign affairs. In April he was lecturing Eden on the need to replace the League's system of collective security with a new system of regional pacts. In June, acting as a "lightning conductor" for the Cabinet, he declared to the 1900 Club that, with the disappearance of the Abyssinian Government, it was "the very midsummer of madness" to continue sanctions against Italy. His diary admits that he did not consult Eden "because he would have been bound to beg me not to say what I proposed", but it also records that Eden had in Cabinet the same day "suggested that we should ourselves propose the removal of sanctions". In October, he lunched alone with the Japanese Ambassador to "prepare the way" for conversations with Eden. In November, having driven through the fog to a Sunday Cabinet, he arrived to find his colleagues lost in an even thicker fog of indecision about whether to accord belligerent rights to both sides in the Spanish Civil War. On his advice they decided to stick to non-intervention and to introduce legislation preventing British ships from carrying war materials to any Spanish port. "Every day", he wrote to Hilda in the autumn, "one interview or committee succeeds another and in the evening there is generally a box large enough to keep me out of bed till the small hours. It is strenuous work but I suppose I would not willingly change it now for any other."

His position as "heir apparent and acting P.M." was finally acknowledged when he took Baldwin's place at the mass meeting which ended the 1936 Party Conference at Margate. "I am sending for people and endeavouring to conduct business," says his diary for October 7th, "as if I were in fact P.M." Remembering the tricks that Fate had played upon his father and upon Austen (who died early in 1937) he wrote to his sister: "I wonder whether Fate has some dark secret in store to carry out her ironies to the end." For him the ironies were to come later and differently; but for Baldwin Fate had reserved one last momentous duty which, Chamberlain acknowledged, "carried him to the highest pinnacle of his career".

On January 20th, 1936, George V died. This was eight months after the celebration of his Silver Jubilee, when the nation saluted the solid dignity of an upright man and proudly rejoiced in the traditions he embodied.

N.C. to Hilda 12.5.1935.

"I must say the way in which the Jubilee was taken by the people everywhere was infectious and I felt it to be a great experience. In fact my sentiments were admirably expressed by a stout flower stall holder in Strutton Ground who said to Mrs. A. Lyttelton as he handed her her tulips, 'Oh! ma'am, Ain't it glorious to be an Englishman? *This'll teach 'em.*'

"Curiously enough the same phrase was reported from Birmingham by Geoffrey Lloyd. He says the poorest streets in Ladywood were decked with flags and streamers and everywhere he was met by the slogan 'This'll show 'em.' 'Em I conclude means the foreigner, or the Communist or anyone who isn't a true blue John Bull. . . .

"The service was most impressive and moving. I was just in line with the P. of W. and the Yorks and their children, and fairly close to the K. and Q. so I saw everything perfectly, and all the time as I gazed across at the ambassadors on the other side I thought 'This'll show 'em.'"

To the new reign Chamberlain looked forward with undisguised anxiety. "I do hope he 'pulls up his socks' and behaves himself now he has such heavy responsibilities," he wrote after Edward VIII's Accession Council, "for unless he does he will soon pull down the throne."

The Premiership was due to change hands after the Coronation in May, 1937. But those at the centre of affairs quickly saw the Coronation preparations overshadowed by an inescapable constitutional dilemma. Our monarchs are crowned, as Hoare later put it in his memoirs, "in a solemn service of Holy Communion and with the rites of a Church that disapproves of the marriage of divorced persons". Edward VIII, however, was openly associating with, and apparently intent upon marrying, a woman who was about to pass through the divorce courts, although as the innocent party, for a second time. On October 20th Baldwin gave his first private warning.

Diary, 25.10.1936.
> "S.B. told me it had passed off in a friendly manner. The King
> ... listened carefully to S.B. on the danger to his throne if he did
> not observe greater precaution but gave no promise or under-
> taking."

Baldwin now marked time, hoping, says his biographer, "though with no great confidence, that the thoughts he had lodged in the King's mind would take root and bear". Chamberlain grew more and more uneasy, and on November 4th he drafted a formal submission to the King advising him to re-order his private life. A meeting of senior Ministers—Baldwin, Chamberlain, Halifax, Simon and Runciman—took place on the 13th, and Chamberlain handed round copies of two documents which he had prepared. The first was a formal advice to the King from the Prime Minister to put an end to his association with Mrs. Simpson; the second was an informal letter saying that the formal document was ready and that, if it were tendered and the advice not taken, it would mean the resignation of the Cabinet. Baldwin asked for no formal expression of opinion on these documents, and merely said he would take them to Chequers and think over them. He appears not to have told his colleagues that on the same day the King's Private Secretary, Hardinge, had, with his approval, addressed a letter to the King warning him of the constitutional position. This letter[1] brought matters to a head and on November 16th the King informed Baldwin that he definitely intended to marry Mrs. Simpson as soon as she was free. If he could do so as King, well and good; if on the other hand the Government opposed the marriage, he was prepared to go.

The issue was complicated and delayed by two new and related ideas which now marched upon the scene.

Diary, 25.11.1936.

"I learned... that the K. had now swung round and had taken up the position that he would contract a morganatic marriage to be legalised by Act of Parliament. This was confirmed at our meeting [of Ministers] this afternoon when it further transpired that the moving spirit had been Esmond Harmsworth, who was in close touch with the King and Mrs. S., with Winston Churchill moving mysteriously in the background and, it is suggested, expressing willingness to form a Government if there should be any refusal on our part to agree. It was agreed that we must act cautiously, and find out attitude of Opposition and of Dominions before committing ourselves. S.B. should point out various difficulties but not turn anything down. I have no doubt that if it were possible to arrange the morganatic marriage this would only be the prelude to the further step of making Mrs. S. Queen with full rights."

Responses from Attlee and from the Dominion Governments (particularly Australia) were emphatically against the morganatic plan, and the Cabinet turned it down on December 2nd. The other proposal, emanating from Mrs. Simpson herself, was that the King should broadcast to the Empire. A draft broadcast was actually read to the Cabinet on December 4th and, in the words of Chamberlain's diary, "proved to be an appeal to the people of the Empire to allow him to make a morganatic marriage. It was unanimously decided that it would be impossible to allow the King, while he was King, to broadcast or make any public utterance which had not been approved by his Ministers, since constitutionally they must be responsible for his words." The Prime Minister therefore decided that he must tell the King that matters could not be allowed to drag on and that, now the situation had resolved itself into a choice between renunciation of Mrs. Simpson

[1] Reproduced in the Duchess of Windsor's memoirs *The Heart has its Reasons* (Michael Joseph, 1936), pp. 244–245.

or renunciation of the throne, a decision must be reached by midnight the following day.

Later that day, however, Chamberlain had conversations with Hoare, who had lunched with Beaverbrook, and with Margesson, who had lunched with Churchill. As a result, and after further Ministerial discussions, Baldwin decided to modify his demand. The need for no long delay was still to be stressed; for constitutional uncertainty was "holding up business and employment" and "paralysing our foreign policy", but no ultimatum was to be delivered. It was certainly not the Government's wish to force abdication. Though Chamberlain admitted, "I have felt all through that we should never be safe with this K.", he believed that the solution the country wanted was the renunciation of the marriage. As late as December 7th his diary still expressed some hope of this. The King's determination, however, proved unalterable.

Walter Monckton, who was acting as the King's personal adviser and liasion officer with Downing Street, now suggested that special legislation should be passed, at the same time as the Abdication Bill, to make Mrs. Simpson's divorce absolute forthwith. His argument, recalls the ex-King, was that "since I should now ease the pressure upon the Prime Minister and the Cabinet by giving them the speedy answer which they wanted they might in the name of humanity show me equal consideration in the one matter that most affected me".[1] Baldwin was well disposed and Chamberlain, though entertaining scruples, thought it might be arranged if the appearance of a deal were avoided. However, records his diary, the more Ministers looked at the proposal, the less they liked it, "because (1) it could not be denied that the K. regarded the Bill as a condition of abdication and it would therefore be denounced as an unholy bargain, (2) it would irretrievably damage the moral authority of the Government at home and in the Empire, (3) it would be looked on as an injury to the marriage law in general, (4) it would injure the respect for the monarchy".

Thus it was not until June 3rd, 1937, that the wedding of the ex-King took place in France—three weeks after the Coronation of his brother, and six days after Neville Chamberlain had kissed hands as Prime Minister.

[1] Duke of Windsor, *A King's Story* (Cassell, 1951), p. 387.

12

PRIME MINISTER

(May 1937 – February 1938)

HIS first thoughts on assuming the Premiership were characteristically for his family.

N.C. to Hilda 30.5.1937.

"You will be wondering what my own feelings are on actually taking up this post which ought to have come to the two senior members of the family and only failed to do so because the luck was against them in forcing them to choose between their natural ambition and their principles. It has come to me without my raising a finger to obtain it, because there is no-one else and perhaps because I have not made enemies by looking after myself rather than the common cause. But there is another contributory factor which is perhaps more important. I should never have been P.M. if I hadn't had Annie to help me. It isn't only that she charms everyone into good humour and makes them think that a man can't be so bad who has a wife like that. She has undoubtedly made countless friends and supporters . . . and she has kept many who might have left me if I had been alone but are devoted to her. . . .

"I am grieved that so many have gone to whom this amends to Father and Austen would have given unqualified pleasure and satisfaction. I don't regret so much that Austen just missed the actual consummation—he knew it was coming. But I wish our Bee could have lived to be aware of it, for it would have meant an enormous lot to her."

He was entering upon the duties and responsibilities of the Premiership, Chamberlain told the Party meeting which elected him its leader, "at an age when most people are thinking of retiring from active work"; but, he added amid laughter, he had hitherto led "a sober and a temperate life" and was consequently "sound in wind and limb". Gladstone once said that sixty should be the maximum age for Prime Ministers, though he himself when he formed his last Government was in his eighties. At sixty-seven, Chamberlain was, with the single exception of Campbell-Bannerman, the oldest statesman of our century to reach No. 10 for the first time. In small things and in great he was very much a product of the years in which he grew to manhood. "The late Victorian age for me," he declared in the 1920s, "before the days of motors and telephones;" and even so simple an amenity as a modern fountain pen he found an instrument of torture, preferring all his life to write letters, diaries and speeches with a plain steel nib. The fastidiousness and formality of his dress recalled his father and his father's day, but so too did the cast of his mind. Liberal imperialism and radical philosophy remained the twin pillars of his political faith. His intellectual curiosity was perennially fascinated by Darwin's challenge to revelation; but, though not springing from any dogmatic religious position, his moral standards were stern. Stern, and Victorian also, were his judgements on the artistic *avant-couriers*. Of Stanley Spencer's "hideous, distorted, grotesque productions", he wrote in 1934, "It rouses me to fury to think that ... any otherwise intelligent person should be fool enough to try to admire it;" and next year he felt sure that Epstein's *Christ* must be a joke produced "for the cynical satisfaction of hearing fools exhaust their vocabulary of admiration over it." This strength of conservative conviction was entirely characteristic, and in politics it tended, in combination with his reserved nature, to divorce him from many of the younger minds in the Party whom he was inclined to dismiss as a disappointing lot.

Robust and physically tireless he remained in these later years, despite the recurrent affliction of gout. Few Prime Ministers since Peel can have worked harder. He was Leader of the House of Commons and, after Eden's resignation, bore the brunt of advocacy and questioning on foreign affairs. From the start, he decided to take the chair of all Cabinet Committees which had to make recommendations on matters of major domestic policy. He demanded of his Ministers that they draw up two-year programmes, with an eye not only to the King's Speeches of 1937 and 1938, but to what would be left for the Election Manifesto of 1939 or 1940. Simon's memoirs record how Chamberlain would go into every difficulty his colleagues brought him as though it was his personal problem, and Ernest Brown, his Minister of Labour, wrote of "the comfort it had been to hard-pressed departmental Ministers to know that, when their subjects have to be discussed, whoever else has not read their papers and digested them, one man had—the Prime Minister".

Outside his work, his chief interests lay in activities, often strenuous activities, in the open air. Approaching his seventieth year and after a heavy parliamentary session, he could take one of his Chequers policeman a six mile walk, "up hill and down dale, through the woods and along the roads, and never turned a hair". He was an average but enthusiastic shot, and "of course for a Cabinet Minister to hit anything is considered very extraordinary, so one gets more than one's share of credit". Fishing, which he had taken to in middle age, was his favourite sport, and he was both expert and generous. "That was a noble fish!" exclaims a grateful letter from Baldwin in 1935. "We had him for dinner on Wednesday, lunch on Thursday, and more will appear at our Sunday evening meal. Our blessings on you and your rod." He was well-versed in natural history, and found endless delight in the garden and park at Chequers, which he improved. To *The Countryman* he would contribute an occasional article on botany. One charming letter to the *Daily Telegraph* recounted the imitative habits of a blackbird in the garden of Number 11, and another to *The Times* the unexpected appearance of a grey wagtail in St. James's Park where it was Chamberlain's custom to take his morning constitutional.

For more popular pastimes he had no inclination, and he was too honest to affect an interest he did not feel. As Prime Minister he would not accept suggestions to show himself at the Derby or at Lords, and indeed resented the attentions of press photographers who pursued him on his fishing holidays. Between his private and his public life, his shy dignity set up a barrier which certainly weakened his effectiveness as a democratic leader. Unlike Baldwin, he never felt able to bring into his speeches a breath of the English countryside that he so much loved. Save for a ready and apt resort to Shakespearean quotation, these speeches reflect little or nothing of his wide reading, nor did the dry voice and matter-of-fact delivery very easily suggest the man whom the melodies and rhythms of Beethoven could carry into another world. His mastery of facts, his incisive intelligence, and the tough austerity and confidence of his bearing, were apparent enough. But lack of colour, or *panache*, or even eccentricity, and a temperamental inability to project very deep emotions or appeal to the heart or rouse a rabble, gave the impression of an altogether plainer and bleaker man than is remembered by his family or the few friends who knew him best.

He was aware of these shortcomings. "I suppose it is a good thing to see oneself as others see us, but it is a very painful process," he wrote, part ruefully, part jocularly, after seeing himself in a film in 1937, "... if I had not previously seen the person who addressed us from the screen, I should call him pompous, insufferably slow in diction and unspeakably repellent in person!" More seriously, the moving tribute to his wife which he wrote on becoming Prime Minister acknowledged that "she has softened or smoothed my natural impatience and dislike of anything with a whiff of humbug about it, and I know she has saved me often from making an impression of harshness that was not intended". Such critical self-analysis, including the inestimable capacity to laugh at himself, is to be found again and again in his private papers. Unfortunately, it did not penetrate to a sufficiently wide circle. "You can't know Mr. Chamberlain till you have been with him five years," was his chauffeur's comment to Hoare. Churchill declared that "amid all the business we did together over nearly twenty years", he could remember only one intimate social conversation with Neville Chamberlain.[1] Those who were closest to him in public life found the real man. The King, says George VI's biographer "had boundless confidence in Mr. Chamberlain, whose personality he found agreeable and assuring".[2]

[1] *The Second World War* (Cassell, 1948), Vol. I, p. 389.
[2] J. W. Wheeler-Bennett, *King George VI* (Macmillan, 1958), p. 328.

Halifax and Hoare in particular sought in their memoirs to correct the contemporary mis-reading of his character. In his own Party, men who had frequent opportunity to meet him privately or in small gatherings recall kindness as well as integrity, sensibility as well as good sense. With the Opposition it was different. "Ungregarious by nature," wrote Duff Cooper, "he never frequented the Smoking Room of the House of Commons, where Stanley Baldwin and Winston Churchill were familiar figures, often in the centre of groups which included political opponents."[1] In the House he was too rarely conciliatory and too often combative; ready enough with the devastating retort which delighted his supporters, but not with the soft (or humorous) answer which turneth away the wrath of opponents. Baldwin had begged him in 1927 to remember that he was addressing a meeting of gentlemen: "I always gave him the impression, he said, when I spoke in the House of Commons, that I looked on the Labour Party as dirt." The impression was shared by the Labour Party, and they deeply resented it.[2] What was insufficiently, if at all, understood was that beneath the tough exterior lay an exceptionally sensitive character, which because of its sensitivity was inclined to judge criticism more hardly than it deserved. Hence unflinching honesty of mind was only too frequently misinterpreted as obstinate arrogance of disposition.

If the lot had fallen unto him in a fair ground, I think in time his reforming fervour would surely have softened these personal antipathies. No Conservative statesman in office in the inter-war years spoke more steadfastly in the accents of social progress. No speeches demonstrate more clearly than his that the so-called "New Conservatism" of the post-war era, was not a miraculous transformation but a natural development. "I did not seek to enter the House of Commons when I was nearly fifty years of age", he told a constituency audience in Birmingham in July 1937, "for the sake of making a career for myself or because I had idle time on my hands that I did not know how to fill up. I went because I was brought up in a house where public service seemed to be a natural part of a man's life . . . I have seen in this great city of ours

[1] *Old Men Forget* (Rupert Hart-Davis, 1953), p. 188.
[2] See Chapter 7, p. 119, *supra.*

how many people there were who were deprived of that full enjoyment of life which everybody ought to have, because of bad housing, bad health, or insufficient medical attendance for themselves and their families, or for want of sufficient income to keep these families in comfort." The way forward, he declared, lay in "better education", "full employment" and "old people free from anxiety". A few days later, at a National Government demonstration in the Albert Hall, he struck a deeper note: "When I speak of the conditions of life I am not thinking only of material considerations. It is no part of my creed that everybody ought to have the same income, for that would not guarantee that everybody would be equally happy. Happiness springs from within, not from without, but it may be fostered or starved by external conditions, and in the model State that all of us are striving after we would like to see conditions so framed as to enable its subjects to create happiness for themselves. If we are to achieve those conditions the people must be strong and healthy. If they should fall victim to accident or disease they should have available the best of medical science. They should be able to command an income sufficient to keep themselves and their families at any rate in a minimum standard of comfort. They should have leisure for refreshment and recreation. They should be able to cultivate a taste for beautiful things, whether in nature or in art, and to open their minds to the wisdom that is to be found in books. They should be free from fear or violence or injustice. They should be able to express their thoughts and to satisfy their spiritual and moral needs without hindrance and without persecution."

These sentiments may seem trite or obvious enough in the 1960's, but remember the time and the circumstances in which they were expressed. A commitment to "full employment", in a year when there were one and a half million still out of work. A projection of the "minimum standard" Welfare State, five years before the Beveridge Report. An acknowledgment of the challenge of leisure, two decades before positive proposals featured in any Party manifesto. A reaffirmation of the tradition of even-handed justice and religious tolerance, when Fascists marched in London and persecution held sway in Europe. Inevitably the harvest of this Government was small, but they sowed good seed. A comprehensive Factories Act, promised for years, at last found its way on to the Statute Book. The pensions scheme was extended on a voluntary basis to black-coated workers. Overcrowding was to be tackled under a new Housing Act which, but for the war, would also have completed the clearance of the slums within five or six years. A six-months' campaign was inaugurated to encourage a wider use of the national health services. Chamberlain's ideas for improving the national physique found expression in the Physical Training and Recreation Act. Hoare's Criminal Justice Bill anticipated by nine years the Labour Government's Act of 1948. Finally, we know from his papers that the Prime Minister's mind was already revolving schemes for further reform of local government and for the control of building and other development in the interests of amenity and agriculture.

It is not true, as has sometimes been said, that this was a one-man Government. Chamberlain dominated it, of course, as he had also dominated the last administrations of Ramsay MacDonald and Baldwin, with the difference that now he could give and did give a firmer lead. But he relied upon and consulted continually the judgement of Halifax, Simon and Hoare, whilst in Swinton, Hore-Belisha, Malcom MacDonald and Kingsley Wood, he had Ministers of very high executive ability.[1] Certainly on the Conservative benches of the House of Commons in these years there were some men of ripe distinction like Churchill and more of clear promise like Macmillan who would have strengthened the administration. Chamberlain's Cabinet-making was extremely cautious—too cautious. He neglected Hoare's advice to "make your new Government as unlike the old as you can", and made relatively few and unexciting changes between 1937 and the outbreak of war. Meanwhile, not only the main development of foreign policy, but the attempted appeasement of Eire (which involved the abandonment of the Treaty Ports), and of Palestine

[1] In Chamberlain's pre-war Government, Simon was Chancellor of the Exchequer; Hoare Home Secretary; Halifax Lord President, and then Foreign Secretary after Eden's resignation in February 1938; Swinton Secretary of State for Air until May 1938, when he was succeeded by the Minister of Health, Kingsley Wood; Hore-Belisha Secretary of State for War; Malcolm MacDonald held either the Dominions Secretaryship or the Colonial Secretaryship, and for a period both.

(which involved the limitation of Jewish immigration) drew the Government and its greatest critic further apart.

It is in a sense an irony of pre-war history that a man of Chamberlain's temperament and opinions should have become the archpriest of appeasement. Throughout his life he had disliked and distrusted Germany. A phrase he used when on holiday in the Black Forest in 1930, "on the whole I loathe Germans", echoed countless others which are to be found in his papers during the First World War and long before that when the Kaiser was wooing the Boers. The first twelve months of Hitler's regime had convinced him that an aggressive Germany was up to her old tricks again, "instigating, suggesting, encouraging bloodshed and assassination, for her own selfish aggrandisement and pride". His private comments on the Nazi leaders were incisive. Hitler was "a lunatic" or "half mad"; Goebbels "a vulgar common little mind"; Ribbentrop "so stupid, so shallow, so self-centred and self-satisfied, so totally devoid of intellectual capacity that he never seems to take in what is said to him". In 1936, for economy's sake, he let his London house in Eaton Square to the Ribbentrops, commenting "I think it is very amusing considering my affections for Germans in general and R. in particular." The excesses of the Nazi regime scandalised and angered him. In particular, "I am horrified by the German behaviour to the Jews." A speech on Empire unity in December 1937, gave him an opportunity to contrast unfavourably "the voluntary subjection of individual liberty of speech and of thought and of action to the direction of the State, or perhaps of a single man" with the democracy we and the Dominions enjoyed and intended to maintain. "For the preservation of democracy, which means the preservation of our liberty," he told the House of Commons in March, 1938, "I myself would fight, and I believe that the people of this country would fight."

No Minister, as we have seen, had done more, no-one had done as much, to make the country ready. "When the late Government were at length convinced of the urgent need to rearm," Churchill acknowledged in 1937, ". . . no one was more active than Mr. Chamberlain." The Defence White Papers of 1936 and 1937 were shaped by his mind. But rearmament had started late, and the level from which it climbed upwards was extremely low. A gap yawned between blue-print and finished product. Estimates varied as to how long it would be before we could fight on more or less equal terms, but even in the summer of 1938 the experts still said one or two years. In the meantime, what hope did we have of stopping the dictators? "At the last election," Chamberlain declared in the debate after Eden's resignation, "it was still possible to hope that the League might afford collective security. I believed it myself. I do not believe it now . . . I say we must not try to delude ourselves, and still more, we must not try to delude small weak nations, into thinking that they will be protected by the League against aggression and acting accordingly, when we know that nothing of the kind can be expected."[1] Reliance upon the anti-Axis sentiments of America would be just as much a delusion, Chamberlain believed. President Roosevelt was struggling against a strong isolationist tide which was actually strengthened by the famous Chicago speech of October 1937, in which he urged that aggressors should be "quarantined". If Japanese planes could shell and sink an American gunboat with impunity and General Franco obtain three-quarters of his oil from American producers, reiteration of American moral principles was unlikely to make rulers tremble in Berlin or Rome.

To France, of course, we were linked both by common ideals and reciprocal alliance. But France, debilitated on account of industrial unrest and flights from the franc, had then two other faults which, Chamberlain wrote privately in January 1938, destroyed half her value as a friend: "She never can keep a secret for more than half an hour, nor a government for more than nine months! Therefore our people see," he went on in this letter to Mrs. Morton Prince, his stepmother's American cousin, "that in the absence of any powerful ally, and until our armaments are completed, we must adjust our foreign policy to our circumstances, and even bear with patience and good humour actions which we should like to treat in very different fashion." To this extent, necessity was the mother of appeasement.

But of course it is also true that the policy marched not only with his practical assessment of the situation but with some of the

[1] February 22nd, 1938, *Hansard*, Vol. 332, c. 227.

deepest impulses of his nature. The very philanthropy that had
brought him into politics and still kept him a radical recoiled from
the waste of war. "To me," he told his Birmingham constituents
in April 1938, "the very idea that the hard-won savings of our
people, which ought to be devoted to the alleviation of suffering
and to the opening out of fresh interests and recreation, to the care
of the old and the development of the minds and bodies of the
young—to think that all these savings should have to be dissipated
on the construction of weapons of war is hateful and damnable."
The very business-like efficiency which made it impossible for
him to see any problem without searching for its solution attracted him to the methodical removal of the principal sources of
friction in the world. If it were possible to achieve a general
settlement giving us a secure prospect, he argued, it would be
wrong to set one's face against peaceful and negotiated changes in
the arrangements of Versailles. These arrangements, as they
affected Germany, still had two principal defects. First, that Germany was, in Lloyd George's famous phrase, "surrounded by a
mob of small states, many of them consisting of peoples who have
never previously set up a stable government for themselves, but
each of them containing large masses of Germans". Secondly,
that President Wilson's fifth "point", namely "an absolutely im-
partial adjustment of all colonial claims", had plainly not been
fulfilled. Therefore, he wrote to his sisters in November 1937,
"I don't see why we shouldn't say to Germany, 'Give us satisfactory assurances that you won't use force to deal with the
Austrians and Czechoslovakians and we will give you similar
assurances that we won't use force to prevent the changes you
want if you can get them by peaceful means.'" Further, as a result of
Halifax's visit to Germany and conversation with Hitler in November 1937, he arrived at the conclusion, as he wrote in his diary,
"that any satisfactory settlement would involve the handing over
of Tanganyika [German East Africa prior to the First World War]
though very probably some adjustments of boundaries might be
agreed upon". That such appeasement of Germany, at this point
of history, rested upon falsely optimistic assumptions about the
measure of Nazi ambitions is now undeniable. We know from
the Nuremberg trial documents that Hitler was insatiable, war

inevitable and appeasement therefore a forlorn hope. But since those who pursued appeasement lacked the benefit of hindsight, it was neither a foolish nor an ignoble hope. The case for appeasement thus rested on the proposition, not merely that it would have been folly to incur war without adequate defences or reliable allies, but morally wrong to accept it as inevitable unless every attempt had been made to redress legitimate grievances peacefully.

Chamberlain must certainly bear the chief responsibility for the policy of appeasement. He himself told the Party meeting which elected him leader that "in all the perplexities and the problems which rise up day after day in front of any Government in these troublesome times, the ultimate responsibility of the final decision must rest upon the shoulders of the Prime Minister . . . and if things go wrong he can never escape the reflection 'I might have prevented this if I had thought or acted differently'." Nevertheless, the policy is not correctly identified with one man alone. The Prime Minister, Hoare insists in his memoirs, "was not an autocrat who imposed his views upon doubting or hostile colleagues. Appeasement was not his personal policy. Not only was it supported by his colleagues; it expressed the general desire of the British people.[1] This is a fundamental consideration in judging his action. Nothing is further from the truth than the myth that has been invented of his intolerant omnipotence. Whilst the prime mover, he was never the dictator of the Government's policy."[2]

This judgement is important to any estimate of Chamberlain's relations with his first Foreign Secretary, Anthony Eden. It is quite clear that the new Prime Minister, in marked contrast with his predecessors, took the closest possible interest in foreign affairs and continually intervened in the making of policy. It is equally clear that, whatever Eden's private feelings may have been on this score, he failed to express either irritation or dissent. On the

---

[1] Cf., "It had the greater part of the Press behind it: in particular *The Times* (which was often ahead of the game), the *Daily Express* of Lord Beaverbrook and the *Daily Mail* of Lord Rothermere, and the fulminations of J. L. Garvin in the *Observer*. . . . In retrospect everyone was against appeasement; at the time not so many." C. L. Mowat, *Britain between the Wars* (Methuen, 1955), p. 591.

[2] *Nine Troubled Years* (Collins, 1954), p. 375.

contrary, as late as January 9th, 1938, he wrote to Chamberlain from the south of France, where he was on holiday, in the following terms: "I do hope that you will never for an instant feel that any interest you take in foreign affairs, however close, could ever be resented by me. I know, of course, that there will always be some who will seek to pretend that the Foreign Secretary has had his nose put out of joint, but that is of no account beside the very real gain of close collaboration between Foreign Secretary and Prime Minister which, I am sure, is the only way that foreign affairs can be run in our country." Chamberlain's papers in this, as in earlier periods, show high respect and regard for Eden, though not for the Foreign Office. They record that while Vansittart argued against Halifax's visit to Germany, ostensibly for an international exhibition of hunting but with the prospect of conversations with Hitler, Eden expressed himself as "quite happy".[1] They also record that Vansittart's promotion in the New Year from permanent head of the Foreign Office to the honorific post of chief diplomatic adviser to the Government was Eden's wish every bit as much as it was Chamberlain's.[2] Though words may mean different things in different mouths, "appeasement" had been Eden's own definition of his foreign policy even before Chamberlain became Prime Minister. "I assure the House," he had said in 1936 after the remilitarisation of the Rhineland, "that it is the appeasement of Europe as a whole that we have constantly before us." Thus when Chamberlain broached the idea of dividing the Axis powers and achieving "peaceful co-existence"[3] with Italy, it was the Foreign Office who "persisted in seeing Musso only as a sort of Machiavelli", whilst "I must say A.E. is awfully good in accepting my suggestions without grumbling".

The Prime Minister's own version of the very real differences

[1] This was confirmed in the memoirs of Halifax, *Fulness of Days* (Collins, 1957), p. 184.

[2] Cf., "Anthony and I were divided, and I fully understood his desire for change", Vansittart, *The Mist Procession* (Hutchinson, 1958), p. 549.

[3] This suggestive phrase is not anachronistic. It occurs in Mussolini's "very cordial reply" referred to in the Diary entry below. This letter, dated July 31st, 1937, states: "The interests of Italy and Great Britain are not opposed to each other either in the Mediterranean or elsewhere. On the contrary, through their peaceful co-existence (*la loro pacifica coesistenza*) they can be responsible for a more active spur to the development of our relations."

that arose between the two men in February should precede
further comment, since it makes clear much that has hitherto
been conjectural and contradicts much that has hitherto been
accepted.

Diary, 19 to 27.2.1938.

"In July I had a meeting with Grandi [the Italian Ambassador] in the
course of which I wrote a letter to Mussolini in friendly terms and
this was followed by a very cordial reply from him in which he
declared his readiness to open conversations with a view to the
removal of all points of difference. I did not show my letter to the
Foreign Secretary for I had the feeling that he would object to it.
Nevertheless, he made no complaint and the F.O. authorised our
Ambassador, Drummond, to say that we hoped the conversations
would begin in September. At that time Eden and I both recognised
(and the Italians apparently agreed) that the formal recognition of
their Abyssinian conquest, to which they attached great importance,
must follow on some declaration by the League that Abyssinia was
no longer an independent State and that members of the League
were therefore at liberty to recognise the conquest if they chose.
We thought then that the League might if conversations went well
be willing to make such a declaration at their next meeting, but
unfortunately during the holiday months Mussolini sent a message
to Franco boasting of his share in F.'s victories and a series of sub-
marine attacks (probably Italian) were made on shipping in the
Mediterranean, which produced such a bad effect on public opinion
that any hope of a League declaration vanished for the time. . . .

"In late December before we separated for Christmas I spoke to
Anthony about the Italian situation. By that time Musso had given
notice of his intention to leave the League. Our relations had steadily
deteriorated. The Bari station was pouring out streams of anti-
British propaganda, the press was hostile, anti-British intrigue was
going on in Egypt, Palestine and Arabia, the Berlin-Rome Axis had
been greatly strengthened, Germany had signed an Anti-Comintern
Pact with Japan, and Italy had joined it. I told A. that I feared we
were getting ourselves into a deadlock, if we stuck to it that we
could not open conversations till the League had given us permission, since the League and Italy were again at daggers drawn. I
therefore asked him to study the question and make some suggestion
for a way out. He raised no objection, in fact he agreed with my
view, and he then went for a brief holiday in France, leaving me to

take charge of the Foreign Office during his absence. Soon afterwards I received from him 2 memoranda and a covering letter in which he said that following our conversations he had instructed the F.O. to study the question and they had produced a memo A, according to which we should trade *de jure* recognition off against sundry concessions by Italy dealing with Spain, Libya, Pantellaria, Arabia, etc. He did not like the idea, however, of setting high moral principles against material advantages, and he had instructed the F.O. to produce alternative B which he preferred. According to B he would go to Geneva and endeavour to obtain the support of Delbos [the French Foreign Minister] for a declaration to be made jointly that the time had come to give recognition of the Abyssinian conquest *de jure*. Then, having got that out of the way, we could enter on conversations with a clean conscience. I replied that I must reject B. We should be giving away our best card for nothing and we should draw down on ourselves a condemnation more scathing than that aroused by the Hoare-Laval proposals. But I did not like A because it was wrongly presented. We should approach the matter from the angle of obtaining general appeasement to which each must make its contribution and justify *de jure* on that ground which was of interest to all Mediterranean nations and, since that sea was a danger spot, to the whole world.

"Soon after this letter had been despatched Roosevelt sprang a surprise by informing us that he proposed to issue a sort of world appeal to end international tension by a general agreement to abide by international law and order. . . . If this proposal had a favourable reception he would summon to Washington representatives of various small nations . . . to formulate a plan for submission to a subsequent conference. He said he would not publish unless by the 17th Jan. (I got this on the 13th) I could assure him of whole-hearted support and co-operation. I was in a dilemma. The plan appeared to me fantastic and likely to excite the derision of Germany and Italy. They might even use it to postpone conversations with us, and if we were associated with it they would see in it another attempt on the part of the democratic bloc to put the dictators in the wrong. There was no time to consult Anthony, for in view of secrecy on which Roosevelt insisted in emphatic terms I did not dare to telephone. Therefore, after consultation with Wilson and Cadogan, I sent a reply deprecating immediate publication. . . . This produced a somewhat sulky acquiescence in postponement and some strongly worded warnings against shocking public opinion by giving *de jure* to Italy.

On Sunday [January 16th] Anthony got back from France and hurried to Chequers. He did not like my reply and without consulting me sent a fresh wire to R. Lindsay in Washington saying I had not exactly meant what I said. He proposed to me that we should at once call off the idea of Italian conversations lest we should offend U.S.A., but I objected, and as we could not agree I summoned the Foreign Affairs Committee of the Cabinet and laid the position before them. As a result we agreed on a compromise reply in which we elucidated our position and made it clear that *de jure* was only to be given as a factor in general appeasement. Subsequent despatches from Lindsay showed that this had the effect desired by me. The course proposed 'entirely met the President's views' and there was no reason why we should not proceed. During the discussions on this matter A. had suggested resignation but I had pointed out the impossibility of doing this since Roosevelt had enjoined complete secrecy upon us.

"Looking back now I cannot recall accurately the changes in Anthony's attitude towards the conversations. During this time Ivy [Sir Austen Chamberlain's widow] was in Rome and had been fêted and made much of. She had seen Mussolini and Ciano and had met practically all the Italians who counted as well as diplomats and other foreigners. She had written to me of the strong dislike and distrust with which Eden was regarded and the general belief that he did not want better relations. She said she had argued that the delays were due to Italian not British action and that she herself had been assured by Eden before she left London that he wanted to talk as soon as the coast was clear. All seemed in vain. One day she met Ciano and he taxed her with not really believing what she said. It happened she had just received a letter from me in which I had praised her efforts and said I was going to try again to overcome difficulties. The letter was meant for her alone but she read it to Ciano. The effect was magical for he was at last convinced. He reported what he had heard to Mussolini . . . [who] sent a message to me by Ivy assuring me of his genuine desire to settle everything between us. Unfortunately this episode seemed to produce in Anthony only further suspicion. If the Italians wanted talks there must be some catch in it, and we had better hang back. Early in February, Grandi came back from his holiday and asked to see me and the Foreign Secretary. It was some time before the latter informed me that Grandi wanted to see me and even then he did not suggest that I should meet his wishes. He did, however, see him himself and once more things appeared to be

213

moving. Anthony discussed subjects of conversation including *de jure* about which he did not appear to think there would be any difficulty or delay in getting League sanction. Yet still no date was fixed for contact and this time it was suggested that we must get further with the settlement of the Spanish situation and the withdrawal of volunteers.

"At last there came another surprise from Germany. . . . Schuschnigg the Austrian Chancellor was suddenly summoned to Berchtesgaden where he was outrageously bullied by Hitler and faced with a series of demands to which he was obliged to yield, since on this occasion Mussolini gave him no support. Very soon afterwards Ciano told Perth [the British Ambassador in Rome] that he had instructed Grandi to press for an early start of the conversations in view of 'possible future happenings' . . . I suggested that now was the time when we should both interview him. This was on Thursday morning the 17th. Anthony agreed and said he would ask Grandi to call at Number 10 next morning when we might try and extract from him the real meaning of Ciano's words. Both A. and I lunched that day with P. Sassoon [the First Commissioner of Works]. . . . A. who sat next to me explained that Cadogan had suggested that it might be better that A. should see Grandi alone and *if necessary* bring him afterwards to see me. I resisted this as I was convinced it was intended to prevent my seeing Grandi lest that should bring the conversations nearer. . . . In the course of the evening, however, a final effort was made by Anthony who sent me a note begging me very earnestly not to commit us to any talks when I met Grandi.

"This note convinced me that the issue between us must be faced and faced at once. In my view, to intimate now to Grandi that this was not the moment for conversations would be to convince Musso that he must consider talks with us 'off' and act accordingly. I had no doubt at all that in his disappointment and exasperation at having been fooled with, as he would think, so long, Italian public opinion would be raised to a white heat against us. There might indeed be some overt act of hostility, and in any case the dictatorships would be driven closer together, the last shreds of Austrian independence would be lost, the Balkan countries would feel compelled to turn towards their powerful neighbours, Czechoslovakia would be swallowed, France would either have to submit to German domination or fight in which case we should almost certainly be drawn in. I could not face the responsibility for allowing such a series of catastrophes to happen and I told Horace Wilson on Friday morning

[February 18th] that I was determined to stand firm even though it meant losing my Foreign Secretary. After this events moved swiftly to a crisis. Grandi met Eden and myself in the Cabinet room at 11 ... he denied emphatically that any agreement concerning Austria had been made between Hitler and Mussolini but he said that if we had started conversations before the recent Austrian coup the latter's attitude would have been very different. How could he move troops to the Brenner as he did before, if he felt that Great Britain was a potential enemy and that the Mediterranean at his back was not secure? 'And now?' I asked, 'It is too late to undo what is done, but what effect would conversations have now on M.'s attitude to Austria.' 'It would encourage him,' G. replied, 'to take a stronger and more independent line.' He declared that M. was ready to discuss anything we chose to mention which might affect our relations: Spain would not be a serious difficulty, nor would propaganda.

"In view of Anthony's note I said finally to Grandi that I thought he had better leave the F.S. and myself to talk and return at 3 o'clock and accordingly he withdrew. I said at once that I had no doubt as to what we ought to say to Grandi when he returned. We should say that conversations should begin at once and we would get Perth back for instructions. Anthony, however, objected. Since M. was so ready for conversations, this was a reason for withdrawal on our part. We ought not to trust him. He believed there was a German-Italian agreement, he did not believe in Grandi's assurances. If Italy was in earnest she would at least make a gesture; she might indeed have accepted the British formula for the withdrawal of volunteers [from Spain]. . . . I asked if Italian acceptance now of the formula would overcome his scruples. He had made a lot of the want of any sign of good faith, but rather inconsistently now declared that acceptance would make no difference whatever. It was clear that the issue was profound and vital. Ostensibly it was whether talks should begin now, really it was whether they should ever begin. There was no accommodation possible and for the first time I could not refrain from reproaches. I told A.E. that he had missed one opportunity after another of advancing towards peace; he had one more chance, probably the last, and he was wanting to throw it away. It was all in vain; I could not move him, so when Grandi returned I told him that I could not give him a final answer then. 'I am calling my Cabinet for tomorrow,' I said, 'in order to consult them. Let there be no mistake; I am not at this moment, committing myself to Yes or No'. . . . I said, however, that it would be helpful to our presentation of the case for talks, should that be our decision, if he could get his Government to accept the formula [on withdrawal of volunteers]. . . .

"I began [at the Cabinet next day, February 19th] by putting my case at some length and on the broadest grounds and Anthony replied rather ineffectively I thought. I then invited each member of the Cabinet to give his views in turn. . . . I marked them as they spoke. Twenty of us were present. . . . Taking out Anthony and myself, 14 supported me without qualification, 4 . . . with some qualification or reserve. None supported Anthony. When invited to reply he said he could not accept the decision and must resign, whereupon there was a gasp of horror. . . . I thought it necessary to say clearly that I could not accept any decision in the opposite sense. Seeing, however, how my colleagues had been taken aback I proposed adjournment. . . . On Sunday [the 20th] I asked A. to have a private talk before the Cabinet. . . . This time we were able to agree that the difference between us was vital and unbridgeable. . . . After long discussions in full Cabinet, we suspended our sitting to allow a committee of mediators . . . to try and accommodate our differences. They however made no attempt to induce me to alter my views, their efforts were directed to convincing Anthony that the differences were less than he made out and that he could with a clear conscience accept the Cabinet's decision and proceed with the talks, merely *warning* Grandi that a Spanish settlement was essential to an agreement and that the Italians must implement their promise to accept the formula and abstain from reinforcements. Anthony, thus bombarded from all sides and very tired, at last begged for an hour's respite to think over his position and we agreed that the Committee should wait to hear his decision. About 7 o'clock he came and, greatly to his credit as I think, he informed us that nothing that had been said could shake his decision. Accordingly he went off to write his letter of resignation. . . .

"I need not now [Feb. 27] recite the sequel which is public property, but I may note that on Sunday morning Horace Wilson gave me a note without any name on it saying that the Italian Government's response would be favourable and Horace Wilson said that this came indirectly from Grandi. Later in the day and before the Cabinet he gave me a second similar note saying that Grandi had now given formal assurance that the response was all right and at the Cabinet, before resignation had taken place, I repeated this in the same words. Anthony repeated then what he had said before to me, that it made no difference to him. I did not ask H.W. who the intermediary was and he did not actually tell me, but I assume it was Joseph Ball who has once or twice before given me information of what Grandi, whom he knows well, was doing or thinking."

The interpretation to be put upon this crisis is still uncertain in detail, but the broad lines should now be clear. It is not true that Chamberlain interfered more with Foreign Office business than is natural for a Prime Minister at a time when foreign affairs are the dominant issue in politics. The two major decisions he made against Eden's judgement were, first, the rejection of Roosevelt's proposal,[1] and second, the decision to begin talks with Italy. The former decision was taken at a time when Eden was out of the country and in circumstances in which it was impossible to communicate with him; the latter was taken with the otherwise unanimous approval of the Cabinet. It is true, however, that for Chamberlain's degree of interference to be tolerable, there must be a much more genuine trust, sympathy and accord between Prime Minister and Foreign Secretary than ever existed between these two. The conclusion is inescapable that Eden was far too loath to make his doubts and resentments explicit and Chamberlain far too ready to ignore his Foreign Secretary's mute discomfort or to accept his polite reassurances. Chamberlain in his papers always shows himself full of admiration for his youthful, talented Foreign Secretary. But perhaps the wide difference in years and the Prime Minister's shy reserve built barriers that neither could leap. Because Eden spoke out so very late, the strength of his conviction came as a surprise to his chief. Though resignation had been mentioned over the Roosevelt issue, Chamberlain wrote to his sisters as late as February 13th denying as "mendacious and vicious" the newspaper reports of a split between himself and Eden. Only on the night of the 17th was he convinced that the

[1] "We must regard its rejection as the loss of the last frail chance to save the world from tyranny otherwise than by war," Churchill, *op. cit.*, p. 199; but, "I am satisfied that on neither count is it possible to maintain the argument that has been advanced to support the conclusion either that the President felt resentment at the reception accorded his initiative, or that his initiative if differently handled, might have had the effect of preventing the war", Halifax, *op. cit.*, p. 194.

situation was critical and only on the 18th, two days before the end, did he finally decide that he must stand firm "even though it meant losing my Foreign Secretary".

Eden's own account of these events has still to be published and will properly command great attention and respect. The weight of evidence now available is against those who would put an unworthy construction on Chamberlain's motives and actions at this time. Even some responsible historians assert that he "thought fit to transact business of State through his sister-in-law" and that he "was in constant touch with Grandi through unofficial intermediaries, behind Mr. Eden's back".[1] But the first of these statements is untrue, and the second rests only on an unsubstantiated dispatch from Grandi printed in Ciano's fascinating but unreliable diplomatic papers.

Lady Chamberlain's stay in Rome during the winter of 1937-38 was not undertaken at her brother-in-law's behest or on his behalf. She had spoken to Eden before she left England, and her letters home record her transparently sincere efforts to dispel Italian animosity against him. Chamberlain's personal letter, which she showed to Ciano and Mussolini and which evoked a cordial response, was never intended for other eyes than hers. This is clear not only from the diary entry quoted above, but from what Lady Chamberlain wrote to the Prime Minister on January 2nd: "I hope you will forgive me for showing your letter." It is certain that her private conversations in Rome, made possible by the Duce's warm memory of her husband, were exasperating to the Foreign Office hierarchy. But she did not act behind their backs or as her brother-in-law's agent.

It seems scarcely less perverse to cast Sir Joseph Ball, the director of the Conservative Research Department, in this melodramatic role. Grandi's despatch to Ciano on February 19th depicted Ball as a daily intermediary between Number 10 and the Italian Embassy and Chamberlain as conspiring through this "secret agent" to worst Eden and then oust him. His story was filled out with a number of circumstantial details, of which the most bizarre was an assignation with Ball in a public taxi-cab to receive Chamberlain's "cordial greetings". Duff Cooper, for one, ac-

---

[1] L.B. Namier, *Europe in Decay* (Macmillan, 1950), p. 119.

cepted all this quite uncritically and without even troubling to ask Ball for his version. On the other hand, Hoare and Amery, two statesmen with very differing views about Chamberlain's policy, both consulted Ball, as I did, and both rejected the veracity of Grandi's account. The English editor of Ciano's papers, Malcolm Muggeridge, whilst taking the contrary view, is constrained to admit that, "Reporting is, in all conceivable circumstances, done with an eye to the reader or readers for whom it is primarily intended . . . Under totalitarian conditions even archives are liable to provide grounds for a charge of lack of zeal, or even unorthodoxy—which means disloyalty. Totalitarian reporting, therefore, tends to be as obsequious as totalitarian oratory. . . . Grandi had to be shown as calling the tune, not only to satisfy his personal vanity, but also because Mussolini had to be made to feel that his representative in London could call the tune."[1]

Grandi did very occasionally use his personal acquaintance with Ball to air views he expected would reach Chamberlain. Scraps of information were also conveyed to Ball through a British subject called Dingli who was acting as a legal adviser to the Italian Embassy. The Prime Minister himself was unaware of the man's existence, but Ball had thought it wise in the summer of 1937 to inform the Foreign Office of his contact and had received a reply from Eden's P.P.S., J.P.L. Thomas, minimising its importance but asking him to pass on to the Foreign Office any genuine information derived from it. This letter is still in existence. It was Dingli who got Ball up from the country on February 20th to acquaint him with the Italian response on the withdrawal of troops from Spain. The two men met at Waterloo Station and drove in a taxi to the offices of the Research Department in Old Queen Street. There the information was given to Ball who immediately passed it on to the Prime Minister's private office—hoping, he wrote at the time, that Chamberlain "might be able to use it in such a way as to prevent Eden resigning". This account squares with Ball's reputation as a man of honour and distinction.[2] It is on all

[1] *Ciano's Diplomatic Papers*, the English edition of *L'Europa Verso La Catastrofe* (Odhams, 1948), pp. xxi-xxii. The Grandi dispatch is on pp. 164–184.
[2] Ball, knighted in 1936, was Deputy Chairman of the Security Executive from 1940 to 1942.

fours with the frankly matter-of-fact entry in Chamberlain's private diary, quoted above. It is also easy to see how Grandi, desiring to ingratiate himself with a régime which suspected his political sympathies, spun what amounted to a highly coloured fiction out of the bare threads of truth. (Even the taxi-cab, it will be seen, was not wholly invented; only Ball's travelling companion and the nature of the errand were altered.)

Eden was succeeded as Foreign Secretary by Lord Halifax. The Opposition objected to a peer; but the Prime Minister undertook, with the aid of R. A. Butler, to answer for the Foreign Office himself in the House of Commons. From now onwards his personal control of the shape and direction of foreign policy became unquestionable. Halifax, no less than his predecessor, was a man with a mind of his own, but it was a mind far more perfectly attuned to that of his chief, and also unusually oblivious to considerations of political status. There is no indication that he even thought it odd, as it certainly appears in retrospect, to have been excluded from all Chamberlain's subsequent meetings with Hitler. Over and over again the Prime Minister's papers record relief and gratitude for a "steady, unruffled Foreign Secretary who never causes me any worry".

It was alleged at the time, and has been repeated since, that Chamberlain deliberately circumvented the Foreign Office; preferring the advice of his own man, Sir Horace Wilson. Wilson, the Government's Chief Industrial Adviser, had in fact been seconded to the Prime Minister's personal service not by Chamberlain but by Baldwin. He would himself deny that the footpath across Downing Street was ever obstructed, the relationship with Cadogan ever anything but close and comradely. But it is certain that Chamberlain found this reserved and extremely able civil servant both congenial and useful. They had qualities in common —tidiness of mind, impatience of humbug, indefatigable industry—and no clashing ambitions. Wilson became the Prime Minister's confidant, and later his emissary; but he was no grey eminence. Chamberlain was never the kind of man to take his policy from somebody else. In essence, that was why Eden had to go.

13

THE ROAD TO MUNICH

(February – September 1938)

THE proposed talks with Italy which had precipitated Eden's resignation began a few weeks later. They were brought to a successful conclusion on April 16th when an agreement was signed in Rome by Ciano and Perth. This dealt, as Chamberlain observed, "in a very careful and comprehensive manner with the possible sources of difference between the Italian Government and ourselves" in the Mediterranean, Africa and the Middle East. In addition it included a declaration that neither Government would employ propaganda to injure the interests of the other. Its most important and controversial features were the undertakings regarding Abyssinia and Spain. For her part, Italy disclaimed any territorial or economic ambitions in Spanish mainland or overseas possessions, and confirmed her adherence to the British proposal for the evacuation of foreign "volunteers" from Spain. At the same time Britain sought to remove Italy's chief grievance by promising to raise the recognition of the Italian conquest of Abyssinia at Geneva. Chamberlain made clear, however, that "the only circumstances in which [British] recognition could be morally justified would be if it was shown to be an essential feature of a general appeasement"—and that in turn depended on a settlement being reached in Spain. Accordingly, the agreement itself, together with the recognition of the Italian conquest, were made contingent on such a settlement. In the months that followed, Chamberlain insisted on this link. It was not until November that the agreement was brought into force. By that time we were the only great power apart from Russia that had not yet accorded *de jure* recognition of Italian Ethiopia. But by that time also, the Spanish Civil War was within four months of its end and Chamberlain could write, "I don't believe that Spain is a menace to European peace any longer."

It was never in any other light than as a menace to European peace that he had viewed the Civil War. With Eden's opinion that British intervention would be "bad humanity and bad politics" and Churchill's that we must at all costs keep out of "this dismal welter", Chamberlain was in full accord, as was his entire Cabinet. Both sides in Spain, nationalist and republican, were receiving foreign help; the danger was that the war would spread and become international. The policy of the Government was therefore consistently directed to confining the war to Spain—even, in the end, at the cost of seeing British ships bombarded when they unloaded in the fighting zone. "I have been through every possible form of retaliation," Chamberlain wrote to his sisters, "and it is abundantly clear that none of them can be effective unless we are prepared to go to war with Franco, which might quite possibly lead to war with Italy and Germany, and in any case would cut right across my policy of general appeasement. Of course it may come to that, if Franco were foolish enough." On this uncomfortable but practical basis his policy rested. To the British Left, however, the Spanish issue appeared in an entirely different light. No episode in the inter-war period so excited the passion of the Labour and Liberal Parties. And so inevitably Chamberlain's unyielding and logical defence of non-intervention throughout 1937 and 1938 hardened their feelings against him, already strong, into a bitter personal animosity. His friends warned him, and he himself recognised, "that the Socialists may succeed in creating a legend about me". With considerable heat he repudiated their attacks.

N.C. Hansard 7.3.1938.

"Because I do not share the views of the Opposition that one has to take sides with the party they favour in Spain, they charge me with having a bias towards dictators. There is no foundation for the charge. But I have to deal with a world in which dictatorships exist. I have no interest in other forms of government, except in so far as they react on other countries. I have no bias in favour of Nazism, Fascism or Bolshevism, because all of them seem to me to be inconsistent with what is all-important to me, because it is the root of my political creed, and that is individual liberty."

Chamberlain himself believed that if the Italian negotiations had taken place earlier Hitler's forcible annexation of Austria in March 1938 might have been prevented. Certainly as late as February 18th Grandi had assured Chamberlain and Eden that no prior agreement on Austria had been made between the two dictators. This was confirmed by Hitler's hysterical relief when Mussolini accepted the annexation as a *fait accompli* ("tell Mussolini I will never forget him for this . . . never, never, never, whatever happens"). All the same, by 1938 there was scarcely any prospect that Mussolini would move troops to the Brenner as he had done four years earlier.[1] If the Italians regarded negotiations with Britain as urgent in February, in view of "possible future happenings", it was not because they hoped to deter the *Anschluss*. It was because, once the *Anschluss* had taken place, a subsequent agreement to talk with the British might be interpreted "as a journey to Canossa under German pressure".[2]

Chamberlain heard the news from Austria in ironic circumstances. He was giving a luncheon party at No. 10 in honour of Ribbentrop who had just replaced Neurath as German Foreign Minister. Churchill, as he relates in his memoirs, was also present. Having spent twenty minutes after lunch talking to Ribbentrop "about a better understanding and mutual contribution to peace by Germany and ourselves", the Prime Minister went into the drawing room and was immediately handed telegrams recounting Hitler's ultimatum to the Austrian Chancellor Schuschnigg. He called Ribbentrop into his room downstairs, asked him before it was too late to get his chief to hold his hand, and stressed the deplorable effect that this development must have on the future tenor of Anglo-German relations. The Government, as he told

[1] Mussolini had told Goering as much in January 1937, though he had shown no pleasure at the prospect, *Documents on German Foreign Policy 1918–1945* (H.M.S.O., 1949) Series D, Vol. 1, pp. 384–385, 387.
[2] Ciano to Grandi, February 16th, 1938, *Ciano's Diplomatic Papers* (Odhams, 1948), pp. 161–162.

Parliament a few days later, had always recognised the close affinity between Germany and Austria, but had always made equally plain that it would "strongly disapprove of the application to the solution of these problems of violent methods". Ribbentrop, however, he wrote to his sisters, appeared totally unable to comprehend this objection: "force is the only argument Germany understands", he added. In this mood he ended his Commons statement on a grimly realistic note. "Nothing could have arrested this action by Germany unless we and others with us had been prepared to use force to prevent it." The new situation must be considered coolly but quickly, and a fresh review of our defence programmes would be instituted forthwith.

Meanwhile we must continue to eat of the bitter fruit of military weakness. "If Austria goes", Austen Chamberlain had warned in 1936, "Czechoslovakia is indefensible." Two years later this was the considered and consistent verdict of the Committee of Imperial Defence and the Chiefs of Staff, and of the Foreign Office experts to whom the question was submitted.

N.C. to Ida 20.3.1938.

"You have only to look at the map to see that nothing that France or we could do could possibly save Czechoslovakia from being overrun by the Germans if they wanted to do it. The Austrian frontier is practically open; the great Skoda munition works are within easy bombing distance of the German aerodromes, the railways all pass through German territory, Russia is 100 miles away. Therefore we could not help Czechoslovakia—she would simply be a pretext for going to war with Germany. That we could not think of unless we had a reasonable prospect of being able to beat her to her knees in a reasonable time, and of that I see no sign. I have therefore abandoned any idea of giving guarantees to Czechoslovakia, or to France in connection with her obligations to that country."

In the House of Commons on March 24th the Prime Minister outlined afresh the circumstances in which Britain would fight, other than in her own defence or that of the British Commonwealth. They were: first of all, in accordance with Locarno and our traditional foreign policy, the defence of France and Belgium against unprovoked aggression; secondly, the fulfilment of our specific treaty obligations, to Portugal, Iraq and Egypt; thirdly,

Right. Mrs. Neville Chamberlain

Below. Trout fishing with the dry fly

At Heston airport on his second flight to Germany

Signing the Munich Agreement

the assisting of a victim of aggression when in our judgement this
would be proper under the provisions of the Covenant of the
League of Nations. The last case, he pointed out, might cover
Czechoslovakia. But we could accept no automatic military obligation in any area where our vital interests were not concerned.
Neither could we give an automatic promise to assist France if she
were called upon to help Czechoslovakia under the terms of the
Franco-Czech Treaty of 1925. At the same time, he added this:
"Where peace and war are concerned, legal obligations are not
alone involved, and, if war broke out, it would be unlikely to be
confined to those who have assumed such obligations. It would be
quite impossible to say where it would end and what Governments might become involved. The inexorable pressure of facts
might well prove more powerful than formal pronouncements,
and in that event it would be well within the bounds of probability that other countries, besides those which were parties to the
original dispute, would almost immediately become involved.
This is especially true in the case of two countries like Great
Britain and France, with long associations of friendship, with interests closely interwoven, devoted to the same ideas of democratic
liberty, and determined to uphold them."

This impressive statement, which was well received in the
House and not ill-received by the Czechs, was subsequently criticised on two main grounds. In the first place, it brushed aside
altogether a proposal made by the Russian Government in the
previous week for a conference of powers inside or outside the
League of Nations. The aim, as defined by the Soviet Foreign
Minister, Litvinov, was collective action which would aim at
checking further aggression, with special reference to Czechoslovakia. Chamberlain objected to this because, as he told Parliament, its purpose appeared to be the negotiation of just such
mutual undertakings in advance as the British Government had
ruled out. More compelling still were his private and unspoken
suspicions of Soviet capacity and motive. In the months that
followed, Maisky, the Russian Ambassador in London, continued
to fish in these troubled Czech waters. It has subsequently been
argued that the cold-shouldering of Russia played a decisive
part in the ultimate tragedy. This is not very likely. Russia

had no common frontier with Czechoslovakia, and the "barrier" policy of Poland and Roumania stood in the way of any assistance she might have wished to give. What assistance Russia was in fact prepared to give was always in doubt. As late as September 23rd, our Foreign Under-Secretary, R. A. Butler, who was at Geneva, could get nothing more precise out of Litvinov than that if the French came to the assistance of the Czechs the Russians "would take action" and "might desire to raise the matter in the League".[1] Time and again, the appreciations arriving at the Foreign Office from our Embassy in Moscow warned that the great purges of 1937 had had a "disastrous effect on the morale and also on the efficiency of the Red Army" and that "it is unlikely that the Soviet Union will go to war in defence of Czechoslovakia".[2] Precisely similar appreciations were reaching Berlin from the German Ambassador, who reported that the overwhelming conviction of the diplomatic corps in Moscow was that the Soviet would do as little as possible.[3] A post-war historian of Soviet foreign policy confirms that there is very little evidence that in the summer of 1938 the Russians were preparing their own people for the possibility that they would be involved in war.[4] Chamberlain's own view was that Stalin was "stealthily and cunningly pulling all the strings behind the scenes to get us involved in war with Germany", a war in which he hoped to be the *tertius gaudens*. Soviet policy when Germany attacked Poland next year scarcely contradicted this diagnosis.

A second and more substantial criticism of Chamberlain's diplomacy was made by Daladier, the new French Prime Minister, who came to London at the end of April to urge "that war could only be avoided if Great Britain and France made their determination quite clear to maintain the peace of Europe by respecting the liberties and the rights of independent peoples".[5]

[1] *Documents on British Foreign Policy 1919–1939* (H.M.S.O., 1949), Third Series, Vol. 2, pp. 497–498.

[2] *Ibid.*, Vol. 1, April 19th, pp. 161–165, May 16th, pp. 303–307, May 22nd, p. 346, May 31st, pp. 419–424; Vol. 2, September 4th, pp. 229–230.

[3] *Documents on German Foreign Policy*, Series D, Vol. 2, May 30th, pp. 363–364, June 22nd, pp. 423–426, August 26th, pp. 629–631.

[4] Max Beloff, *The Foreign Policy of Soviet Russia* (Oxford, 1949), Vol. 2, pp. 120–166.

[5] *Documents on British Foreign Policy*, Third Series, Vol. 1, p. 217.

There were great attractions in such a declaration if it could be implemented, but whether Daladier spoke for his Cabinet, let alone for France, was more than doubtful. Strang, then head of the Central Department of the Foreign Office, recalls that "unlike the British Government, the French Government were deeply divided, with Georges Mandel and his friends all for resistance and Georges Bonnet and his like all for surrender, and with Edouard Daladier . . . torn between the two, leaning towards a robust policy but lacking the resolution to hold to it. The result was that, while the declared policy of France was to stand by her obligation, a very different impression was given by what French Ministers said behind the scenes, whether in social gatherings or to foreign representatives."[1] They were inevitably conscious of the military and moral weaknesses of the nation at their back. The brunt of the war would fall first upon the French. Yet La Chambre, who was Air Minister at the time, stated without contradiction at the Riom Trials that it was impossible for the French air forces in 1938 to carry out effectively even the very limited duties laid down by the General Staff.[2] The French had a clear treaty obligation to the Czechs; for them a point of honour, not simply a point of strategy, was involved. Yet *Gringoire*'s celebrated headline, *'Veux-tu mourir pour le Tchecoslovaquie?'* was typical of the pacifism of their press from the start. On April 8th the German Ambassador in Paris, Welczeck, reported that the declarations of the French Government found little echo in press or public opinion.[3] By the eve of the Munich Conference our own Ambassador in Paris, Sir Eric Phipps, was reporting: "All that is best in France is against war, *almost* at any price (hence the really deep and pathetic gratitude shown to our Prime Minister)." Phipps added: "To embark upon what will presumably be the biggest conflict in history with our ally, who will fight, if fight she must, without eyes (air force) and without real heart must surely give us furiously to think. It may be asked why I have not reported sooner in the above sense. The answer is that up to the

[1] *Home and Abroad* (Deutsch, 1956), pp. 134–135.
[2] Quoted by Viscount Maugham, *The Truth about the Munich Crisis* (Heinemann, 1944), pp. 26–27.
[3] *Documents on German Foreign Policy*, Series D, Vol. 2, pp. 217–223.

last hour the French had hypnotised themselves into believing that peace depended upon Great Britain, and not upon Herr Hitler. They were convinced, that is to say, that if Great Britain spoke with sufficient firmness Herr Hitler would collapse."[1] Chamberlain was never prepared to act on this assumption. Later that summer he was fortified in his attitude by reading Professor Harold Temperley's book on the foreign policy of Canning, who had laid it down repeatedly, "that you should never menace unless you are in a position to carry out your threats". This in effect was what Chamberlain had said to Daladier on April 29th.

"If he had understood M. Daladier correctly," says the official record,[2] "the latter was of the opinion that, if, at this juncture, we were to speak to the German Government with sufficient firmness, then there would be no war, for either Germany would not be able or would not care to brave the united forces of France, Great Britain and Czechoslovakia, and such assistance as might be obtainable from outside sources. He considered that this was what the Americans in their card games called bluff. It amounted to advancing a certain declaration in the hope that that declaration would prevent the events we did not wish to occur. But it was not a certainty that such action would be successful. It might be true that the chances against war were 100-1, but so long as that one chance existed we must consider carefully what our attitude must be, and how we should be prepared to act in the event of war. . . . If a war arose after such a declaration, he himself could not see any possibility of saving Czechoslovakia, of avoiding the destruction of that country, or of its being overrun by the aggressor. . . . In such a situation, were we to say to Germany that we would not tolerate her continued progress in Europe and that the moment had come to call a halt; and that, if Germany were to take certain steps, we would then declare war? We would then be casting the die and deciding that, in our view, this was, from the military point of view, the opportune moment to declare war on Germany with the object of bringing about her defeat. When listening to M. Daladier, he had himself felt corresponding

[1] *Documents on British Foreign Policy*, Third Series, Vol. 2, p. 51.
[2] *Ibid.*, Vol. 1, pp. 220–221.

emotions. It made his blood boil to see Germany getting away with it time after time and increasing her domination over free peoples.[1] But such sentimental considerations were dangerous, and he must remember, as M. Daladier would also have to remember, the forces with which we were playing. Whatever the odds might be in favour of peace or war, it was not money but men with which we were gambling, and he could not lightly enter into a conflict which might mean such frightful results for innumerable families, men, women and children, of our own race. We must therefore consider with the greatest care whether, if the attitude he had just outlined towards Germany were adopted, we—and in this connexion he was thinking of His Majesty's Government and the French Government, since we could not count on any outside support—were sufficiently powerful to make victory certain. Frankly, he did not think we were."

To this piece of rigorous reasoning he added, if only implicitly, a consideration of almost equal importance. It was true, he said to the French, that at some time we might be compelled to go to war. "Circumstances might arise in which things more precious would be at stake than wealth, or life, or property." The Czechoslovak crisis, to his mind, did not fulfil these conditions of last resort.

The problem, as Mussolini pithily put it in a speech at Treviso in September, was that Czechoslovakia was not just Czechoslovakia, but "Czecho-Germano-Polono-Magyaro-Rutheno-Roumano-Slovakia". Its boundaries had been drawn by the Treaty of Versailles in defiance of the doctrine of self-determination, and it reproduced in miniature the whole racial jigsaw of the old Habsburg Empire.[2] Lloyd George had had "serious misgivings" about this, but the persuasive Benes had won the day by promising the Peace Conference to organise the minorities on a cantonal system analogous to that of Switzerland. This promise was not fulfilled. A centralised State was established instead, and the resultant racial bitterness was exacerbated by the great economic depression

[1] Cf., his letter to Hilda Chamberlain, dated March 13th: ". . . those wretched Germans. I wished them at the bottom of the sea; instead of which they are on top of the land, drat 'em!"

[2] According to the census figures of 1930, its composition was as follows: Czechs, 7,477,000, Germans, 3,231,000, Slovaks, 2,309,000, Magyars, 691,000, Ruthenians 549,000, Poles 81,000.

which hit the German industrialised areas of the country (the Sudetenland) with particular severity.

It has been claimed, probably truly, that the minorities in Czechoslovakia were better treated than in any other succession State. But that is not saying very much. Today we are re-learning in other contexts and continents than Europe the difficulties and complexities of creating a multi-racial community from disparate and even hostile elements. It requires a genuine and fundamental spirit of partnership and an abundant measure of tolerance and tact. These qualities were not evinced by the Czechs. When Runciman studied the situation on the spot in the summer of 1938 he reported that "Czechoslovak rule in the Sudeten areas for the last twenty years, though not actively oppressive, and certainly not 'terroristic', has been marked by tactlessness, lack of understanding, petty intolerance and discrimination, to a point where the resentment of the German population was inevitably moving in the direction of revolt."[1] Poles and Magyars were scarcely less dissatisfied, but the Germans had the hardest lot. "Czech officials and Czech police, speaking little or no German, were appointed in large numbers to purely German districts; Czech agricultural colonists were encouraged to settle on land transferred under the Land Reform in the middle of German populations; for the children of these Czech invaders Czech schools were built on a large scale; there is a very general belief that Czech firms were favoured as against German firms in the allocation of State contracts and that the State provided work and relief for Czechs more readily than for Germans. I believe these complaints to be in the main justified," wrote Runciman. "Even as late as the time of my Mission, I could find no readiness on the part of the Czechoslovak Government to remedy them on anything like an adequate scale." In the elections of 1935 the Sudeten German Party had polled more votes than any other, and in 1938 it was the largest Party in the State Parliament. It could, however, always be outvoted. These grievances, large and small, were inevitably exaggerated and exploited by the Nazis. All the same, Runciman concluded that it was a natural development in the circumstances

[1] The text of Runciman's report is reprinted in *Documents on British Foreign Policy*, Third Series, Vol. 2, pp. 675–679.

for the Sudeten Germans to turn for help towards their kinsmen and eventually desire to join the Reich.

This pronouncement was perhaps the most authoritative but certainly not the first of its kind to reach the Foreign Office. To go no further back than the week of the *Anschluss*, we find Basil Newton, our Ambassador in Prague, arguing in a dispatch that the *status quo* in Czechoslovakia had already proved unacceptable and could not be perpetuated even after a victorious war.[1] "If I am right in thinking that, having regard to her geographical situation, her history and the racial divisions of her population, Czechoslovakia's present position is not permanently tenable," Newton wrote on March 15th, "it will be no kindness in the long run to try to maintain her in it. We should rather make it as easy for her as possible to adjust her position to the circumstances of post-war Europe while she can still do so in more favourable conditions than will obtain later."[2] This realistic appraisal, from one who sympathised with the Czechs and hated Hitler, contributed to Chamberlain's belief that on this issue it was sensible to think in terms of concession rather than in terms of war. Such a belief inevitably ruled out a more definite commitment to Czechoslovakia than he had given in March.

The main result of the Anglo-French conversations in April was therefore a decision to make a joint *démarche* at Prague to secure "the maximum concessions from Dr. Benes". A fortnight later there appeared in certain American and Canadian newspapers the report of an "off the record" statement made by the Prime Minister to their London correspondents at a party at Lady Astor's. This was to the effect that the Czechoslovak State could not continue to exist in its present form, but that the integrity of Czechoslovakia within adjusted boundaries should be guaranteed by a four-power pact. It seems clear that the report was broadly, if not in detail, correct. Its first proposition echoes Newton's dispatch and its second, the idea of the joint guarantee, was mentioned by Chamberlain in a letter to his sisters immediately after the *An-*

[1] Lord Strang points out how in 1945 the German minority was driven out of Czechoslovakia and herded into Germany, "a process which the Potsdam Conference was fain to recognise and into which it tried, without great success, to bring some degree of order and humanity". *Op. cit.*, p. 132.

[2] *Documents on British Foreign Policy*, Third Series, Vol. 1, pp. 55–56.

schluss. It shows the undeviating line of Chamberlain's thought from beginning to end of this crisis.

But if he was bent from first to last on a settlement by concession, he was also bent from first to last on resisting a settlement by force. It was agreed at the Anglo-French talks that the British should inform the Germans of their action at Prague and ask for German co-operation in reaching a peaceful settlement. If necessary, they would warn the German Government of the consequences of aggression against Czechoslovakia, on the lines of Chamberlain's statement in Parliament on March 24th. It did, in fact, become necessary to give such a warning during the crisis weekend of May 19th–22nd when there appeared to be evidence that the Germans intended a *coup* against Czechoslovakia.

N.C. to Ida 28.5.1938.

> "The more I hear about last weekend the more I feel what a 'd——d close-run thing' it was. . . . I cannot doubt in my own mind (1) that the German Government made all preparations for a *coup*, (2) that in the end they decided after getting our warnings that the risks were too great, (3) that the general view that this was just what had happened made them conscious that they had lost prestige, and (4) that they are venting their spite on us because they feel that we have got the credit for having given them a check. . . . But the incident shows how utterly untrustworthy and dishonest the German Government is and it illuminates the difficulties in the way of the peacemaker."

The Germans denied any intention of a *putsch* that weekend. However, before the end of the month Hitler was giving secret orders that the Sudeten German question must be settled by October 1st even if this involved a European war. At the same time, in order to insure himself against possible attack on the French front, he ordered an accelerated expansion of the fortifications of the West Wall or Siegfried Line.

Whilst thus preparing for war, the Germans spoke smooth words to the British. Captain Wiedemann, a confidant of Hitler, arrived in London in July to explore the possibility of a visit from Goering. He gave "the most binding assurance—in fact he was authorised to do so—that in present circumstances the German Government were planning no kind of forcible action", though he could not answer for the consequences if incidents occurred in which "a number of the Sudeten Deutsch were massacred". The British were not reassured by this. On the same day as he saw Wiedemann, the Foreign Secretary gave instructions that the question of the Runciman Mission should be broached with the Czechs, and later that week the Prime Minister informed Dirksen, the German Ambassador, that incidents such as Wiedemann had mentioned, however provocative, would not be accepted by us as a pretext for force.

Dirksen, indeed, was impressed by the mood of Chamberlain's Cabinet. He reported home that, whilst it was ready to make sacrifices to satisfy Germany's legitimate demands, nevertheless, "If Germany should resort to military means to reach these objectives, then England would without any doubt resort to war at the side of France."[1] He added: "Preparations in both the military and the economic fields have advanced far enough for this"—a piece of intelligence that was far from accurate, since Arthur Robinson of the Supply Board told Chamberlain in this same July that it would be a year before we were ready.

As the summer wore on and Runciman went about his thankless task in Prague, reports reached this country of military preparations in Germany on an extensive scale. The Chamberlain Government sought by repeated warnings, each time a little stiffer, to restrain Hitler, whilst at the same time they endeavoured to persuade the Czechs to offer terms which would satisfy reasonable demands from the Sudeten Germans. These efforts were all in vain. By September 13th the Sudeten leaders, Henlein and Frank, had flung Benes's concessions back in his face and Hitler's speech to his assembled legions at Nuremberg had provoked hand-to-hand fighting in the Sudetenland.

"In these circumstances", Chamberlain later reported to Parliament, "I decided that the time had come to put into operation a plan which I had had in my mind for a considerable period as a last resort. One of the principal difficulties in dealing with totalitarian Governments is the lack of any means of establishing contact with the personalities in whose hands lie the final decisions for the country. So I resolved to go to Germany myself to interview

[1] *Documents on German Foreign Policy*, Series D, Vol. 1, p. 1159.

Herr Hitler and find out in personal conversation whether there was yet any hope of saving the peace."

To-day, in an era of personal diplomacy and "summitry", exchanges of visits between democratic and totalitarian leaders are taken almost as a matter of course. But what Chamberlain proposed to do in September 1938, was then a startling and audacious innovation. When Halifax first heard of it, "it rather took his breath away." Hitler, if gleeful, was also amazed: *"Ich bin vom Himmel gefallen."* Not a few objected that Chamberlain was detracting from the dignity of a British Prime Minister. But for the great mass of public opinion Chamberlain's gesture appealed to larger and deeper instincts. There was admiration for "the courage of a man of nearly seventy setting out on his first flight to beard the dragon in his den".[1] There was a sportsmanlike enthusiasm for qualities of verve and dash that most people did not realise he had in him—though the knowing ones with long memories said, "It's Joe over again—it's what Joe would have done." Above all, there was hope.

> *As Priam to Achilles for his son,*
> *So you, into the night, divinely led,*
> *To ask that young men's bodies, not yet dead,*
> *Be given from the battle not begun.*

So wrote the Laureate in *The Times*; and even the spokesman of his severest critics, the *Daily Herald*, admitted, "It is an effort to stave off war which has seemed to be growing dreadfully near, and, as such, it must win the sympathy of opinion everywhere, irrespective of Party."

Irrespective of country too, one may add, if one recalls not only the millions who acclaimed him as he left home, but the messages from abroad that sped him on his way, and, not least, the humble German crowds who waited in the rain to "heil" him in the streets of Munich and at the crossings, the stations, and the windows of the houses, all the way to Berchtesgaden.

N.C. to Ida 19.9.1938.

"We drove to the Brown House a good deal higher up the mountain. The entrance of the house is on one side opening on to a sort

[1] J. W. Wheeler-Bennett, *Munich: Prologue to Tragedy* (Macmillan, 1948), pp. 106–107.

of terrace from which a flight of steps descends to the road. Half way down these steps stood the Führer bareheaded and dressed in a khaki-coloured coat of broadcloth with a red armlet and a swastika on it and the military cross on his breast. He wore black trousers such as we wear in the evening and black patent-leather lace-up shoes. His hair is brown, not black, his eyes blue, his expression rather disagreeable, especially in repose, and altogether he looks entirely undistinguished. You would never notice him in a crowd and would take him for the house painter he once was. After saying some words of welcome he took me up the steps and introduced me to a number of people among whom I only distinguished General Keitel, a youngish pleasant-faced smart-looking soldier. We then entered the house and passed along a very bare passage through a small room to the celebrated chamber or rather hall, one end of which is entirely occupied by a vast window. The view, towards Salzburg, must be magnificent but this day there were only the valley and the bottoms of the mountains to be seen.

"At the opposite end was a raised dais on which a large round table was laid for tea, while near the window was a second table for the inferior officials. On the walls were a number of pictures by old German and Italian masters. Just behind me was a huge Italian nude!

"We sat down, I next to Hitler with the interpreter [Dr. Paul Schmidt] on his other side. H. seemed very shy and his features did not relax while I endeavoured to find small talk.

"I. I have often heard of this room but it is much larger than I expected.

"H. It is you who have the big rooms in England.

"I. You must come and see them some time.

"H. I should be received with demonstrations of disapproval.

"I. Well perhaps it would be wise to choose the moment.

"At this H. permitted himself the shadow of a smile.

"After we had finished tea H. asked abruptly what procedure I proposed. Would I like to have two or three present at our talk. I replied that if convenient to him I would prefer a *tête-à-tête*.

"Thereupon he rose and he and I and the interpreter left the party and walked upstairs and through a long room with more pictures (and more nudes) till we arrived at his own room. This was completely bare of ornament. There wasn't even a clock, only a stove, small table with 2 bottles of mineral water (which he didn't offer me), 3 chairs and a sofa. Here we sat and talked for 3 hours."

The Prime Minister began the conversation[1] by expressing his anxiety for an improvement in Anglo-German relations. Many people in England, he said, completely distrusted Hitler's intentions. He therefore suggested that they should first have a frank talk of a general character, so that each might know exactly where the other stood, leaving the problem of Czechoslovakia till the next day. Hitler demurred to this procedure, emphasising that the Czech question was urgent and must be dealt with at once. "All right," said Chamberlain, "go ahead"; whereupon, to his surprise, the Führer launched into a long historical retrospect of his pacific attitude towards Germany's various neighbours. To this harangue Chamberlain listened patiently until there was mention of the Anglo-German Naval Treaty, which limited the German Fleet to a third of the British. Then he interrupted, drawing from Hitler a clear statement that "unless there was an understanding on both sides that in no circumstances would we go to war with one another, in his opinion it would be impossible that the Treaty should stand". At the time Chamberlain did no more than point out that Hitler might have real cause for complaint "if I allowed him to think that in no circumstances would we go to war, when in fact there might well be conditions when we might have to come in". But this exchange stuck in his mind, and a fortnight later at Munich he personally wrote into Strang's draft declaration on the future of Anglo-German relations this central sentence: "We regard the agreement signed last night and the Anglo-German Naval Agreement as symbolic of the desire of our two peoples never to go to war with one another again." This was one of many occasions during the September negotiations when Chamberlain insisted on getting things on the record.

The next matter to be discussed was Czechoslovakia itself. The Führer now developed at length, and with growing animation, his views on racial unity, his lifelong ideal of bringing all Ger-

[1] The sources are Chamberlain's Minute, *Documents on British Foreign Policy*, Third Series, Vol. 2, pp. 338–341, his account at the Anglo-French talks, *ibid.*, pp. 374–378, his private letter to Ida Chamberlain, dated September 19th, and his statement in the House of Commons on September 28th; and also Schmidt's notes, *Documents on British Foreign Policy*, Third Series, Vol. 2, pp. 342–351, *Documents on German Foreign Policy*, Series D, Vol. 2, pp. 786–798 and his memoirs, *Hitler's Interpreter* (Heinemann, 1951) pp. 90–95.

mans back into the Reich, his realisation that this was possible only where they were living in territories adjacent to Germany, his success in incorporating the seven million Germans of Austria, his overwhelming preoccupation now with the three million in the Sudetenland. "Hold on a minute," Chamberlain exclaimed breaking in upon this excited monologue, "there is one point on which I want to be clear and I will explain why: you say that the three million Sudeten Germans must be included in the Reich; would you be satisfied with that and is there nothing more that you want? I ask because there are many people who think that is not all; that you wish to dismember Czechoslovakia." This plain speaking was apparently not resented. Hitler replied that he certainly did not want a lot of Czechs; on the other hand, he would not feel safe so long as the military treaty betwen Czechoslovakia and Russia remained. However, if the Sudeten Germans came into the Reich, other minorities would secede, and "what was left would be so small that he would not bother his head about it". The Prime Minister was so anxious that this point should be clearly on the record that he restated it and Hitler confirmed it. It appears both in Chamberlain's own Minute of the conversation and in the account he later gave to Daladier and the French. However, a few days after the Berchtesgaden meeting, Ribbentrop offensively refused to allow the British Government to have a copy of Schmidt's record of the conversation. A strong protest was made and, after much equivocation, a record was prepared for the Prime Minister which, wrote Ribbentrop, "naturally cannot be binding on either side".[1] It was not received at the Foreign Office until Chamberlain was back in Germany at the Godesberg meeting. Schmidt's version said, not that the secession of minorities would leave Czechoslovakia so small that Hitler would not bother his head about it, but that it would mean that "Czechoslovakia would, in any case, cease to exist after a time".[2] This episode, too, had its sequel at Munich where, in an Annex to the main Agreement drafted by Sir William Malkin, Germany bound herself to

[1] *Documents on British Foreign Policy*, Third Series, Vol. 2, pp. 400–401, 428, 430–431.
[2] The corresponding document in the German archives contains neither phrase; the relevant sentence is not included.

give a guarantee to Czechoslovakia when the question of the Polish and Hungarian minorities had been settled.

Finally, in this first meeting at Berchtesgaden, the Prime Minister raised the considerable practical difficulties he foresaw in any secession of the Sudeten Germans. Would it not involve transfers of population as well as changes of boundary? With petulant anger Hitler brushed such questions aside as "academic": "I want to get down to realities. Three hundred Sudetens have been killed and things of that kind cannot go on; the thing has got to be settled at once: I am determined to settle it: I do not care whether there is a world war or not: I am determined to settle it and to settle it soon and I am prepared to risk a world war rather than allow this to drag on." At this outburst Chamberlain became extremely indignant, enquiring with asperity why the Führer had allowed him to come all the way to Berchtesgaden if in fact he were determined to reach a settlement by force. If Hitler was not prepared to discuss matters, the Prime Minister might as well leave at once. If, on the other hand, his objection was that conversations were impossible while "incidents" were taking place, he would propose a joint appeal, signed by the two of them, asking both sides to refrain from such incidents. Hitler replied emphatically that he could not be expected to address reprimands to what he called "the victims of Czechoslovak persecution". In that case, observed Chamberlain, unless the Führer had something further to suggest, there seemed nothing else to be done. There was a moment's hesitation, and then Hitler's whole manner changed.

N.C. to Ida 19.9.1938 (continued).

"He quietened down then, said if I could assure him that the British Government accepted the principle of self-determination (which he had not invented) he was prepared to discuss ways and means. I said I could give no such assurance without consultation [with the Cabinet, the French and Runciman]. My personal opinion was that on principle I didn't care two hoots whether the Sudetens were in the Reich or out of it according to their own wishes, but I saw immense practical difficulties in a plebiscite. I could, however, break off our talk now, go back and hold my consultations and meet him again. That is a possible procedure, he said, but I am very sorry that you should have to make two journeys. However, next time I shall

238

come to meet you somewhere near Cologne. Then I asked him how the situation was to be held in the meantime and he promised not to give the order to march unless some outrageous incident forced his hand."

Chamberlain told this to the French Ministers on September 18th adding, with regard to Hitler's promise, that he had derived the impression that "he would be better rather than worse than his word, and that he could be relied upon unless something quite unexpected occurred". To his sisters the next day he wrote: "I got the impression that here was a man who could be relied upon when he had given his word." The similarity in expression, as well as the context, make it clear that neither of these remarks were general comments on Hitler's character, but that both were assessments of his likely conduct in the next few days pending the reopening of negotiations. They were shrewd assessments, since we know now that Hitler's deadline for invasion was not until October 1st.

On his Cabinet and on the French, as later on the House, Chamberlain impressed his conviction that "with the German troops in the positions they then occupied there was nothing that anybody could do that would prevent that invasion unless the right of self-determination were granted to the Sudeten Germans, and that quickly". That was the sole hope, he declared, of a peaceful solution. Henderson's dispatches from Berlin confirmed the Prime Minister's view, and it was further fortified by Runciman's report. This advised that the frontier districts where the Sudeten population was an important majority should be given full right of self-determination at once. The six hours of Anglo-French talks on the 18th ended after midnight with agreement to accept such self-determination. Areas with over 50 per cent of German inhabitants would be ceded, frontier adjustments and population transfers would be arranged through an international body including a Czech representative, and the existing Czech military alliances with France and Russia would be replaced by an international guarantee in which Britain would join. The Czechs first decided to refuse these proposals, were then told to think again or accept the consequences of isolation and finally, "forced by circumstances and by excessively urgent pressure", gave in on the 21st.

The documents we have accumulated since the war make plain the unwavering persistence with which Chamberlain pushed through this policy. His mind, once made up, was always extremely hard to alter, and on this issue it was made up early. Either there had to be concessions, or else we had to go to war. But how *could* we go to war, when we ourselves were unready, when the French were blowing hot and cold, when the Russians could not be relied upon, and when the Dominions—South Africa, Australia and Canada—were divided? And why *need* we go to war, on account of "a quarrel in a far-away country between people of whom we know nothing", in the absence of any direct treaty obligation on our part, and in order to compel three million Germans to remain Czechoslovak subjects against their interest and will?

But, ask the critics, was the choice really as simple and clear-cut as Chamberlain thought? Was there not behind the brazen front which Germany presented to the world an element of bluff or internal stress which a firmer British policy could have exploited? Would an ultimatum over Czechoslovakia have stopped Hitler in his tracks or led to his overthrow by his own military leaders? Chamberlain certainly had an inkling of dissension in the German camp. He knew, from the Foreign Office telegrams, that General Beck had resigned after a stormy interview with Hitler, because he declined to participate in an attack on a friendly State.[1] He had also read the account of Vansittart's private conversation with a Herr von Kleist who came to England in August with, it was said, the approval of the German War Office, as "a representative of the old German Conservative Party" and "an emissary of the moderates in the General Staff". "He reminds me", wrote Chamberlain to Halifax, "of the Jacobites at the court of France in King William's time and I think we must discount a good deal of what he says."[2] Would, or should, his attitude have been different had he actually got wind of General Halder's now celebrated plot to arrest Hitler in the event of Czechoslovakia being invaded? "All conspiracies are difficult", replied Sir Lewis Namier, scarcely a friendly witness so far as Chamberlain is concerned, "and this

[1] *Documents on British Foreign Policy*, Third Series, Vol. 2, p. 242.
[2] *Ibid.*, Vol. 2, pp. 683–687.

Right. With Hitler at Godesberg, September 1938

Below. The War Cabinet, September 1939. *Back row, left to right*, Sir Kingsley Wood, Winston Churchill, Leslie Hore-Belisha, Lord Hankey.
Front row, Lord Halifax, Sir John Simon, Neville Chamberlain, Sir Samuel Hoare, Lord Chatfield

Left. H.M. King George VI
visits No. 10 Downing Street,
September 1939

Below. Presenting a farewell
gift to Earl Baldwin on his
retirement in 1937

one must be counted among the unhatched chickens. Moreover, the German generals seem to have been singularly inept at conspiracy; never before had they practised that manœuvre, and now it was too late to learn it."[1] This view is closely confirmed in Sir John Wheeler-Bennett's brilliant history of the German Army, which records the conclusion that "there is no evidence but the flimsiest assertion that, had Mr. Chamberlain never gone to Berchtesgaden or to Godesberg or to Munich, the conspirators would have been sufficiently prepared or resolute to strike.[2] As for Hitler himself, there is no ground at all for supposing that he was bluffing or, therefore, that Chamberlain could successfully have "called his bluff". "On the contrary," concludes Sir Ivone Kirkpatrick, who was then First Secretary in the Berlin Embassy, "he was not only resolved on war but was actually looking forward to it."[3] The proof of this was given at Godesberg.

[1] "Munich Survey: A Summing Up", *Listener*, December 2nd, 1948.
[2] *The Nemesis of Power* (Macmillan, 1953), p. 424.
[3] *The Inner Circle* (Macmillan, 1959), p. 132.

14

MUNICH

(September – October 1938)

AS he left for his second conference with Hitler on September 22nd, the Prime Minister made a statement to the assembled newspaper men at Heston airport. "A peaceful solution of the Czechoslovakia problem", he said, "is an essential preliminary to a better understanding between the British and German peoples; and that, in turn, is the indispensable foundation of European peace. European peace is what I am aiming at, and I hope this journey may open the way to get it." At Berchtesgaden Hitler had told him that if the principle of self-determination were accepted for the Sudeten Germans he would discuss the ways and means of carrying it out. Chamberlain had rapidly succeeded in getting, not only his colleagues, but the French Government and also the Czechoslovak Government to agree to the principle and to a procedure for implementing it. At Cologne airport he was greeted by a galaxy of dignitaries, a guard of honour was drawn up for his inspection and a band provided by the Leibstandarte Adolf Hitler played "God Save the King". The streets, decorated with swastikas and Union Jacks, were lined with cheering people, and the famous Petersberg Hotel provided luxurious accommodation and a splendid view across the Rhine to Godesberg. There at the Hotel Dreesen, where he had planned the "blood-bath" of 1934, Hitler waited.

During the afternoon, the British party—including Kirkpatrick, who was this time to be responsible for our official record[1]—were ferried across under the eyes of thousands of spectators. They found the Führer in an ugly mood. To Chamberlain's prepared statement on the Anglo-French proposals, he replied brusquely that he was sorry but all that was no longer of any use (*"Es tut mir leid, aber das geht nicht mehr"*). Czechoslovakia, he declared, was an artificial construction whose creation had done a great wrong to a number of other countries. Representatives of Poland and Hungary had recently visited him and said that they would not in any circumstances agree to their nationals remaining under Czech rule. These claims had his full sympathy, and peace could not be firmly established until they had been settled. A Cabinet crisis in Czechoslovakia itself and armed clashes on the frontier had brought the problem to a critical stage. No delay was possible: a settlement must be reached within a few days.

This peremptory outburst, which constituted in effect a breach of the Berchtesgaden understanding, was a grievous surprise and disappointment to the Prime Minister. He described himself as "profoundly shocked"; Schmidt's memoirs described him as flushing with anger. He had succeeded in getting agreement to exactly what the Führer had said he wanted, and without, as he put it, "the expenditure of a drop of German blood". Now the Führer said he wanted something different. Of course, there were Hungarian and Polish claims; but on Hitler's own showing they had not the same urgency as the Sudeten question. Of course, there were incidents and faults on both sides; but the whole point of his own efforts was "to show the world that the orderly operation of treaty revision could be achieved by peaceful means". What proposals had the Führer to make to this end?

Hitler now declared that there was only one possibility: the Czechs must withdraw their army, police and all State organs from German-speaking areas forthwith; the ceded territory would at once be occupied by German troops; the frontier line could subsequently be modified by plebiscite. He rejected the Czech right to indemnification for State property, and he refused to

[1] *Documents on British Foreign Policy 1919–1939* (H.M.S.O., 1949), Third Series, Vol. 2, pp. 463–473, 499–508. The other primary source is the record in *Documents on German Foreign Policy 1918–1945* (H.M.S.O., 1949), Series D, Vol. 2, pp. 870–879, 898–908. See also, Chamberlain's statement in the House of Commons on September 28th.

consider a non-aggression pact with the new Czechoslovakia so long as the Polish and Hungarian minorities remained unsatisfied. It was Chamberlain's turn to retort that these proposals, particularly those relating to immediate military occupation of the Sudetenland, were unacceptable. An acrimonious and desultory debate followed, with Hitler urging the necessity of speed, fulminating against Czech "outrages" and threatening "a military solution", and Chamberlain at a loss to understand "why, if Herr Hitler could obtain all that he wanted by peaceful means with complete certainty, he should elect to adopt a course which involved the loss of German lives and a certain element of risk". Neither was prepared to compromise, though neither seemed ready to provoke a rupture. Finally, after three hours of talk and an inspection of maps showing the language boundaries, the conference adjourned in deadlock.

Early next morning the Prime Minister despatched a letter across the river.

N.C. to Adolf Hitler 23.9.1938.

". . . The difficulty I see about the proposal you put to me yesterday afternoon arises from the suggestion that the areas should in the immediate future be occupied by German troops. . . . I do not think you have realised the impossibility of my agreeing to put forward any plan unless I have reason to suppose that it will be considered by public opinion in my country, in France and, indeed, in the world generally, as carrying out the principles already agreed upon in an orderly fashion and free from the threat of force. . . .

"Even if I felt it right to put this proposal to the Czech Government, I am convinced that they would not regard it as being in the spirit of the arrangement which we and the French Government urged them to accept and which they have accepted. In the event of German troops moving into the areas as you propose, there is no doubt that the Czech Government would have no option but to order their forces to resist. . . .

"It being agreed in principle that the Sudeten German areas are to join the Reich, the immediate question before us is how to maintain law and order pending the final settlement of the arrangements for the transfer. There must surely be alternatives to your proposal which would not be open to the objections I have pointed out. For instance, I could ask the Czech Government whether they think there could be an arrangement under which the maintenance of law and order in certain agreed Sudeten German areas would be entrusted to the Sudeten Germans themselves—by the creation of a suitable force, or by the use of forces already in existence, possibly acting under the supervision of neutral observers. . . ."

Hours passed before there was any reaction from the opposite bank. At the Petersberg, Chamberlain and Nevile Henderson, our Ambassador in Berlin, anxiously paced the balcony; at the Dreesen, Schmidt recalls "feverish discussions" between Hitler, Ribbentrop and their advisers. Well on in the afternoon came the Führer's reply, containing no modification of his previous position, giving a flat *non possumus* to Chamberlain's compromise proposal, and adding a generous measure of vulgar abuse of the Czechs. Kirkpatrick says that in discussing the next move a rupture was considered. Eventually, however, "Mr. Chamberlain decided to send Sir Horace Wilson and Henderson to give Ribbentrop a written request that the full German proposals should be set forth in a document. Apart from keeping the door open the Prime Minister was rightly anxious to have in the event of a breakdown an official statement of the German demands, which hitherto had been made verbally and could consequently have been modified or misrepresented later."[1]

It was arranged that there should be a final meeting to discuss the German document. This began at 10.30 p.m. and went on into the small hours. The Führer's manner was friendlier than on the previous day, but the so-called "memorandum" was, if anything, worse than expected. It demanded that the occupation of the Sudetenland by German troops should begin on September 26th and be completed by September 29th, and that the evacuated territory should be handed over in its existing condition without so much as the removal of a peasant's cow. It added that the German Government "agreed to permit" a plebiscite before November 25th to settle the definitive frontier. This, said Hitler, represented his last word. In that case, Chamberlain replied, there was no purpose in negotiating any further. He would go home "with a heavy heart, since he saw the final wreck of all his hopes for the peace of Europe". But his conscience was clear; he had

[1] *The Inner Circle* (Macmillan, 1959), p. 119.

done everything possible for peace; unfortunately he had found no echo in the Führer, whom he bitterly reproached for his failure to respond. The proposals he had been handed he declared to be nothing less than an ultimatum, a *diktat*. At this, Kirkpatrick recalls, Hitler looked pained. "Mr. Chamberlain, you are grievously mistaken; this is not a *diktat*," he said. "If you will look at the document again, you will see that it is headed by the word 'Memorandum.' "[1] The Prime Minister acidly retorted that he was more impressed by the contents than by the title. The way in which the proposals were put would inevitably make people say that Hitler was behaving like a conqueror. No time was given for the slightest discussion nor even for the practical execution of the necessary measures. They were ostensibly negotiating a peaceful settlement, yet the whole tone of the document was imperious and aggressive.

These objections were not without some effect. Hitler agreed, first to tone down the asperity of the document by a number of minor alterations which he pencilled into his copy, and secondly, to extend the time limit for German occupation of the Sudetenland to (what had always been his ultimate deadline) October 1st. "You are the only man to whom I have ever made a concession," he said grumpily. Chamberlain acknowledged these improvements in the form of the document, but pointed out that they in no way affected its substance. He added that it was not for him to accept or reject the German proposals, but as an intermediary he would see that they were submitted to the Czechoslovak Government.

The Prime Minister flew back to London later on the 24th and the Cabinet met that night. According to the memoirs of Duff Cooper (who was on the eve of resignation) and of Leo Amery, Chamberlain was prepared to recommend to the Czechs that they should accept the Godesberg terms.[2] This story is flatly contradicted by Hoare, who was much closer to the events and who says that an immediate meeting of the "Big Four"—Chamberlain, Halifax, Simon and himself—decided that Hitler's demands

[1] *Op. cit.*, p. 121.
[2] *Old Men Forget* (Rupert Hart-Davis, 1953), p. 234; *My Political Life* (Hutchinson, 1955), Vol. III, p. 268.

were unacceptable, and that this view was subsequently confirmed by the Cabinet.[1] Chamberlain's own papers are silent on the point, since he was not keeping a diary and the pressure of events had forced a fortnight's gap in his correspondence. However, it is not difficult to sense in his public words and actions the tug of two conflicting sets of arguments. On the one hand there was no denying that public opinion had at this time hardened against further appeasement. Halifax had advised Chamberlain of this by telegram on the night of the 23rd, and mass-observation surveys show that his estimate was sound.[2] The British Press came out in full cry against the Godesberg memorandum. On the 25th, the Czech Government rejected it as "absolutely and unconditionally unacceptable". This, after all, was in line with the Prime Minister's own reaction when first faced with the proposals. Emergency measures now began to operate. During the week-end the air-raid precautions system was put on a war footing, and later in the week the Fleet was mobilised, on Chamberlain's own initiative,[3] and the Auxiliary Air Force called up. War looked unavoidable.

On the other hand, none of the practical arguments for avoiding war had been weakened. The pitiful little slit trenches being dug in the parks and the single anti-aircraft guns mounted on Horse Guards Parade and Westminster Bridge testified to our own unreadiness. Discouraging telegrams were arriving from Australia and South Africa. On the night of the 25th, Daladier, writhing under an inquisition from the "Big Four", was eloquent about the moral obligations of France but unconvincing on how she would fulfil them. Next day, General Gamelin told his British colleagues that, if the Germans invaded, Czechoslovakia's resistance was likely to be of "extremely brief duration". From Geneva,

[1] *Nine Troubled Years* (Collins, 1954), p. 312.

[2] C. Madge and T. Harrison, *Britain by Mass-Observation* (Penguin, 1939), pp. 65, 74–75, 101. This indicates, in brief, that anti-Chamberlain sentiments were expressed by 10 per cent at the time of the Berchtesgaden meeting and immediately after Munich, but by 40 per cent on September 21st–22nd.

[3] Hoare says that Chamberlain gave the order to the First Sea Lord at the end of one of the meetings of the "Big Four" and that Duff Cooper was subsequently informed (*Nine Troubled Years*, p. 317). Duff Cooper's memoirs do not claim that his own role extended beyond ensuring announcement of the news forthwith, which was expected to have a deterrent effect on Hitler (*Old Men Forget*, p. 240).

R. A. Butler had already reported the imprecision of Russian intentions. Thus the Foreign Office statement on the night of the 26th that if Czechoslovakia were attacked France would be bound to come to her assistance, "and Great Britain and Russia will certainly stand by France" was, if not the "clever lie" which the *Matin* called it, at any rate little more than a brave bluff. Moreover, the case for going to war in defence of the territorial *status quo* in Czechoslovakia had been rejected from the first, and the principle of self-determination and the ceding of territory had already been accepted at Berchtesgaden. It therefore seemed quite unreasonable to Chamberlain, as he said in a broadcast message to the nation and the Empire on the night of the 27th, that "a quarrel which has already been settled in principle should be the subject of war". He could well understand, he added, the Czech rejection of the German memorandum; yet he believed that if only time were allowed, "it ought to be possible for the arrangements for transferring the territory that the Czech Government has agreed to give to Germany to be settled by agreement, under conditions which would assure fair treatment to the population concerned". He would not abandon his efforts for peace as long as any chance remained, and "I would not hesitate to pay even a third visit to Germany if I thought it would do any good".

Chamberlain saw clearly enough that the issue might go far deeper than the future of the Sudetenland. "If I were convinced" he said in this same broadcast, "that any nation had made up its mind to dominate the world by fear of its force, I should feel that it must be resisted. Under such a domination life for people who believe in liberty would not be worth living."

On the 26th and 27th Horace Wilson was in Berlin as Chamberlain's personal emissary to make a fresh appeal to Hitler. At first the Führer was unmoved, except to anger, but on the night of the 27th a personal letter was received from him which opened a new chink of hope. In this letter Hitler gave certain assurances about the German military occupation of the Sudetenland and the subsequent plebiscite, and offered to join in a guarantee of the frontiers of the new Czechoslovakia. The Prime Minister, making what he later described to his sisters as "the last desperate

248

snatch at the last tuft of grass on the very edge of the precipice",
thereupon drafted a reply proposing "to come to Berlin myself
at once to discuss arrangements for transfer with you and representatives of the Czech Government, together with representatives of France and Italy if you desire". At the same time, with a
very sure touch, he wrote a personal message to Mussolini: "I trust
your Excellency will inform German Chancellor that you are
willing to be represented and urge him to agree to my proposal
which will keep all our peoples out of war."

Now from the Anglo-Italian Agreement of April some reward
was reaped. The Duce next morning, September 28th, ordered
Attolico, his Ambassador in Berlin, to advise Hitler to postpone
mobilisation for twenty-four hours and to accept Chamberlain's
scheme for a conference. At a quarter past four that afternoon,
the Prime Minister was coming to the end of an eighty-minute
speech in the House of Commons on the Czechoslovak crisis and
his own efforts for peace, when an urgent message arrived for
Lord Halifax who was sitting in the peers' gallery. A few moments
later, Chamberlain's Parliamentary Private Secretary (Lord Dun-
glass, now Lord Home) passed a note along the Treasury Bench to
Sir John Simon. It was handed to the Prime Minister just at the
point in his account where he was welcoming Mussolini's re-
straining action. He paused to read the message, and when he
faced the House again he was smiling.

N.C. Hansard 28.9.1938

"That is not all. I have something further to say to the House yet.
I have now been informed by Herr Hitler that he invites me to meet
him at Munich tomorrow morning. He has also invited Signor
Mussolini and M. Daladier. Signor Mussolini has accepted and I
have no doubt M. Daladier will also accept. I need not say what my
answer will be."

"Thank God for the Prime Minister," cried one unidentified
member, who thereby touched off a demonstration of hysterical
relief rarely, if ever, paralleled in Parliamentary history. "From
all sides," recalled Simon in his memoirs, "there was impetuous
cheering, in which few failed to join, and we adjourned almost at
once by general consent. I saw men, some of whom have since

spoken slightingly of what Chamberlain was trying to do, cross the floor in tears and with unrestrained emotion grasp him by the hand."[1] Early next morning he was at Heston again, quoting the childhood rhyme, "If at first you don't succeed, try, try, try again", and hoping that on his return he might be able to say with Hotspur, "Out of this nettle, danger, we pluck this flower, safety."

The Munich conference assembled at the Führerbau at 12.30 on September 29th and went on, with lunch and dinner breaks, for some fourteen hours.[2] Chamberlain was accompanied by Sir Horace Wilson, and they were later joined by Nevile Henderson and by the legal adviser of the Foreign Office, Sir William Malkin. France was represented by Daladier and Léger, Italy by Mussolini and Ciano, Germany by Hitler, Ribbentrop and Weizsacker. Of course, Chamberlain's original proposal had been for a conference of the four powers *plus* Czechoslovakia, and the opening session at Munich which lasted until three o'clock in the afternoon was punctuated by his persistent demand for the presence of a Czech representative—a demand which was first backed but later abandoned by Daladier.

Early on in this session, Mussolini tabled what he described as a "practical solution" to the Sudeten problem. Italian archives and German memoirs have now revealed that the Duce's proposals had actually been drafted by Goering, Neurath and Weizsäcker, and then given to Attolico for transmission to Rome.[3] They consisted of five Clauses. The first stated that evacuation of the Sudetenland was to begin on October 1st, and the fifth that occupation by stages of the predominantly German territory by German troops would begin on the same date. Clause 2 read as follows: "The Guarantor Powers, England, France and Italy, will

[1] *Retrospect: The Memoirs of the Rt. Hon. Viscount Simon* (Hutchinson, 1952), p. 247.

[2] The two principal sources, which do not always tally owing to the confusion at the conference, are Sir Horace Wilson's brief account written from memory, *Documents on British Foreign Policy*, Third Series, Vol. 2, pp. 630–635, and the German diplomatic records, *Documents on German Foreign Policy*, Series D, Vol. 2, pp. 1003–1008, 1011, 1014.

[3] M. Toscano, *Le Origini del patto d'acciaio* (Florence, 1948); E. Kordt, *Wahn und Wirklichkeit* (Stuttgart, 1948); L. B. Namier, *Europe in Decay* (Macmillan, 1950), p. 124, 135.

guarantee to Germany that the evacuation of the territory shall be completed by the 10th October, without any existing installations having been destroyed." Clause 3 provided that the conditions governing the evacuation would be laid down in detail by an international committee on which the four powers and Czechoslovakia would be represented. Clause 4 postulated international supervision of the plebiscite and of the final determination of frontiers in "doubtful territories", and the occupation of these territories by international forces until the plebiscite was completed.

Daladier at once said that he accepted this document as a basis for discussion. Chamberlain, while also welcoming the proposals in general, seized on Clause 2 as an excuse for raising the issue of Czech representation. He did not see how Britain could be expected to undertake the guarantee referred to unless we were sure it would be honoured, and we could have no such assurance unless a representative of the Prague Government was available to give it. Hitler replied that if Czech consent had first to be sought on every detail, a solution could not be expected before a fortnight had passed, and such a delay, given the existing state of tension, would be intolerably dangerous. This was a European question, he declared, not simply a German-Czech question, and if the Prague Government was not prepared to accept a document bearing the "moral authority" of their four signatures, this would be a sign that it would accept nothing but force. Chamberlain agreed that delay was undesirable and that the dispute was indeed a European question which the great powers had both a right and a duty to settle. All the same, he insisted, they must see that they exercised their authority in a proper manner. He proposed that they should adjourn for a short time to study Mussolini's document. Meanwhile, however, Daladier, who had begun by agreeing with Chamberlain, had since said that "if the inclusion of a Prague representative would cause difficulties he was ready to forgo this".

When the conference reassembled at 4.30 p.m. it was decided to discuss the so-called Mussolini document point by point.[1]

[1] This follows the German minute. Wilson's account places the beginning of the Clause-by-Clause discussion in the first session of the conference.

Clause 1 was immediately agreed to. But on Clause 2 Chamberlain again expressed his doubts on the possibility of giving a guarantee without knowing from an official representative the attitude
of the Czech Government. Daladier dissented, saying that he did
not think Czech agreement was necessary. After much discussion
the point of substance was at last given up and the technical difficulty was got over by a revision of wording.

As the conference went on, its hurried and faulty organisation
grew apparent and its procedure became increasingly muddled
and confused. It broke up into a series of individual discussions,
particularly on the zones to be evacuated and the areas in which a
plebiscite was to be held. In the course of these exchanges, Hitler
was practically driven to distraction by Chamberlain's nagging
concern over the question of compensation for Czech property
in the Sudetenland. "Our time is too valuable to be wasted on
such trivialities," he is said to have shouted at the Prime Minister.[1]
But the Prime Minister characteristically persisted. "During dinner," recalls Wilson, "we had prepared and sent into the Drafting
Committee a short clause (no copy available) providing that
financial and currency questions arising out of the transfer of the
territory should be referred for settlement to a German–Czech
Commission with a neutral Chairman. On returning to the Fuhrer
House I learnt that this was unacceptable to the Germans (Herr
von Ribbentrop in evidence) and that all that Sir William Malkin
had been able to arrange was that the draft clause should come up
to the Conference as a separate paper. When the draft Agreement
came before the Conference this clause was absent. (On enquiry
I was told (a) that it was not agreed and (b) that the draft we had
sent in had been lost.) We took a stand on this, pointing out that
there must be a number of questions—property, currency, outstanding loans, etc.—of the kind contemplated by the draft clause.
Eventually a way out was found by a clause (the Supplementary
Declaration) providing that all questions arising out of the transfer shall be considered as coming within the terms of reference to
the International Commission."[2]

After protracted redrafting and tedious delays, amounting in

[1] P. Schmidt, *Hitler's Interpreter* (Heinemann, 1951), p. 110.
[2] *Documents on British Foreign Policy*, Third Series, Vol. 2, p. 633.

Wilson's words to five hours during which chaos ruled, the moment came for signature of the Agreement. It was then discovered that the pretentious inkpot which had been provided contained no ink.

In retrospect it might be said that the Munich agreement itself was just as empty.[1] At the time, however, even Duff Cooper, the fiercest critic of Munich, acknowledged the "great and important differences" between its terms and those demanded at Godesberg. "It is a great triumph for the Prime Minister," said Duff Cooper in his resignation speech, "that he was able to acquire them." The Godesberg memorandum had been in effect an ultimatum, the Munich Agreement reverted to the original Anglo-French plan and laid down the conditions for its application under international supervision. At Godesberg Hitler had demanded the complete evacuation of the Sudetenland in one operation which would have involved cruel hardship; the Munich decision was that it should be carried out in five clearly defined stages over a period of ten days. The line up to which German troops would enter into occupation was no longer the line laid down in the map attached to the Godesberg memorandum, but was to be fixed by an International Commission. Similarly the plebiscite areas were to defined by the International Commission, and not by Germany, and were to be provisionally occupied by an international force. The objectionable conditions in the Godesberg memorandum which would have forbidden transferred populations to take with them a stick of furniture or a bite of food were withdrawn altogether, and the detailed arrangements for evacuation were to be laid down by the International Commission. Finally, the Munich Agreement included provisions which found no place at all in the Godesberg memorandum: a right of option into or out of transferred territories, international supervision of other questions arising from the transfer of populations, and, subject to settlement of the question of the Polish and Hungarian minorities, German and Italian participation in a joint guarantee against unprovoked aggression on the new boundaries of Czechoslovakia.

There was no disposition on Chamberlain's part to underesti-

[1] The terms of the Agreement are set out in full in the Appendix.

mate the blow to Czech interests and national pride. "We must feel profound sympathy for a small and gallant nation in the hour of their national grief and loss," he told the House of Commons, and Kirkpatrick has testified that when the result of the conference was communicated to the Czech delegation Chamberlain's sympathetic and understanding bearing contrasted markedly with the peremptory and even brutal attitude of Daladier.[1] He claimed no more for this settlement than that it had substituted an orderly for a violent method of carrying out an agreed, if unpalatable, decision. In this way it had avoided war at a time when we were neither materially nor psychologically prepared for war and on an issue where our own vital interests were not felt to be directly at stake.

N.C. Hansard 3.10.1938.

"No doubt I shall have plenty of critics who will say that I am guilty of facile optimism, and that I should disbelieve every word that is uttered by rulers of other great States in Europe. I am too much of a realist to believe that we are going to achieve our paradise in a day. We have only laid the foundations of peace. The superstructure is not even begun."

Before returning to England on September 30th, he had a private talk with Hitler at the Führer's flat in Munich.[2] The conversation ranged over Spain, where Hitler denied that he had ever had any territorial ambitions but stressed the necessity to stop the Communist "infection" spreading, over South-Eastern Europe, where he defined Germany's interest, as economic and not political, and, at greatest length, over disarmament. The Prime Minister described himself as being "oppressed by the thought of the increasing burden which was being imposed upon all countries by the expenditure upon armaments, which was eating up the capital which ought to be employed on building houses, on better food and on improving the health of the people". To this Hitler replied logically but negatively, that where disarmament was concerned "if a single nation refuses to agree, all the others have to follow her

[1] *Op. cit.*, pp. 129–130.
[2] A record was written by Hitler's interpreter, Schmidt, and is printed in *Documents on British Foreign Policy*, Third Series, Vol. 2, pp. 635–640.

example"; and from this conversation, as from the Munich settlement itself, Chamberlain drew a realistic conclusion:

N.C. Hansard 3.10.1938 (continued).

"For a long period now we have been engaged in this country in a great programme of rearmament, which is daily increasing in pace and in volume. Let no-one think that because we have signed this agreement between these four Powers at Munich we can afford to relax our efforts in regard to that programme at this moment. Disarmament on the part of this country can never be unilateral again."

At the end of this conversation at Munich, the last occasion on which the two men ever met, the Prime Minister said, according to Schmidt's record, "that he thought it would be a pity if this meeting passed off with nothing more than the settlement of the Czech question, which had been agreed upon yesterday. What he had in mind was to suggest to Herr Hitler that it would be helpful to both countries and to the world in general if they could issue some statement which showed the agreement between them on the desirability of better Anglo-German relations, leading to a greater European stability. Accordingly, he had ventured to draft a short statement which he would now ask Herr Hitler to read and to consider whether he would be disposed to issue such a statement over the signatures of himself and the Prime Minister to the public. As these observations were translated to Herr Hitler he ejaculated at intervals 'Ja! Ja!' and when it was finished he said he would certainly agree to sign this document. When did the Prime Minister wish to do so? The Prime Minister: Immediately. Herr Hitler: Then let us sign. At this point, they both rose, went to a writing table and, without any further words, appended their signature to the document." It read as follows:

"We, the German Führer and Chancellor and the British Prime Minister, have had a further meeting to-day and are agreed in recognising that the question of Anglo-German relations is of the first importance for the two countries and for Europe.

"We regard the Agreement signed last night and the Anglo-German Naval Agreement as symbolic of the desire of our two peoples never to go to war with one another again.

"We are resolved that the method of consultation shall be the method adopted to deal with any other questions that may concern our two countries, and we are determined to continue our efforts to remove possible sources of difference and thus to contribute to assure the peace of Europe."

Chamberlain had a clear purpose in securing Hitler's signature to this. Lord Home recalls that at breakfast that morning Chamberlain had shown him the document and said, "If he signs it and sticks to it that will be fine, but if he breaks it that will convince the Americans of the kind of man he is"; and he had added, "I will give the maximum publicity to it when I return to London". This, then, was the scrap of paper which he flourished to the Press men on his arrival at Heston later in the day and whose terms he broadcast before leaving the airfield. That night from the window at Downing Street he allowed himself, in a mental and emotional condition close to breaking point, to use a phrase which he quickly regretted and later half retracted: "This is the second time in our history that there has come back from Germany to Downing Street peace with honour. I believe it is peace for our time." But with this must be read his more measured words to the House of Commons:

N.C. Hansard 6.10.1938.

"I hope hon. Members will not be disposed to read into words used in a moment of some emotion, after a long and exhausting day, after I had driven through miles of excited, enthusiastic, cheering people —I hope they will not read into those words more than they were intended to convey. I do indeed believe that we may yet secure peace for our time, but I never meant to suggest that we should do that by disarmament, until we can induce others to disarm too. . . . I realise that diplomacy cannot be effective unless the consciousness exists, not here alone, but elsewhere, that behind the diplomacy is the strength to give effect to it."

15

THE AFTERMATH OF MUNICH

(October 1938 – September 1939)

THE arguments about Munich will continue, but it is possible now that the archives have been opened and so many private accounts published to judge them in perspective. Few people seriously claim now that a League of Nations with more than half the great powers outside it would have or could have stopped the Second World War. No-one seriously claims who has studied their speeches, particularly in the General Election of 1935, that the Labour Party would have pushed rearmament ahead faster, or indeed anything like so fast, as Chamberlain did in 1936 and 1937. In their television appearance together in the autumn of 1959, on the occasion of Mr. Eisenhower's visit to London, both Mr. Macmillan and Mr. Eisenhower agreed that the Second World War was inevitable because Hitler was determined on it, and the evidence that this was in fact so is now overwhelming.[1] Should then Britain have fought in October 1938 rather than September 1939? Was the year's respite a gain on balance to Great Britain or the Axis Powers? And here one of the most interesting witnesses is Mr. John F. Kennedy, the President of the United States. His father was at the time the American Ambassador at the Court of St. James, and felt deep despondency in 1940 about Britain's chances of survival. His son

[1] Though accepted by every other historian of authority, this view has been challenged —unconvincingly, I think—in *The Origins of the Second World War*, by A. J. P. Taylor (Hamish Hamilton, 1961) which was published whilst this biography was in proof.

did not share this view and (aged 23) put forward his own. This is his judgement:

"[People] felt and many still do feel that Hitler in 1938 was merely bluffing . . . Many in England shared this belief even in August 1939. There, people felt Chamberlain was badly taken in, but I think a study of the position of the two countries will show that Chamberlain could not have fought even if he had wanted to. I do not claim that Munich was simply the result of British inability to fight as set forth by Baron von Neurath.[1] I believe that Chamberlain was sincere in thinking that a great step had been taken towards healing one of Europe's fever sores. I believe that English public opinion was not sufficiently aroused to back him in a war. Most people in England felt 'It's not worth a war to prevent the Sudeten Germans from going back to Germany'. They failed at that time to see the larger issue, involving the domination of Europe. But though all these factors played a part in the settlement of Munich, I feel that Munich was inevitable on the grounds of lack of armaments alone."[2]

It is not at Munich but at the locust years, 1934 and 1935, that the finger of criticism should be pointed. Too little was done, even though Chamberlain was the most valiant for rearmament in the Government—so much so that the contrast of his tough attitude with Baldwin's more pliant one brought stern condemnation from *The Economist* in October 1935:

"It is certainly a regrettable departure from British tradition that the Chancellor of the Exchequer should himself be the foremost advocate of increased expenditure on armaments. And it certainly will not help to promote national agreement on foreign policy if collective security is to be used as an excuse for unilateral rearmament by Great Britain."

It is fair to add, as Mr. Kennedy does, that *The Economist* later

---

[1] Mr. Kennedy quotes the former German Minister of Foreign Affairs to this effect: "Immediately after his return to London Mr. Chamberlain announced a huge programme of rearmament. At the same time the defects of Britain's military preparedness became plainly visible. It was then no longer possible to conceal the true reason for her 'peaceful' attitude at Munich. She had simply been unable to embark on a European war at that time."

[2] John F. Kennedy, *Why England Slept* (Hutchinson, 1940), pp.195–196.

changed its mind, but also, again following Mr. Kennedy, that rearmament policies cannot change as swiftly as editorial views.

We can now check Mr. Kennedy's assessment against the known facts and figures of military production at the time.

Eleven months separated the Munich Agreement from the outbreak of war. Diplomatically, the period falls into two equal and distinct parts, divided by the death blow which Hitler delivered to Czechoslovakia and to the policy of appeasement in March 1939. "A new epoch in the course of our foreign policy," to use Chamberlain's own description, opened after the occupation of Prague. The military turning point, however, antedated the diplomatic. "A new epoch in the history of rearmament," to quote the echoing phrase of the historian of British war production, "began in the autumn of 1938 and ended in the summer of 1940."[1] After Munich, that is to say, rearmament was "definitely geared to eventual military action", and the last strong hopes of peace were not allowed to hold back our accelerating preparations against war.

"One good thing, at any rate, has come out of this emergency through which we have passed," said Chamberlain at the end of the Munich debate in the House of Commons. "It has thrown a vivid light upon our preparations for defence, on their strength and on their weakness. I should not think we were doing our duty if we had not already ordered that a prompt and thorough inquiry should be made to cover the whole of our preparations, military and civil, in order to see, in the light of what has happened during these hectic days, what further steps may be necessary to make good our deficiencies in the shortest possible time."

The deficiency upon which public and Parliamentary attention chiefly and rightly focused was in our defence against air attack, including civil defence. The Munich crisis had found us still with barely 10 per cent. of the estimated "ideal" requirement of A.A. guns, and most of those we had were not the newer 3.7- and 4.5-inch guns but 3-inch conversions. Only 1,430 searchlights were available out of an approved programme of 4,128, only 140 barrage balloons out of 450, and, as Chamberlain told Baldwin in

[1] M. M. Postan, *British War Production* (History of the Second World War: United Kingdom Civil Series, H.M.S.O. and Longmans, 1952), p. 53.

the last weeks of his life, only 60 fire pumps in the whole of London. Expert scepticism and official parsimony had had a particularly damping effect on the progress of civilian A.R.P. What is more, Hoare wrote to Chamberlain in October, "the burden of A.R.P. is too heavy for me with all my other work". At Hoare's suggestion, therefore, John Anderson was that month appointed Lord Privy Seal and took over the administration of the Air Raid Precautions Department at the Home Office together with the co-ordination of policy on all aspects of civil defence. Estimates of expenditure on A.R.P. now shot up from £9¼ million in the current year to £42 million in the financial year 1939–40, plus another £9 million aid for emergency fire-fighting purposes. A campaign for voluntary national service (which included the Regular Forces as well as the several branches of civil defence) was launched in a broadcast by the Prime Minister in January 1939, and a handbook on the subject was distributed to every household in the land. "Anderson" shelters were constructed to protect ten million people in their own homes and gardens. Walter Elliot's plans for evacuating schoolchildren and finding emergency beds in hospitals were perfected. All this took place in the year after Munich. At the same time, the last Defence White Paper of the peace, published in February 1939, announced a substantial strengthening of our ground defences against air attack. By the time war broke out, the provision of A.A. guns had increased fourfold to 1,653, of which more than half were the larger guns, and balloon defence had been completed in London and extended outside. More important still, the chain of radar stations which during the Munich crisis had been in operation only in the Thames estuary now guarded Britain from the Orkneys to the Isle of Wight.

The year's breathing-space was also vital for the modernization and expansion of our air power. Here the Government was not so much taking fresh decisions as reaping the harvest of Swinton's brilliant tenure of the Air Ministry. This had come to an end in May 1938 for the straightforward political reason, confirmed in Chamberlain's papers, "that when a Department is under such continuous bombardment as the Air Ministry has been it is impossible to maintain its position with the head in 'another place'".

"It's a cruel job" he wrote afterwards to Hilda, "to tell one's friend that he would do well to give up . . . I said to him that he would never have a fair chance while he remained at the Ministry but the moment he left people would begin to recognise the worth of what he had done." This was certainly how it turned out. Some two weeks before Swinton's resignation the Cabinet had given authority to a new programme, known as Scheme L, which for the first time and in accordance with the Prime Minister's personal view defined Air Force expansion not in terms of finance, but simply in terms of industrial capacity. Great additions to this capacity had been sponsored by Swinton and the 12,000 modern aircraft in two years which were now contemplated would be of types he and his Ministry colleagues had ordered off the drawing-board.[1] At the time of Munich, of course, Scheme L had just got under way. In September 1938, the R.A.F. had only one operational fighter squadron equipped with Spitfires and five in process of being equipped with Hurricanes; by the summer of 1939, however, it had 26 squadrons of modern eight-gun fighters, and a year later during the Battle of Britain it was to have on average 47. The new types of bombers, particularly the "heavies", took longer to reach the squadrons, though when they came they would be decisively better than the corresponding German machines. Meanwhile the resources of the aircraft industry, with output climbing from a monthly average of 240 in 1938 to 660 in 1939, were stretched to the peace-time limit, and at the turn of the year the office of Director of Planning of War Production was set up to crystallize plans for expansion under wartime conditions.

Though the numerical increase in the total strength of the Luftwaffe during this period was at least as great as that of the R.A.F., the extent to which we caught up with the Germans in modernising the quality of our fighter force has been authoritatively described as "the most important achievement of rearma-

[1] Cf., "It would have been easy to produce large quantities of aircraft of the types then in production. Firms would have been only too happy to do so. We could have produced a fine balance sheet of numbers; and we should have lost the Battle of Britain. Few people realise (or did then) how heartbreaking are the delays in getting out a new type." Viscount Swinton, *I Remember* (Hutchinson, 1948), p. 110.

ment between Munich and the outbreak of war".[1] This great gain was freely admitted by Churchill in *The Gathering Storm*. But Churchill went on to make a powerful argument that 1938 nevertheless presented us with a more favourable military situation than 1939, since the Germans would have found it less easy then to win bases in France and the Low Countries from which to raid Britain with decisive effect.[2] I doubt, however, if he gives sufficient weight to contemporary estimates of the vulnerability of London and other nerve centres in 1938. More important, the argument rests upon assumptions of Allied, or rather French, military superiority at that date which are, to say the least, controversial. The contrary considerations are economically deployed in an entry in Hore-Belisha's diary a few days before the Munich settlement: "The P.M. yesterday spoke to us of the horrors of war, of German bombers over London and of his horror in allowing our people to suffer all the miseries of war in our present state. No-one is more conscious than I am of our present deficiencies. Chiefs of Staff view—to take offensive against Germany now would be like 'a man attacking a tiger before he has loaded his gun'."[3]

It is true, and was frankly recognised after Munich, that with every month that passed the Reichswehr would become stronger and the challenge to the French Army correspondingly greater. For this reason, a radical change was made in the policy governing the role and size of the British Army. We have seen how, in February 1937, the War Office capitulated to Chamberlain's argument that, if only on grounds of manpower shortage, this country must "renounce all idea of a Continental Army on the scale of 1914–18 and continue to concentrate resources on building up the Air Force and Navy". In the November after Munich, Anglo-French conversations took place at the Quai d'Orsay during which Daladier impressed upon Chamberlain the need for a larger British contribution to land fighting. Hore-Belisha, supported by Halifax, now weighed in with a proposal that the fundamental doctrine of the Army's "limited liability" should be drop-

---

[1] M. M. Postan, *op. cit.*, p. 108.
[2] *The Second World War* (Cassell, 1948), Vol. I, pp. 264–265.
[3] R. J. Minney, *The Private Papers of Hore-Belisha* (Collins, 1960), p. 146.

ped, and in February 1939 the Prime Minister recommended this course to the Cabinet. In March, it was agreed in staff talks with the French to raise our Army to 32 divisions, and before the end of the month Chamberlain announced in the House of Commons that the Territorial Field Force would be brought up to war establishment and then doubled.

This break with past policy inevitably, and almost at once, led to two further developments against which the Prime Minister had hitherto set his face. First, in order to convince the French that we meant business and the Territorial volunteer that he was not being asked to make sacrifices that others were allowed to shirk, a measure of compulsory military service was introduced for the first time in Britain in a period of peace. Secondly, in order to cope with the vast administrative and industrial problems caused by the sudden expansion of the Army programme, steps were taken to set up a Ministry of Supply. Both these decisions were announced by Chamberlain in April, though the Ministry of Supply did not begin work until August, on the very eve of war.

Conscription was voted against by the Opposition in Parliament. ("Looking back," wrote Attlee long after the war, "I think that our attitude was a mistake."[1]) It was also denounced by the Trade Union leaders, Citrine and Bevin, at a stormy interview in Downing Street. This reaction had been clearly foreseen by the Prime Minister. Indeed, his reluctance to antagonise those upon whom the rearmament programme so largely depended for success was particularly noted by Hore-Belisha in the course of persuading him to change his mind. A similar thought had prompted Chamberlain's steady objection to appointing a Minister of Supply. "If you are really to produce any substantial result—and even then it could not come at once—you would have to arm such a Minister with compulsory powers," was the point he had made again and again in the House. "I am not satisfied that we cannot get what we want by voluntary co-operation of employers and trade unionists. When we find that we still cannot fill our requirements, then it will be time enough to talk about a Minister of Supply." Though the Opposition did not accept his argument

---

[1] *As It Happened* (Heinemann, 1954), p. 103. "I agree with him," wrote Dalton in his memoirs, *The Fateful Years* (Frederick Muller, 1957), p. 250.

against the Ministry, they and the T.U.C. certainly concurred in ruling out compulsion. In this period, and even beyond, it was simply not "on" politically to enforce transfers of skilled labour or to increase the supply by dilution or upgrading. These were among the handicaps to full economic mobilisation that must be kept in mind when assessing the progress that was made in the output of war-stores.

Where a peace-time industry could be drawn upon without much need for expansion or adaptation, the tasks of re-equipment were achieved with remarkable despatch. Lord Woolton, for example, was appointed Adviser on Army Clothing at the end of April 1939 and by the beginning of September he was able to write to Chamberlain: "I am glad you let me help in getting the Army clothed: it is ready." Even so, he described this, twenty years after, as the most difficult and worrying job of his life.[1] How much more difficult must it have been to accelerate the pace of weapon production by industries unused to the work and requiring additional capacity, tooling up, and (above all) experienced manpower. This does not mean that the extra year after Munich was not useful in terms of current production. "If in October 1938," says the official History of British war production, "this country was not able to put into the field more than two fully-armed divisions, it disposed in September 1939 of sufficient equipment for about five divisions more or less adequately equipped."[2] The rub, however, lies in the words "more or less adequately"; for assuredly, it was less rather then more. In the early war summer of 1940, Chamberlain was to write to his sisters: "We have plenty of man-power, but it is neither trained nor equipped. We are short of many weapons of offence and defence"; and, from Gort's dispatches to Montgomery's memoirs, this has been the general judgement. What Chamberlain's critics were not satisfied to allow, and he himself did not live to see confirmed, was that "not only was an ever-growing flow of munitions finding its way into the hands of the fighting men, but the country was also acquiring the industrial capacity, organisation and experience which a year or two later was to give forth a supply of war-stores more

[1] *The Memoirs of the Rt. Hon. The Earl of Woolton* (Cassell, 1959), p. 159.
[2] M. M. Postan, *op. cit.*, p. 109.

abundant than that at any point in the First World War".[1] The
eleven months saved at Munich were eleven months in which this
industrial momentum could pick up, and they brought the Army
that much closer to the fuller flow of tanks, artillery, machine-
guns, rifles and ammunition which would reduce Hitler's superiority in the field.

So far as the Navy was concerned, there was never any question
of inferiority to the Germans. Our effective strength, a quarter of
which had been either newly built or brought up to date between
1935 and 1938, was overwhelming. "It would be unjust to the
Chamberlain Administration and their Service advisers to suggest
that the Navy had not been adequately prepared for a war with
Germany, or with Germany and Italy," wrote Churchill in
describing the situation when he took over the Admiralty in
1939. "The effective defence of Australasia and India in the face
of a simultaneous attack by Japan raised more serious difficulties,"
he added, "but in this case—which was at the moment unlikely—
such an assault might well have involved the United States. I
therefore felt, when I entered upon my duties, that I had at my
disposal what was undoubtedly the finest-tempered instrument of
naval war in the world, and I was sure that time would be granted
to make good the oversights of peace and to cope with the
equally certain unpleasant surprises of war."[2] In fact, a decision to
plan for a "two-power standard"—that is to say, the naval force
needed to protect our interests simultaneously against Japan in
the Far East and Germany in Europe—was taken before war broke
out as a result of discussions following the Munich crisis. This decision was certainly not of immediate importance; what was really
urgent after Munich was to make good the deficiency in destroyers and smaller vessels for convoy-escort and anti-submarine
duties. Accordingly, the naval building programme for 1939 included two destroyer flotillas and twenty fast escort vessels of a
new type, as well as some other smaller craft, and preparations
were completed to take up many of the largest trawlers and equip
them with Asdics.

To sum up: by September 1939, Britain was still very far from
having completed her preparations for war, but in the preceding

[1] *Ibid.*, p. 102.   [2] *The Second World War*, Vol. I, p. 322.

year these preparations had greatly increased in scale and in urgency. We had improved our absolute strength in every respect, and in air power we had improved our relative strength. The capital of the Empire and the centres of armament production had had their nakedness covered. Our civil defences had been put in order. Far more fighter squadrons had been remounted on the modern aircraft that were to win the Battle of Britain. At the Admiralty, programmes had been pressed ahead to counter the menace of the U-boat. A fundamental revision of Army policy had enabled a sizable British Expeditionary Force to be planned. Output of war-stores had risen and at quickening rates, and so had our industrial potential for war.

All these gains are matters of historical fact. On the other hand, many of the "losses" by which critics have supposed the gains to be outweighed are highly conjectural. Thus it is said that between 1938 and 1939 we "lost" France's opportunity to strike at German unpreparedness in the West, Czechoslovakia's 36 divisions and famous arsenal, and Russia's adhesion to the common cause. But to say this is to assume that, had we gone to war in 1938, the French would not have betrayed the Maginot mentality, the Czechs would not have collapsed like the Poles, the Skoda works lying close to their frontier would not have changed hands anyway, and the Russians would not have behaved as they did the following year with characteristically cynical opportunism. These assumptions crumple under analysis. The true argument to be met is Churchill's observation that munitions production on a nation-wide plan is a four years' task—"The first year yields nothing; the second very little; the third a lot, and the fourth a flood."[1] It follows that Germany, already in the third or fourth year of intense preparation, added more to her total armaments between 1938 and 1939 than we did ourselves. This is an important point, but it is by no means conclusive; for, unless Allied strength at the time of Munich was unquestionably sufficient to enable us at once to strike a fatal blow at Germany's industrial heart (and it was not), the logical conclusion of Churchill's argument cannot be that we should have fought Hitler in 1938. The logical conclusion must be, either that we should have fought him

[1] *Ibid.*, p. 263.

266

much earlier before his rearmament programme had got under way, or else that we should have avoided fighting him until much later when the full flood of our own rearmament programme had reduced the ratios of his superiority. Strategically 1938 was about two years too late and 1939 was about two years too soon.[1]

Military considerations, however, can only be part of the argument. Whatever view one may take of the military consequences of the "Munich year", of its effect on the will to fight of the country and the Empire there can be no doubt. In 1936, the year of the Rhineland crisis, when we might have stopped Hitler in his tracks, the representative British view was that the Germans were "only going into their own back garden". In 1938, a denial of self-determination to three million Germans living under alien rule was not considered either here or in the Empire to be something "that Britons should be asked to die for". In 1939, on the other hand, it had become plain beyond doubt that the ambitions of Nazism stretched far beyond the ethnic frontiers of Germany, that it had indeed "made up its mind to dominate the world by fear of its force".[2] Here, far more than in the precise stages to which German rearmament or our rearmament had advanced, we may discern what determined the date of our declaration of war. At the heart of Chamberlain's policy lay the fundamental proposition he expressed at the end of the Munich debate in a moving passage on the dread features of modern warfare. "You cannot ask people to accept a prospect of that kind, you cannot force them into a position that they have got to accept it," he declared, "unless you feel yourself, and can make them feel, that the cause for which they are going to fight is a vital cause—a cause that transcends all the human values, a cause to which you can point, if some day you win the victory, and say, 'That cause is safe'." This was certainly what the nation did feel in the autumn of 1939 and did not feel at the time of Munich. As Lord Halifax put it: " . . . when all has been said, one fact remains dominant

[1] Cf., the similar conclusion of the military historian Cyril Falls, *Listener*, November 11th, 1948.
[2] From Chamberlain's broadcast on the eve of Munich, September 27th, 1938, to which he frequently harked back. The famous phrase about the Rhineland was Lord Lothian's, that about the Sudetenland is from a letter to Chamberlain by Lord Kennet, formerly Hilton Young.

and unchallengeable. When war did come a year later it found a country and Commonwealth wholly united within itself, convinced to the foundations of soul and conscience that every conceivable effort had been made to find the way of sparing Europe the ordeal of war, and that no alternative remained. And that was the big thing that Chamberlain did."[1]

No-one can dispute that the avoidance of war in 1938 was in accord with the overwhelming sentiment of British opinion. Chamberlain returned from Germany to a hero's welcome. "Come straight to Buckingham Palace," bade the King, "so that I can express to you personally my most heartfelt congratulations on the success of your visit to Munich." All the way from Heston airport to the palace, the streets, as the Prime Minister described to his sisters, "were lined from one end to the other with people of every class, shouting themselves hoarse, leaping on the running board, banging on the windows, and thrusting their hands into the car to be shaken". A tremendous ovation awaited him when he and Mrs. Chamberlain appeared on the Palace balcony with the King and Queen, and later under his windows in Downing Street densely packed crowds sang "For he's a jolly good fellow". The week-end Press, London and provincial, dailies and Sundays, broke into a chorus of almost unanimous thankfulness.[2] "No conqueror returning from a victory on the battlefield," thundered *The Times*, "has come home adorned with nobler laurels." "The gratitude of millions of mothers, wives, sweethearts, pours out to feed a flood which will sweep Mr. Neville Chamberlain to a high pinnacle in history," forecast the *Sunday Dispatch*. From the *Birmingham Daily Gazette* came a special tribute: "Birmingham is proud that the peace of Europe, when all but lost, has been saved by a cool-brained and determined Birmingham man." Newspapers such as the *Manchester Guardian*, which stressed the high price paid for peace, nevertheless admitted that this could not be measured "against the horrors that might have extinguished not only Czechoslovakia, but the whole of Western civilization". Even the *Daily Herald* hesitated to condemn out-

[1] *Fulness of Days* (Collins 1957), p. 198.
[2] For a detailed survey, see W. W. Hadley, *Munich: Before and After* (Cassell, 1944), pp. 93–110.

right: "Summing up, we must say that this plan is open to grave criticism on a number of important points. Nevertheless Herr Hitler has had to abandon the most brutal of his Godesberg terms. For the first time he has had to realise that there are forces in the world more powerful than the absolute will of a dictator."

The British Press was certainly reflecting the mood of the nation. Argument grew hotter as time went on but it has been very properly pointed out that in the Commons debate after Munich the Opposition virtually evaded the issue of peace and war: "Just as, on September 28th, no one of them had interrupted Mr. Chamberlain's speech to protest against the acceptance of the Berchtesgaden terms, so now, with one exception—Mr. Duff Cooper—no Member of the House was sufficiently certain of himself to stand up in his place and say that the terms of the Munich Agreement should have been rejected at the price of war, because no Member of the House was sufficiently assured that the people of Britain would have endorsed such a rejection."[1] Nor would the people of the Dominions have endorsed such a rejection. "No-one who sat in this place, as I did during the autumn of '38, with almost daily visitations from eminent Canadians and Australians, could fail to realise that war with Germany at that time would have been misunderstood and resented from end to end of the Empire"—this was written by Geoffrey Dawson, editor of *The Times*, in a letter to Chamberlain which arrived the day after he died. Mackenzie King of Canada told Churchill during the war "that he very much doubted whether his country would have rallied to us at once".[2] Though the Australian Government considered that constitutionally it was not possible for Australia to be neutral in a British war, the Opposition were flatly against involvement in 1938. So far as South Africa was concerned, Hertzog and Smuts were agreed on a policy of non-belligerency.[3] The telegrams which Chamberlain received from the Dominion Prime Ministers after Munich really speak for themselves:

[1] J. W. Wheeler-Bennett, *Munich: Prologue to Tragedy* (Macmillan, 1948), p. 184.
[2] *The Memoirs of Lord Ismay* (Heinemann, 1960), p. 92.
[3] J. W. Wheeler-Bennett, *King George VI* (Macmillan, 195 409n.

"The heart of Canada is rejoicing tonight at the success which has crowned your unremitting efforts for peace. May I convey to you the warm congratulations of the Canadian people, and with them, an expression of their gratitude, which is felt from one end of the Dominion to the other. My colleagues in the Government join with me in unbounded admiration of the service you have rendered mankind."

J. A. Lyons to N. C. 30.9.1938.

"My colleagues and I desire to express our warmest congratulations at the outcome of the negotiations at Munich. Australians in common with all other peoples of the British Empire owe a deep debt of gratitude to you for your unceasing efforts to preserve peace."

General Hertzog to N. C. 30.9.1938.

"The news of the outcome of the Conference at Munich was received in the Union with immense relief. May I convey to you my most hearty congratulations on the success of your efforts and those of the other statesmen who took part in it in saving Europe from a conflagration the consequences of which one shudders to contemplate."

Not only from all over Britain and the Dominions but from all over the world the tributes poured into Downing Street. Within three weeks of Munich he had received more than 40,000 letters and his wife another 12,000 and not until after Christmas did this tide show much abatement. Accompanying the messages came flowers, and some poems, and gifts galore—with a strong emphasis, as might be expected, on fishing rods and salmon flies. Four thousand tulips arrived from Holland, cases of Alsatian wines from France, and from Greece a request for a piece of his umbrella to make a relic in an icon. King Haakon of Norway cabled his congratulations and King Leopold of the Belgians wrote in his own hand. From countless Englishmen in public life we may take two quotations. "You have done a most wonderful piece of work and done it under the guidance and providence of God," declared George Lansbury who once had led the Labour Party; and the Archbishop of Canterbury wrote: "You have been enabled to do a great thing in a great way at a time of almost unexampled crisis. I thank God for it." More impressive still were the letters from

humbler folk, from total strangers, from private soldiers of the First World War, from those who had been unemployed for years yet still managed to send him a present in gratitude. Most touching of all were the thoughts of the women with most to lose. From Hampshire: "I feel with God's help that you have given me back my boys, at one time it seemed as if we must lose all three of them"; from Northumberland: "I thank you a thousand times from the depth of my heart, the mother of five sons": from Paris: "Il n'y a pas une épouse, pas une maman de France qui, à l'heure présente, ne vous vénère et prie pour vous et ceux que vous aimez"; and from Rome: "Mister Chamberlain! God may bless your white head! I am an Italian mother who wishes express you all her devotion."

This is what that great-hearted Socialist James Maxton meant when he said during the Munich debate that the Prime Minister had done "something that the mass of the common people in the world wanted done". From his very different standpoint, Anthony Eden meant the same thing when he counted among the influences that had averted war, "that genuine desire for peace among all peoples. German and Italian, as well as French and British." Wherever Chamberlain went in the months that followed the truth of these observations was underlined. In the towns and villages of South Wales—scarcely a Conservative stronghold— "I never heard a solitary boo"; on the contrary "the streets were lined with people cheering and shouting 'Good old Neville' and 'God bless you' with the most evident sincerity and heartiness." In Paris, in November, and still more in Rome, in January, the warmth of his reception was particularly remarkable.

Eden, during the Munich debate, had acknowledged the significance of the spontaneous ovations which Chamberlain had been accorded in Germany. "It was clearly a manifestation of the deep desire of the German people for peace," he said; and added, "the fact that it has at last found expression may be a real signpost on the road to peace." This was Chamberlain's thought too; and, if he erred, it was in holding to this thought too obsessively, too obstinately, hoping against hope, even when every other signpost began to point the other way. It is not true that he trusted too much in Hitler; what he trusted in too much were the many deterrent and persuasive forces that might have been expected to hold Hitler back.

He trusted in the gathering pace of British rearmament, and in February we find him writing that Hitler had "missed the bus" at the time of Munich, since "they could not make nearly such a mess of us now as they could have done then, while we could make much more of a mess of them". He trusted in the difficulties created by economic crisis in Germany, as revealed by experienced travellers and, indeed, Nazi leaders themselves. "They might take it," he told a City luncheon party in the House of Commons, "that when the German statesmen—he would not say the German people—reflected on the possible consequences of a conflict, if it ever arose, they would think not only of our armaments but of our great financial resources which in a war of long duration, might well prove to be a deciding factor."[1] He trusted in the deterrent influence of the United States, and cordially and publicly welcomed Roosevelt's strong speeches to Congress in January and to the Board of the Pan-American Union in April. He trusted in the persuasive influence of Mussolini. By far the most important single feature of his conversations in Rome was the warning he tried to give Hitler *via* his ally that "it would be a terrible tragedy if aggressive action were taken under a misapprehension as to what lengths the democracies might be prepared to go to". The Duce, however, had his own aggressive intentions towards Albania, and, Chamberlain noted, "made no direct reply to this remark".[2]

Even when the assurances given at Munich had been thrown to the winds by Hitler, and Prague occupied, Chamberlain still refused to accept the view that war was inevitable. He trusted rather in the deterrent effect of the guarantees now made to Poland, Roumania, Greece and Turkey. He trusted, as ever, in the restraints of more moderate opinion inside Germany.

Since the Prime Minister was not thinking even at this stage in terms of an inevitable war, he was little attracted to the idea of an

[1] As reported in *The Times*, December 16th, 1938. Chamberlain believed himself to be speaking "off the record".
[2] *Documents on British Foreign Policy 1919–1939* (H.M.S.O., 1950), Third Series, Vol. 3, p. 529.

alliance with Soviet Russia. He agreed with Beck, the Polish Foreign Minister, that "such an association might lead Hitler to make an attack which otherwise he hoped it might still be possible to avoid". He also feared that it would make any subsequent negotiation or discussion with Germany and Italy difficult, if not impossible.

Of course, in a practical military context, the guarantees to the border states of Central and Eastern Europe could not have much meaning unless there was an agreement with their neighbour, Russia. But the great obstacle to such an agreement, as Churchill has pointed out, was "the terror of these same border countries of receiving Soviet help in the shape of Soviet armies marching through their territories to defend them from the Germans, and incidentally incorporating them in the Soviet-Communist system of which they were the most vehement opponents."[1] They hardly knew which to fear most—German attack or Russian rescue. Chamberlain shared this deep and justifiable emotion. He had as little taste for what he called "the Bolshies" as he had for the Nazis. He distrusted their motives "which seem to me to have little connection with our ideas of liberty and to be concerned only with getting everyone else by the ears", and he suspected that "they are chiefly concerned to see the 'capitalist' Powers tear each other to pieces whilst they stay out themselves". His political judgement made him doubt Russia's willingness to defend the common cause; less reliably, his advisers provided him with a consistently low assessment of her military capacity to do so.

For all these reasons, Chamberlain was reluctant to acquiesce in the opening of negotiations with the Soviet. He did so only under strong pressure from the French Government and from public opinion at home as reflected in the Press, in Parliament and in the anxieties of his Cabinet colleagues. He was neither elated when the negotiations seemed to be going well, nor cast down when they seemed to be going badly, nor shaken when the Communist preference for an accommodation with the Nazis became apparent.

In face of the Russo-German non-aggression pact at the end of August, the Chamberlain Cabinet stood absolutely firm to its

[1] *The Second World War*, Vol. I, p. 283.

obligations. The world was told so in an immediate communique, and Hitler himself in a personal letter from the Prime Minister.

N.C. to Adolf Hitler 22.8.1939.

"... It has been alleged that if His Majesty's Government had made their position more clear in 1914, the great catastrophe would have been avoided. Whether or not there is any force in that allegation, His Majesty's Government are resolved that on this occasion there shall be no such tragic misunderstanding. If the need should arise, they are resolved and prepared to employ without delay all the forces at their command, and it is impossible to foresee the end of hostilities once engaged. It would be a dangerous delusion to think that, if war once starts, it will come to an early end, even if a success on any one of the several fronts on which it will be engaged should have been secured ..."

Throughout these final months, indeed, he never allowed the survival of hope to cloud his expression of the national resolve. At Birmingham, two days after the annexation of Czechoslovakia, he declared: "I am convinced that after Munich the great majority of British people shared my hope, and ardently desired that that policy should be carried further. But to-day I share their disappointment, their indignation, that those hopes have been so wantonly shattered ... I do not believe there is anyone who will question my sincerity when I say there is hardly anything I would not sacrifice for peace. But there is one thing I must except, and that is the liberty that we have enjoyed for hundreds of years, and which we will never surrender ... no greater mistake could be made than to suppose that, because it believes war to be a senseless and cruel thing, this nation has so lost its fibre that it will not take part to the utmost of its power, resisting such a challenge if it ever were made. For that declaration I am convinced that I have not merely the support, the sympathy, the confidence of my fellow countrymen and countrywomen, but I shall have also the approval of the whole British Empire and of all other nations who value peace indeed, but who value freedom even more." To the House, following on the pledge to Poland, and later to the Women's Conference of the National Union, he spoke in equally forthright terms—"I trust that our action, begun but not concluded, will prove to be the turning point not towards war, which wins nothing, cures nothing, ends nothing, but towards a more wholesome era when reason will take the place of force"; "I want to make it equally plain that we are not prepared to see the independence of one country after another successively destroyed."

It was, however, at Cardiff in June, during his happy tour of South Wales, that he spoke in his most characteristic mood. Again, of course, there was the firm reference to "protecting the independence of the small States whose faith in their own security has been shaken by watching the fate of others". But the greater part of the speech harked back, for the last time in public, to the themes which were closest to his heart. First this, from Joe Chamberlain's son: "We act as trustee for those countries which we administer with the intention of helping the more backward races gradually to improve their own conditions, and to take an increasing part in the work of government until some day they may be able to stand alone and govern themselves with no help from outside". And then this, from the ex-Chancellor: "It has been my privilege to see for myself some of the work which has been done out of this [Special Areas] expenditure in the way of industrial development and land settlement. I have visited the Treforest Trading Estate and the Boverton Co-operative Farm, and I came away greatly heartened and encouraged by what I saw. I am convinced that in these two experiments we have made a real advance in the direction that we wanted to go, and that they will prove to be only the beginning of further work in the same direction." Finally this, a decade after leaving the Ministry of Health: "Quite recently, in the medical examination of the militiamen, we have at last got some figures upon which we can rely . . . Only 2·7 per cent have been definitely rejected as unfit. It would appear from that that, instead of being a C3 nation, as we have been told, the younger generation at any rate (I am not talking about the old ones!) are becoming an A1 nation . . . That is good and welcome news for all those who care about the welfare of the country, and those who have devoted many years to the improvement of our health services must, I think, feel to-day that their work has been justified." Liberal imperialism, full employment and social reform—the philosophy of a man trained and capable of being a notable

Prime Minister in peace and fated instead to lead only in the shadows or twilight of war.

Hitler's armies drove into Poland at dawn on September 1st; the British ultimatum, which was delayed principally because it had been hoped to synchronise it with the French, expired at eleven o'clock on the 3rd; and later that morning the Prime Minister spoke to the House of Commons in the accents of personal tragedy. "Everything that I have worked for, everything that I have hoped for, everything that I have believed in during my public life, has crashed in ruins "

16

THE LAST YEAR

(September 1939 – November 1940)

THOUGH so much had crashed in ruins, yet hope remained. "I trust," he told the House of Commons, "I may
live to see the day when Hitlerism has been destroyed and a
liberated Europe has been re-established." In fact he lived only to
see Hitlerism triumphant and the greater part of Europe held in
thrall. In September, Poland succumbed to Germany's *blitzkrieg*
and Russia's treachery, and was partitioned between the two.
Inspired by this success and by fear of subsequent German pene-
tration, Russia now compelled the Baltic republics to admit her
garrisons and during the winter wore down the stout resistance
of the Finns by massive force. Our help to Finland was tragi-
cally limited by repeated refusals from Norway and Sweden to
permit the passage of troops through their countries. Then in
April it was Scandinavia's turn to be attacked by the Germans.
Denmark was occupied almost without opposition and forces
were landed by sea and air at several points in Norway. Our own
expeditionary counter-strokes failed or were abandoned largely
owing to lack of air cover, and on May 4th the Norwegian army
surrendered. The following week, the *Wehrmacht* struck lightning blows at Holland and Belgium and swept skilfully and ruth-
lessly into France. At home, the Government fell; and it was as a
member of Churchill's National administration that Chamberlain in the last months of his life saw the epic evacuation of the
B.E.F. from Dunkirk, the separate French armistice, and the

German air offensive on Britain launched as the preliminary to an intended invasion.

This catalogue of catastrophe was punctuated by insidious suggestions that we should sue for a negotiated peace. Such suggestions came from the Germans, from the neutrals, and from the defeatists at home. To all these siren voices Chamberlain turned an obstinate ear. The first moment of danger, as he clearly foresaw, came immediately after the defeat of Poland. The "war twilight" (his own expression) was already trying people's nerves; his post was full of "stop the war" letters; Lloyd George in the House of Commons on October 3rd begged him to take specific proposals for peace into serious consideration; and finally on the 6th Hitler, in a speech to the Reichstag, suggested holding a European conference on problems arising from the collapse of Poland. The Prime Minister's public response, which he drafted with the aid of Halifax, Simon and Churchill, could not have been more forthright. "Past experience has shown that no reliance can be placed upon the promises of the present German Government"—that was the key sentence. His personal reflections were equally sharp and uncompromising:

N.C. to Ida 8.10.1939.

"As you know, I have always been more afraid of a peace offer than of an air raid, but I did feel that if Hitler made it himself it would almost certainly be in such a form as to be plainly unacceptable.

"My view has been that it was too early for any hope of a successful peace negotiation, the Germans not yet being sufficiently convinced that they could not win. I still hold this view and for that reason I did not want an offer which would be sufficiently specious to encourage the peace-at-any-price people. There are a good many more of these than is apparent. For instance in 3 days last week I had 2,450 letters and 1,860 of them were 'stop the war' in one form or another. A considerable proportion showed indications that they were prompted by the Dick Sheppard Peace Pledge Union or by the Bishop of Chelmsford's Peace Council. Others are on the line, 'You stopped war before, surely you can find a way out now, before we are all pushed over the precipice'. I have little doubt that L.G. was encouraged by his correspondence to think that he could get a lot of support for a move that (he hoped) might damage the Government in general and the P.M. in particular.

"He got a proper ticking off in the House[1] which was very angry with him and I have seldom seen a man look more unhappy. . . .

"To return, however, to more important considerations, I was I confess anxious when I read Hitler's clever speech and especially when the first American reaction was reported, viz. that he had made a very attractive series of proposals and that his tone had been surprisingly friendly to Great Britain. I refused to think about the speech that night but next morning I was clear in my own mind that it offered no real advance in mind or spirit towards a reasonable peace and that it must be rejected. . . . The difficulty is that you can't believe anything Hitler says . . . the only chance of peace is the disappearance of Hitler and that is what we are working for."

This view survived the buffetings of fortune, diplomacy and misrepresentation. In November, Leopold of Belgium and Wilhelmina of Holland addressed a joint appeal to the King of England, the President of France and the Chancellor of Germany to discuss terms of peace. "I was much disgusted," wrote Chamberlain to his sisters, contemptuously dismissing the appeal as "a manoeuvre to prevent Hitler's attacking the Low Countries." In February and March of the following year, Sumner Welles, the U.S. Under-Secretary of State, was sent as Roosevelt's special envoy to Germany, Italy, France and Britain to discover the possibilities of a just and permanent peace. "I am proud to serve in your Government," was Churchill's reaction when he saw Chamberlain's reply to the peace suggestions Sumner Welles had gathered.[2]

For a short time in May, after his Government had collapsed, and when the fall of France was imminent and the fate of the B.E.F. uncertain, Chamberlain went through a phase of acute pessimism. Hoping for an intervention by Roosevelt, he did not hesitate to communicate this mood to the even more pessimistic American Ambassador, Joseph Kennedy. But the convergence of their views did not last for more than a few days:

Diary, 1.7.1940.

"Saw Joe Kennedy who says everyone in U.S.A. thinks we shall be beaten before the end of the month. Not one of the American

[1] The "ticking off" came from Duff Cooper and David Grenfell. See Hansard Vol. 351, c. 1870–1883, and Duff Cooper, *Old Men Forget* (Rupert Hart-Davis, 1953), pp. 266–267.
[2] W. S. Churchill, *The Second World War* (Cassell, 1948), Vol. 1, p. 442.

journalists who have been in the Low Countries or France believes we can stand up to the bombing we shall get from the air. *But it seems to me that they don't take account of what our Air Force may do to the bombers.* All reports seem to point to the invasion this week or next. W.C. [Churchill] was very pleased with my broadcast."

The broadcast referred to, which was heard on the B.B.C. Home and Overseas services on June 30th and relayed throughout North America, arose out of a story that Chamberlain and Halifax were intriguing to oust Churchill, in order to negotiate peace terms with Hitler. It was, of course, a lie; and on the radio Chamberlain declared: "Anyone who lends himself to German propaganda by listening to idle talk about disunion among us, or who imagines that any of us would consent to enter upon peace negotiations with the enemy, is just playing the Nazi game. We are a solid and united nation which would rather go down to ruin than admit the domination of the Nazis." How completely his integrity in such matters was trusted, by his colleagues and by reputable American opinion, may be gauged by an offer which reached him in the brief weeks between his resignation and his death, from the then Minister of Information:

Duff Cooper to N.C. 18.10.1940.
". . . As you are aware, Mr. Lloyd George has for long been writing a fortnightly article which is syndicated all over the United States and, as you will readily imagine, the tone of these articles has left very much to be desired.

". . . It has now been suggested by the United Press that a similar fortnightly article should be contributed to their columns by yourself. They point out what is undoubtedly the case, that there is nobody else in England who could perform this service with sufficient authority or to whom they would make the offer. . . ."

Throughout his wartime Premiership, indeed, it was the reverse charge, the charge of over-optimism or of complacency, that was most frequently brought against Chamberlain. In a speech to the Conservative Central Council on April 5th, 1940, he used an expression, "Hitler missed the bus", for which, in the light of the Norwegian campaign afterwards, he was severely criticised. I have already quoted this same colloquialism from his family letters as far back as February 1939, and it occurs in them again in May and December. On each occasion, private and public, the basic reasoning was the same: the longer that war could be put off, and once it began the longer the German attack was delayed, the more time we should have to make good the deficiencies in our own defence preparations. This basic reasoning, though much disputed, was sound. What was not sound, but also never publicly stated, was his private view that Nazism might conceivably be destroyed and Hitler overthrown without a frontal clash between Germany and the Allies. A letter to his sisters late in 1939 dismissed as "very fantastic to my ear" the current rumours about a sudden airborne invasion of Britain, and cast doubts on military prophecies of a major attack on the Maginot Line in the spring:

N.C. to Ida 5.11.1939.
"Well it may be so, but I have a 'hunch' that the war will be over before the spring. It won't be by defeat in the field but by German realisation that they *can't* win and that it isn't worth their while to go on getting thinner and poorer when they might have instant relief and perhaps not have to give up anything they really care about. My belief is that a great many Germans are near that position now and that their number, in the absence of any striking military success, will go on growing with increasing rapidity.
"To my mind it is essential to get rid of Hitler. He must either die, or go to St. Helena, or become a real public works architect, preferably in a 'home.' His entourage must also go, with the possible exception of Goering, who might have some ornamental position in a transitional Government. Having once got rid of the Nazis, I don't think we should find any serious difficulty in Germany over Poland, Czechoslovakia, Jews, disarmament, etc."

A month later he felt obliged by "the general consensus of reports" to believe that German morale, so far from weakening, had been stiffened by Goebbels's propaganda. "I am beginning to wonder," he wrote, "whether we shall do any good with them unless they first get a real hard punch in the stomach." But even as late as March he told Sumner Welles (who did not agree) that he remained sceptical about a German offensive in the spring.
This scepticism, it is clear, sprang more from hope, indeed from

wishful thinking, than from any nice or experienced appreciation of strategic probabilities. By temperament he shrank from a holocaust; therefore he comforted himself with the illusion that victory might be won without. Even in the "phoney" war, which was certainly not phoney for those who fought it at sea and in the air, his heart was seared by every casualty. "You will understand how hateful I find my personal position," he wrote to the Archbishop of Canterbury two days after war broke out. "I simply can't bear to think of those gallant fellows who lost their lives last night in the R.A.F. attack [on the German naval base at Kiel], and of their families who have first been called upon to pay the price. Indeed, I must put such thoughts out of my mind if I am not to be unnerved altogether." Even "the triumph of U-boats destroyed" discomforted him: "If they called in at our ports in peace-time we should probably say what good fellows the officers and men were. And we have to kill one another just to satisfy that accursed madman. I wish he could burn in Hell for as many years as he is costing lives." Time served not to blunt but only to sharpen these feelings. After visiting the B.E.F. in France just before Christmas he wrote to his sisters: "It sickened me to see the barbed wire and pill-boxes and guns and anti-tank obstacles, remembering what they meant in the last war. I was glad when it was over." In the last terrible summer of his life he reflected on the soldiering experiences of his son Frank, "now under canvas to his great satisfaction" and "in roaring spirits!" "One gets a different side of it," he observed sadly, "when one is continually writing letters of sympathy to people who have lost their sons."

"I used to say to Annie before war came," he wrote immediately after his fall, "that if such a thing happened I thought I should have to hand over to someone else, for I knew what agony of mind it would mean for me to give directions that would bring death and mutilation and misery to so many. But the war was so different from what I expected that I found the strain bearable and perhaps it was providential that the revolution which overturned me coincided with the entry of the real thing."

He should have resigned on the outbreak of war. He was too much a man of peace to lead a nation and an Empire effectively in war. Different qualities are needed and it is inevitable that the Lloyd Georges should succeed the Asquiths, and the Churchills the Chamberlains. True if he had resigned at once it would surely have been Halifax and not Churchill who would for a time have been Prime Minister. But Churchill's electric appeal and his wide knowledge of war would surely have taken him presently to the leadership.

As soon as Churchill was installed at the Admiralty in September 1939, a series of almost daily letters, several pages long and ranging well beyond Naval responsibilities, began to descend on the Prime Minister. For some weeks this procedure was accepted philosophically and only one reply was sent. This said: "I can assure you that all your letters are carefully read and considered by me, and if I have not replied to them, it is only because I am seeing you every day and moreover, because as far as I have been able to observe, your views and mine have very closely coincided." At length, on the evening of October 2nd, the Prime Minister sent for the First Lord. He assured him that he did not wish their relations to become purely formal and that he would welcome talks between them as time permitted. But if Churchill were dissatisfied with any aspect of Government policy, the proper course was to raise the matter with the Minister concerned or, if necessary, to put forward a paper to the War Cabinet so that the question could be discussed there and responsibility for the decision shared. To this course Churchill agreed, promised to write no more letters, and swore he was wholeheartedly behind Chamberlain and wanted no extended powers himself. "I believe all this was quite genuine," was the Prime Minister's private comment; and Horace Wilson's minute records that their conversation was "friendly throughout". Next week, they and their wives spent a pleasant social evening together at Admiralty House, an occasion charmingly described in Churchill's memoirs.[1]

Goodwill continued to grow in the months that followed. Occasionally one of Chamberlain's letters will provide some now familiar glimpse of the First Lord idiosyncratically at work— holding forth in Cabinet very volubly "and not always entirely

[1] *Ibid.*, pp. 388–389. The dinner took place on Friday, October 13th; Churchill, in error, says Friday, November 13th.

relevantly," or keeping officers and officials up into the small hours until "they are worn out in arguing with him". "I say to myself," recorded the Prime Minister, "that this is just the price we have to pay for the asset we have in his personality and popularity;" and to this asset his papers add with impressive frequency two other factors which made their relationship especially satisfactory now, as also later when their positions were reversed. The first was that, unexpectedly, their conclusions on matters of policy almost always agreed, "though we haven't always arrived at them by the same road". The second was that there existed between the two men a complete mutual trust: "To me personally Winston is absolutely loyal and I am continually hearing from others of the admiration he expresses for the P.M." As the strains grew greater, their association became closer. In February, for the first time, Churchill accompanied Chamberlain to the Supreme War Council in Paris. ("Winston was in the seventh heaven at being asked to come and declared that he had never enjoyed two days more.") In April, to coincide with Cabinet changes, it was arranged that the First Lord should preside over the Military Co-ordination Committee which superintended the general conduct of the war. ("He has told me that he deeply appreciates the confidence I have given him and that he will endeavour to respond.") Their relations remained always easy and often cordial.

It was with his Secretary of State for War that Chamberlain's relations had really become difficult and delicate. This was surprising, for he had consistently held Hore-Belisha in high regard and esteem. He had sent him to the War Office in 1937 against Inskip's advice, and a few months later delightedly wrote to his sisters: "My new S. of S. is doing what I put him there for and has already stirred the old dry bones up till they fairly rattle." When R. S. Hudson and some other junior Ministers had made a dead set against Hore-Belisha at the end of 1938, the Prime Minister backed him loyally, describing him as the best Secretary of State for War since Haldane.[1] But though he continued to admire his "very exceptional qualities of courage, imagination and drive", he came to see also that "he has the defects of his qualities". Hore-Belisha's eagerness and self-confidence, noted Chamberlain, made

[1] R. J. Minney, *The Private Papers of Hore-Belisha* (Collins, 1960), pp. 162–163.

284

him too assertive, too inconsiderate of opposing points of view, too careless of other people's feelings. In particular, he became too careless of Gort's feelings, and Gort was Commander-in-Chief of the B.E.F. To what extent the friction between the two was aggravated by Hore-Belisha's military or political ill-wishers is far from clear. What is clear is that Gort mistook criticism of the inadequacy of the B.E.F.'s defences, and especially the shortage of pill-boxes, for a lack of confidence in his own generalship.[1] Resentment at the Front and the Commander-in-Chief's threats to resign were reported to the Prime Minister by Ironside, Chief of the Imperial General Staff, and later by the King. This was one important reason for Chamberlain's own visit to France at the end of the year.

He was successful in smoothing things over for the time being:

Lord Gort to N.C. 27.12.1939.

"As I think you know I am personally appreciative of the many good qualities of the Secretary of State and also of the many and varied reforms he has brought about in the Army. The criticisms which are made, some of which are doubtless unfair, are due in the first instance to his temperament and his inability to place himself in the other man's shoes. . . .

"I note you fear it may be difficult to restore the confidence of the Army in him. Whilst I naturally do not know with any exactness the situation in the War Office, I can say of the B.E.F. that since your visit any feeling they had previously of possibly misplaced criticism has wholly disappeared. I am therefore confident that, far from things deteriorating out here, I will be able continually to improve the atmosphere. After your talk with the Secretary of State he doubtless now appreciates that any criticism of an army in the field, which must from time to time be necessary and indeed welcome, should be couched in sympathetic language.

"If not, the very necessary confidence and trust between leaders and led, which we all try so hard to foster in war, may fail us in a critical moment."

However, Chamberlain had not found his talk with the Secretary of State at all reassuring. "I had the feeling," his diary records, "that he did not and could not see where he had gone wrong and

[1] *Ibid.*, pp. 257-264.

285

only thought he had been treated with great injustice and prejudice." For this reason, he concluded that trouble would inevitably break out again and "that if favourable opportunity came to move him from the W. O. I had better take it and not wait for another crisis. In wartime nothing could be worse than perpetual friction and want of confidence between the Secretary of State and the C.-in-C. in the field."

The favourable opportunity quickly presented itself to Chamberlain's mind. The Ministry of Information, then in the charge of Lord Macmillan, had long been under fire. This was a difficult and important post for which Hore-Belisha "appeared to have special qualifications" and about whose conduct he had expressed original ideas. Would it not be a good plan, Chamberlain asked Halifax, to move him there and replace him by Oliver Stanley "as the greatest contrast in temperament I could find"? Halifax in a letter expressed some doubts, though not very strongly, and the Prime Minister therefore sounded a number of his other Cabinet colleagues regarding the Hore-Belisha appointment. He also wrote that he had sounded Attlee, Camrose and the editor of the *Sunday Times*. On the whole, reactions were very favourable. Chamberlain now summoned Hore-Belisha to an appointment at 2.45 on the afternoon of January 4th, intending to offer him the Ministry of Information.

At the eleventh hour, however, this sensible and imaginative appointment was subjected to a virtual veto from the Foreign Office. After the Cabinet on the morning of the 4th Halifax stayed behind and, to Chamberlain's consternation, intimated that he and his advisers were strongly against Hore-Belisha's going to the Ministry of Information. "He thought," wrote Chamberlain to his sisters three days later, "it would have a bad effect on the neutrals both because H.B. was a Jew and because his methods would let down British prestige." In fact, since it had been previously suggested that the appointment of a Jew would discount the Ministry in American eyes, Chamberlain had already consulted Lindsay, our former Ambassador, "who dismissed the suggestion at once as entirely baseless". All the same, in the teeth of this objection he felt he could not go on with the original plan. Only an hour remained before the appointment fixed for that afternoon. Hurriedly, therefore, he accepted Halifax's suggestion that Hore-Belisha should be offered the Board of Trade which would be vacated by Stanley. After painful interviews, and despite the advice of Churchill and the intercession of Kingsley Wood, this offer was refused.[1]

N.C. to Ida 7.1.1940.

"I own that I was relieved when K.W. returned with the news that H.B. would not alter his decision for I did not really think it a good appointment. But I did and do feel very sorry for H.B., for although what has happened is his own fault, his mistakes were not deliberately made and I consider he has done great service. What happens to him now must depend on himself but I hope he won't make it too difficult for me to have him back in some other capacity later on."

The opportunity, of course, did not recur, and to all intents and purposes Hore-Belisha's career was broken. The Ministry of Information went to Lord Reith. It is not to be doubted that Hore-Belisha would have been more effective in this particular post. Whether he would have accepted the Ministry of Information had it been offered, we can only guess. That it was about to be offered he never knew, and the reason why it was not offered has never before been given. To Chamberlain as to Halifax anti-Semitism was alien and repugnant. Yet Halifax clearly felt bound to give this advice, and that it was taken is proof again of the influence which Halifax's opinions and counsel consistently had upon Chamberlain during this concluding period of his power. In March he wrote, "I would rather have Halifax succeed me than Winston." The choice was now not long delayed.

Though there is truth in Disraeli's observation that England does not love coalitions, modern wars can only with the greatest difficulty be prosecuted in an atmosphere of Party bickering and strife. "I cannot pretend that all our Ministers get everything right all at once," Chamberlain wrote at an early stage, "but they are trying very hard to do so and it does not promote national unity to have every effort sneered at and crabbed and every complaint exploited to the uttermost." He had himself, on Halifax's advice, resisted all temptation to make Party capital by holding a

[1] *Ibid.*, pp. 269–278.

General Election in the months after Munich; his motive, he declared, was the desire not to aggravate political differences. He had invited both the Labour and Liberal Oppositions to enter the Government when war broke out; but to no avail. Their brusque refusal was a disappointment, but not a surprise. They rarely left him in any doubt that, whoever else might achieve national unity, it could not be he. His letters speak repeatedly of the burden it was in the midst of war "to be thinking in between whiles of how to ward off Opposition attacks on the Government for doing necessary but unpopular things"; of the House of Commons getting "more and more ill tempered and unreasonable"; of his own speeches being "continually interrupted with shouts, sneers, and derisive laughter"; of his depression being increased "by the partisanship and personal prejudice shown by the Labour Party". They made him the scapegoat for all the failures of the past, they blamed him personally for everything that went wrong in the present, and looking to the future they scorned his liberal-minded generalities and his simple argument that one needed to win the war before one could win the peace. In private consultation their attitude was often more friendly, but their urgent aim was not to counsel him but to get rid of him.

In this aim they were decisively assisted by a growing group of dissident Conservatives. There can be no question that these men, like the leaders of the Labour Party, were motivated by genuine disagreement on public policy rather than by personal ambition or disappointment. Yet it is true that a weakness of Chamberlain's in war, even more than in peace, was that he made insufficient use of the available stock of talent in his Party. When war broke out, Churchill and Eden returned to the fold; but with these exceptions the Prime Minister's good appointments (Woolton as Minister of Food, for example) were not Conservative, and his Conservative appointments (Gilmour as Minister of Shipping, for example) were not good. A small group of anti-Munich Conservatives, under Leo Amery's chairmanship, continued to meet weekly over dinner to discuss the developing situation. Many of them also took a prominent part in the All-Party Action Group which was led by Clement Davies, later to be leader of the Liberals; Boothby was one of its secretaries. Later on, in April 1940, the elder statesman Lord Salisbury convened a score or more of leading Conservative backbenchers in both Houses to form a Watching Committee which met every few days and made private representations to the Government.[1]

All these discussions and discontents came to a head just before Whitsun. Our troops had had to be withdrawn from Namsos and Andalsnes in Norway, and a two-day debate in the House of Commons had been fixed for May 7th and 8th. Amery and Clement Davies now decided to see if they could make of this the occasion for a trial of strength. Not till the morning of the 8th did the Labour Party agree to force a division and the Government issued a three-line whip. The debate then assumed the character of a vote of censure. But the damage had already been done on the opening day. Chamberlain's skilful, if matter-of-fact, defence of the conduct of operations and the structure of the War Cabinet might, perhaps, have served against the mocking of the Opposition backbenchers and the debating of Attlee and Sinclair. It could not withstand the voices from behind the Treasury Bench. Sir Roger Keyes, no orator, but resplendent in the uniform of an Admiral of the Fleet, seemed to many to speak for every serving man and woman who felt that the politicians had let them down. Amery himself, making the speech of the debate and the speech of his life, called with conviction for "a real National Government", impassionedly dismissing the old one with Cromwell's terrible words to the Long Parliament: "You have sat too long here for any good you have been doing. Depart, I say, and let us have done with you. In the name of God, go." That night Chamberlain spoke to the King of reconstructing his Government on the basis of a national coalition in which the Labour Party would join, but he did not yet realise the urgency of the political crisis.

The criticism from his own side he felt very deeply. When Herbert Morrison opened the debate on the second day and announced that the Opposition would divide, he rose in anger and called on "my friends in the House—and I have friends in the House— . . . to support us in the Lobby tonight". No doubt this was badly put, and many have said since that this appeal to Party

[1] On these groupings, see L. S. Amery, *My Political Life* (Hutchinson, 1955), Vol. III, pp. 339 and 355.

or to personal loyalties fell below the level of events. Churchill for one did not think so. Winding up for the Government with a speech of much eloquence and force, he allowed himself a piece of splendid irony: "Exception has been taken because the Prime Minister said he appealed to his friends. He thought he had some friends, and I hope he has some friends. He certainly had a good many when things were going well!" Now, however, things were going too badly for friendship to prevail. When the House divided the Government's majority, normally 200-odd, fell to 81; 33 of its supporters, including 29 Conservatives, voted with the Labour and Liberal Oppositions and more than double that number abstained. Those voting against the Government included ex-Ministers like Amery, Duff Cooper, Hore-Belisha and Winterton, and such future Ministers as Macmillan, Richard Law, Molson and Wolmer. The figures would have been worse had it not been privately intimated to backbenchers beforehand that the Prime Minister was planning to reconstruct his Government. All the same, there were some among those who "rebelled" or abstained who did so with troubled and anguished minds. Duff Cooper saw one young officer in uniform who had been for long a fervent admirer of Chamberlain, walking through the Opposition Lobby with tears streaming down his face.[1] And Hailsham's son Quintin Hogg, who had voted against the Government, wrote to Chamberlain: "God bless you in your great present trouble. Your country is and always will be grateful to you for your devoted service and your splendid courage . . . whatever happens, you can be sure that you *have* your friends even amongst those who did not vote with you."

N.C. to Ida 11.5.1940.

"The debate was a very painful affair to many besides myself, and in particular for its exhibition of personal and Party passion. It was supposed to be about Norway, but I think that it was recognised that the Government had a pretty good case there. . . . But the long period of waiting without any real set-back to German prestige, and then the sudden and bitter disappointment over the hopes that had been so recklessly and unjustifiably fostered by the Press, just boiled up with the accumulated mass of grievances to find expression. The

[1] *Old Men Forget*, p. 279.

serving Members were acutely conscious of various deficiencies, not realising apparently that, though you can double your T.A. with a stroke of the pen, you can't do the same thing with its equipment. The Amerys, Duff Coopers, and their lot are consciously or unconsciously swayed by a sense of frustration because they can only look on, and finally the personal dislike of Simon and Hoare had reached a pitch which I find it difficult to understand but which undoubtedly had a great deal to do with the rebellion.

"A number of those who voted against the Government have since either told me or written to me to say that they had nothing against me except that I had the wrong people in my team. . . . They don't want to believe that the real reason is our comparative weakness because we haven't yet anything like caught up the German start, but as that fact remains whatever the administration, I am afraid they will presently be disappointed again."

So much for the why and wherefore; but the sequel too is best told in his own words:

N.C to Ida 11.5.1940 (continued).

"It did not take me long to make up my mind what to do. I saw that the time had come for a National Government in the broadest sense. I knew that I could not get it, but it was necessary to get an official confirmation of the Opposition attitude, if only to justify my resignation to my own Party. I had conversations with Winston and Halifax who I found agreed with my view, and I sent for Attlee and Greenwood that afternoon [May 9th] to ask the definite question whether the Labour Party would join a Government under me or if not under someone else. I did not name the someone else to them but I had understood that they favoured Halifax,[1] and I had him in mind. He declared, however, that after careful reflection he would find it too difficult, being in the Lords, whereas troubles always arise in the Commons. Later I heard that the Labour Party had changed their minds and were veering towards Winston and I agreed with him and Halifax that I would put Winston's name to the King.

"The two Labour men, with whom my personal relations have for some time been quite friendly, were, as I expected, unable to pledge their Party though their replies indicated their own opin-

[1] This is confirmed by Dalton in his memoirs, *The Fateful Years* (Frederick Muller, 1957), pp. 306–307, 309.

ion in the sense I expected. I therefore asked them to collect the voices at Bournemouth from their Executive Committee and let me know the answer yesterday afternoon [May 10th]. This they did and immediately I went off to the Palace and handed in my resignation. The King was as nice as possible and . . . he expressed what I know were very genuine regrets as well as his own pleasure at my remaining in the new Government. . . .

"I must say that Winston has been most handsome in his appreciation of my willingness to help and my ability to do so. I know that he relies on Halifax and me and, as he put it in a letter, 'My fate depends largely on you.'[1]

"He would have given me the Exchequer if I had been willing to take it. But I saw it was impossible. With Labour's set at me I should soon have seemed the obstacle to all they wanted and they would quickly have been making my position untenable. The only chance of letting their passions die down is to take a place which does not bring me into conflict with them.[2]

"You will be wondering how we are taking it. At present everything is overshadowed by the new aggression [against Holland and Belgium] and until we are freed from the anxieties which that involves everything else seems small and petty. . . .

"I am getting an enormous number of letters and so is Annie. Many of them are very painful reading for the distress they reveal, and almost without exception, they declare their complete and unbroken confidence. I believe this always happens when a well-known Minister resigns and I don't attach any particular importance to it. But it does depress me much more than if they were all letters of abuse.

"It is hard on Annie, but as usual she is standing up to it like a heroine. Winston doesn't want us to move from this house [No. 10] for a month or even longer and then (if the Government still stands) we are to go back to No. 11. But Chequers! I shall have to go there some time to collect my things and say good-bye. It will be a bad wrench to part with that place where I have been so happy."

[1] On his return from the Palace on May 10th, Churchill wrote to Chamberlain: "With your help and counsel and with the support of the great Party of which you are the Leader, I trust that I shall succeed . . . To a very large extent I am in your hands—and I feel no fear of that."

[2] He was offered and accepted the Lord Presidency, and also the Leadership of the House of Commons. The Labour Party objected to his leading the Commons and he "gave it up without a sigh".

This political blow and all it meant in terms of personal distress proved mortal to Neville Chamberlain. He fell from power on May 10th; on June 16th his diary records, for the first time, "considerable pain in the abdomen"; on July 24th X-rays revealed a partial stricture of the bowel and an exploratory operation was ordered; on September 9th he returned to No. 11 "a partially crippled man", knowing that the cancerous growth which had caused the trouble was inoperable and incurable. He resigned from public life on October 3rd, and the following week-end, wishing to make proper provision for the future and the family, he pressed Horder to give him some idea of his expectation of life. After much hesitation "he went so far as to say he would be surprised if I were not here in 3 months time but more surprised if I were here in 12 months". The news was accepted stoically, indeed thankfully, for he was in great misery. But the end came even sooner than he had been told, as perhaps Lord Horder knew it really would. He died on November 9th, and on the 14th, with the War Cabinet as pall-bearers, his ashes were buried in Westminster Abbey next to the tomb of Bonar Law.

Years later another famous doctor was to write this: "I have slowly come to frame in my mind an aphorism that can never be stated as such, because no statistics can be advanced to support it: 'The happy man never gets cancer' . . . The instances where the first recognisable onset of cancer has followed almost immediately on some disaster, a bereavement, the break-up of a relationship, a financial crisis, or an accident, are so numerous that they suggest that some controlling force that has hitherto kept the outbreak . . . in check has been removed."[1] Cause and effect cannot be proved, but in Neville Chamberlain's case the suddenness of physical collapse in a constitution hitherto so tough and wiry could certainly be taken as *prima facie* evidence of the truth of Sir Heneage Ogilvie's aphorism.

Certainly in those final months, and even before the operation, he was desperately unhappy. He shared with all his colleagues and countrymen in the deepening calamities of a summer more anxious than any in our history. Hoare, indeed, believed that it

[1] Sir Heneage Ogilvie, "The Human Heritage" (the Ward Jones lecture, Manchester University), *The Lancet*, July 6th, 1957.

was the fall of France rather than the fall of his Government that finally shattered his friend's spirit.[1] But though for an instant now Chamberlain may have thought he saw the spectre of defeat, the last pages of his diary and of his family correspondence belie this judgement. "We are going to see this b—y thing through," was the spirit in the air-raid shelters as reported by his doctors; and his own spirit responded: "We must just go on fighting as hard as we can in the belief that some time—perhaps sooner than we think —the other side will crack." Not the initial triumph of the Axis, then, but the weight of personal hopelessness was what numbed his will to live. "I frankly envy Austen's peace," he wrote to Hilda in May, and to the same sister in July: "My friends all say I look well. But I have lost my spring and my spirits. All my recreations, flowers, fishing and shooting, country life, have been taken from me—and there is nothing to look forward to."

This state of mind was aggravated and embittered by attacks that continued to be made upon him by the Left-Wing Press in a seemingly concerted effort to drive him from office altogether. It was argued that his presence in the Government militated against national unity and the forthright prosecution of the war. In truth, his presence in the Government at this time guaranteed national unity; for he was still the accepted leader of the majority Party which, on his first entry into the House in his new capacity, rose to a man "and received him in a vehement demonstration of sympathy and regard".[2] Churchill's memoirs pay tribute to the steadfastness of Chamberlain's loyalty and support which buttressed his own political position.[3] This loyalty he certainly stretched to the utmost limit, since, acknowledging that "one cannot refuse anything in times like these to the Prime Minister", Chamberlain even agreed, if the ancient feud were dropped, to serve in Cabinet with Lloyd George. But this trial at least he was spared, for Lloyd George refused the offers that were made to him.

As for the prosecution of the war, he became Chairman of what was henceforth called the Lord President's Committee, "which

[1] *Nine Troubled Years* (Collins, 1954), pp. 432–433.
[2] W. S. Churchill, *The Second World War* (Cassell, 1949), Vol. 2, p. 9.
[3] *Ibid.*, pp. 9 and 287.

consisted of a few senior Ministers who took decisions on a whole range of subjects, especially those relating to the Home Front, without troubling the Cabinet".[1] In this capacity he played a leading part in placing the Emergency Powers (Defence) Bill on the Statute Book. In addition, at Churchill's request and with Malcolm MacDonald's aid, he was responsible in June for a secret and unrewarded endeavour to get Eire to abandon neutrality. At the end of August, when Chamberlain's return to work was under question, the Prime Minister wrote to him to say that, quite apart from general policy developments, there were only too many thorny subjects—he instanced railway fares, the rating problems of local authorities in coastal areas under heavy attack, and war damage compensation—on which he badly needed his predecessor's advice and help. From other colleagues he won golden, and sometimes surprised, opinions. Beaverbrook, with whom his relations were now particularly friendly, sent a warm letter of gratitude for Chamberlain's consistent backing "in my audacious courses" at the Ministry of Aircraft Production. "If you don't mind my saying it as bluntly as I have blurted out things in the past," wrote the Liberal leader, Archibald Sinclair, "I have learned to appreciate the value of your counsel." As for the Labour leaders, Chamberlain believed that they were "finding that I am a very different person from what they supposed". This belief was warranted, as Attlee's retrospective judgement will show: "He was Lord President. Very able and crafty, and free from any of the rancour he might well have felt against us. He worked very hard and well: a good chairman, a good committee man, always very businesslike. You could work with him."[2]

The regard of his colleagues was little reflected in the Press when he resigned in October. Commenting on their short, cold and for the most part depreciatory notices of his role in international politics, he wrote in his diary: "Not one shows the slightest sign of sympathy for the man or even any comprehension that there may be a human tragedy somewhere in the background." However, in the months before, and in the weeks that followed, letters poured in from many hundreds who did indeed

[1] C. R. Attlee, *As It Happened* (Heinemann, 1954), p. 115.
[2] *A Prime Minister Remembers* (Heinemann, 1961), p. 37.

comprehend not only his tragedy, but his gifts, his character, and his achievement. Perhaps they helped him at the time; certainly those who seek to judge Neville Chamberlain should listen to a few at least of these voices.

King George VI to N.C. 8.10.1940.

"You were my Prime Minister in the earliest years of my reign, and I shall ever be grateful for your help and guidance during what was in many ways a very difficult period. For me too it will always be a pleasure to recall our many and intimate talks together. I have sympathised with you very much in seeing your hopes shattered by the lust and violence of a single man; and yet, as I told you once before, your efforts to preserve peace were not in vain, for they established, in the eyes of the civilised world, our entire innocence of the crime which Hitler was determined to commit. For this alone, the country owes you a deep debt of gratitude."

Winston Churchill to N.C. 2.10.1940.

"I and all your colleagues have admired your unshaken nerve and persevering will. The help you have given me since you ceased to be my chief tided us through what may well prove to be the turning point of the war. You did all you could for peace; you did all you could for victory. . . . We have been associated, as our fathers were before us, in the ups and downs of politics, now together, now apart, but I look back upon this stern year of comradeship with feelings of the deepest respect and regard for you."

Malcolm MacDonald to N.C. 8.11.1940.

"Your industry, your incorruptible honesty of purpose, your unflinching devotion to ideals which were yet practicable, your utter fearlessness in pursuing them, will always be an example of right conduct in a public man that I for one amongst the younger generation shall cherish. I shall never have a leader whose private and public character I respect more. I am sure you will not mind my adding that during these last few years (since on entering the Cabinet I first learned, to my surprise, that I was completely wrong in sharing a common view that you were a die-hard Tory!) I have come to feel for you not only a deep admiration but also a genuine affection."

Sir Alexander Cadogan to N.C. 12.10.1940.

"I am not going to write about the events of the last two and more years—I can't presume to usurp the function of the 'historian,' though I do anticipate his judgement. But I do want to say how happy I was to serve you and to enjoy, as I dare to believe, your friendship. I shall always treasure that as a very happy memory, and I shall be very proud of it. I have tried to serve several Ministers and even—at further remove—several Prime Ministers; and I did what I could for a perfectly dizzying succession of Delegates at Geneva! But I have never learnt so much as I did from you, nor felt my loyalty so completely engaged. Nor have I met such sympathy."

Cardinal Hinsley to N.C. 5.10.1940.

"Your efforts to preserve peace gave to our cause a moral strength that can never be disregarded. For this all who have regard for Britain's honour must be profoundly grateful. . . . You will surely receive the reward of those who are promised the blessing of peace-makers."

Some time before he resigned he was offered a peerage, and on his resignation the Garter. He declined both, preferring as he said "to die plain 'Mr. Chamberlain' like my father before me", and taking comfort from the fact that all three Chamberlains were to die Members of the House of Commons. Like his father before him, he had given of his best to his city and his country. Like his father too, he had upheld the progressive cause of Empire, and at Ottawa built well for his day. Like his father again, he had championed and extended social reform; moreover, by prudent finance, by restoring confidence and by assisting recovery, he had strengthened its economic foundations. Finally, like his father, he had failed in his lifetime to realise the dearest of all his hopes. Yet the hope could not have been more noble, nor could it have been pursued with greater courage or capacity; it was frustrated by evil, but it won at least a respite, if not for reason to prevail, then for strength to be gathered. And the noblest of Englishmen who worked so closely with Neville Chamberlain may fittingly be given the last word. As Churchill said to the House of Commons in his great valediction:[1] "The only guide to a man is his conscience; the only shield to his memory is the rectitude and sincerity of his actions. It is very imprudent to walk through life without this shield, because we are so often mocked by the failure of our hopes and the upsetting of our calculations; but with this

[1] Printed in full in the Appendix.

shield, however the fates may play, we march always in the ranks of honour."

Neville Chamberlain died at Heckfield in Hampshire and a simple wall stone in the village church is his memorial. It reads: "Neville Chamberlain. Prime Minister of Great Britain 1937–1940. Write me as one that loves his fellow-men."

THE FAMILY TREE

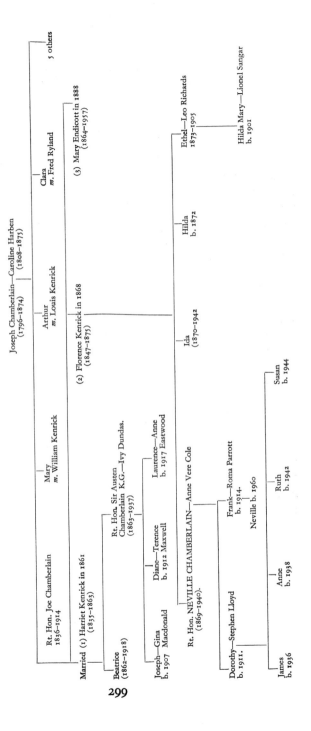

299

APPENDIX B

THE MUNICH AGREEMENT

Germany, the United Kingdom, France and Italy, taking into consideration the agreement which has been already reached in principle for the cession to Germany of the Sudeten German territory, have agreed on the following terms and conditions governing the said cession and the measures consequent thereon, and by this agreement they each hold themselves responsible for the steps necessary to secure its fulfilment:

1. The evacuation will begin on the 1st October.

2. The United Kingdom, France and Italy agree that the evacuation of the territory shall be completed by the 10th October, without any existing installations having been destroyed, and that the Czechoslovak Government will be held responsible for carrying out the evacuation without damage to the said installations.

3. The conditions governing the evacuation will be laid down in detail by an international commission composed of representatives of Germany, the United Kingdom, France, Italy and Czechoslovakia.

4. The occupation by stages of the predominantly German territory by German troops will begin on the 1st October. The four territories marked on the attached map [not reproduced here] will be occupied by German troops in the following order: The territory marked No. I on the 1st and 2nd of October, the territory marked No. II on the 2nd and 3rd of October, the territory marked No. III on the 3rd, 4th and 5th of October, the territory marked No. IV on the 6th and 7th of October. The remaining territory of preponderantly German character will be ascertained by the aforesaid international commission forthwith and be occupied by German troops by the 10th of October.

5. The international commission referred to in paragraph 3 will determine the territories in which a plebiscite is to be held. These territories will be occupied by international bodies until the plebiscite has been completed. The same commission will fix the conditions in which the plebiscite is to be held, taking as a basis the conditions of the

Saar plebiscite. The commission will also fix a date, not later than the end of November, on which the plebiscite will be held.

6. The final determination of the frontiers will be carried out by the international commission. This commission will also be entitled to recommend to the four Powers, Germany, the United Kingdom, France and Italy, in certain exceptional cases minor modifications in the strictly ethnographical determination of the zones which are to be transferred without plebiscite.

7. There will be a right of option into and out of the transferred territories, the option to be exercised within six months from the date of this agreement. A German-Czechoslovak commission shall determine the details of the option, consider ways of facilitating the transfer of population and settle questions of principle arising out of the said transfer.

8. The Czechoslovak Government will, within a period of four weeks from the date of this agreement, release from their military and police forces any Sudeten Germans who may wish to be released, and the Czechoslovak Government will, within the same period, release Sudeten German prisoners who are serving terms of imprisonment for political offences.

ADOLF HITLER
NEVILLE CHAMBERLAIN
ÉDOUARD DALADIER
BENITO MUSSOLINI

Munich,
September 29, 1938.

Annex to the Agreement

His Majesty's Government in the United Kingdom and the French Government have entered into the above agreement on the basis that they stand by the offer, contained in paragraph 6 of the Anglo-French proposals of the 19th September, relating to an international guarantee of the new boundaries of the Czechoslovak State against unprovoked aggression.

When the question of the Polish and Hungarian minorities in Czechoslovakia has been settled, Germany and Italy for their part will give a guarantee to Czechoslovakia.

ADOLF HITLER
NEVILLE CHAMBERLAIN
ÉDOUARD DALADIER
BENITO MUSSOLINI

Munich,
September 29, 1938.

Declaration

The Heads of the Governments of the four Powers declare that the problems of the Polish and Hungarian minorities in Czechoslovakia, if not settled within three months by agreement between the respective Governments, shall form the subject of another meeting of the Heads of the Government of the four Powers here present.

ADOLF HITLER
NEVILLE CHAMBERLAIN
ÉDOUARD DALADIER
BENITO MUSSOLINI

Munich,
September 29, 1938.

Supplementary Declaration

All questions which may arise out of the transfer of the territory shall be considered as coming within the terms of reference to the international commission.

ADOLF HITLER
NEVILLE CHAMBERLAIN
ÉDOUARD DALADIER
BENITO MUSSOLINI

Munich,
September 29, 1938.

Composition of the International Commission

The four Heads of Government here present agree that the international commission provided for in the agreement signed by them to-day, shall consist of the Secretary of State in the German Foreign Office, the British, French and Italian Ambassadors accredited in Berlin, and a representative to be nominated by the Government of Czechoslovakia.

ADOLF HITLER
NEVILLE CHAMBERLAIN
ÉDOUARD DALADIER
BENITO MUSSOLINI

Munich,
September 29, 1938.

APPENDIX C

THE CHURCHILL VALEDICTION

Rt. Hon. Winston Churchill, M.P. Hansard 12.11.1940.

"Since we last met, the House has suffered a very grievous loss in the death of one of its most distinguished Members and of a statesman and public servant who, during the best part of three memorable years, was first Minister of the Crown.

"The fierce and bitter controversies which hung around him in recent times were hushed by the news of his illness and are silenced by his death. In paying a tribute of respect and of regard to an eminent man who has been taken from us, no-one is obliged to alter the opinions which he has formed or expressed upon issues which have become a part of history; but at the Lychgate we may all pass our own conduct and our own judgements under a searching review. It is not given to human beings, happily for them, for otherwise life would be intolerable, to foresee or to predict to any large extent the unfolding course of events. In one phase men seem to have been right, in another they seem to have been wrong. Then again, a few years later, when the perspective of time has lengthened, all stands in a different setting. There is a new proportion. There is another scale of values. History with its flickering lamp stumbles along the trail of the past, trying to reconstruct its scenes, to revive its echoes, and kindle with pale gleams the passion of former days. What is the worth of all this? The only guide to a man is his conscience; the only shield to his memory is the rectitude and sincerity of his actions. It is very imprudent to walk through life without this shield, because we are so often mocked by the failure of our hopes and the upsetting of our calculations; but with this shield, however the fates may play, we march always in the ranks of honour.

"It fell to Neville Chamberlain in one of the supreme crises of the world to be contradicted by events, to be disappointed in his hopes, and to be deceived and cheated by a wicked man. But what were these hopes in which he was disappointed? What were these wishes in which he was frustrated? What was that faith that was abused? They were surely among the most noble and benevolent instincts of the human heart—the love of peace, the toil for peace, the strife for peace, the pursuit of peace, even at great peril and certainly to the utter disdain of popularity or clamour. Whatever else history may or may not say about these terrible, tremendous years, we can be sure that Neville Chamberlain acted with perfect sincerity according to his lights and strove to the utmost of his capacity and authority, which were powerful, to save the world from the awful, devastating struggle in which we are now engaged. This alone will stand him in good stead as far as what is called the verdict of history is concerned.

"But it is also a help to our country and to our whole Empire, and to our decent, faithful way of living that, however long the struggle may last, or however dark may be the clouds which overhang our path, no future generation of English-speaking folks—for that is the tribunal to which we appeal—will doubt that, even at a great cost to ourselves in technical preparation, we were guiltless of the bloodshed, terror and misery which have engulfed so many lands and peoples, and yet seek new victims still. Herr Hitler protests with frantic words and gestures that he has only desired peace. What do these ravings and outpourings count before the silence of Neville Chamberlain's tomb? Long and hard, hazardous years lie before us, but at least we entered upon them united and with clean hearts.

"I do not propose to give an appreciation of Neville Chamberlain's life and character, but there were certain qualities, always admired in these Islands, which he possessed in an altogether exceptional degree. He had a physical and moral toughness of fibre which enabled him all through his varied career to endure misfortune and disappointment without being unduly discouraged or wearied. He had a precision of mind and an aptitude for business which raised him far above the ordinary levels of our generation. He had a firmness of spirit which was not often elated by success, seldom downcast by failure and never swayed by panic. When, contrary to all his hopes, beliefs and exertions, the war came upon him, and when, as he himself said, all that he had worked for was shattered, there was no man more resolved to pursue the unsought quarrel to the death. The same qualities which made him one of the last to enter the war, made him one of the last who would quit it until the full victory of a righteous cause was won.

"I had the singular experience of passing in a day from being one of his most prominent opponents and critics to being one of his principal lieutenants, and on another day of passing from serving under him to become the head of a Government of which, with perfect loyalty, he was content to be a member. Such relationships are unusual in our public life. I have before told the House on the morrow of the Debate which in the early days of May challenged his position, he declared to me and a few other friends that only a National Government could face the storm about to break upon us, and that if he were an obstacle to the formation of such a Government, he would instantly retire. Thereafter, he acted with that singleness of purpose and simplicity of conduct which at all times, and especially in great times, ought to be a model for us all.

"When he returned to duty a few weeks after a most severe operation, the bombardment of London and of the seat of Government had begun. I was a witness during that fortnight of his fortitude under the most grievous and painful bodily afflictions, and I can testify that, although physically only the wreck of a man, his nerve was unshaken and his remarkable mental faculties unimpaired.

"After he left the Government he refused all honours. He would die like his father, plain Mr. Chamberlain. I sought the permission of the King, however, to have him supplied with the Cabinet papers, and until a few days of his death he followed our affairs with keenness, interest and tenacity. He met the approach of death with a steady eye. If he grieved at all, it was that he could not be a spectator of our victory, but I think he died with the comfort of knowing that his country had, at least, turned the corner.

"At this time out thoughts must pass to the gracious and charming lady who shared his days of triumph and adversity with a courage and quality the equal of his own. He was, like his father and his brother, Austen, before him, a famous Member of the House of Commons, and we here assembled this morning, Members of all parties, without a single exception, feel that we do ourselves and our country honour in saluting the memory of one whom Disraeli would have called an 'English worthy.' "

INDEX

Wheatley, John, 93, 103, 105

Wheeler-Bennett, Sir John, 202 (note), 234 (note), 241

Widows, Orphans and Old Age Pensions Act, 113–117

Weidemann, Captain, 232, 233

Wigram, Mr. and Mrs. Ralph, 159

Wilhelmina, Queen of Holland, 279

Wilson, Sir Henry, 86

Wilson, Sir Horace, 212, 214, 216, 220, 245, 248, 250, 251 (note), 252, 253, 283

Wilson, Sir Leslie, 85

Wilson, Tyson, 64

Winterton, Lord, 290

Wolmer, Lord, 134, 290

Wood, Sir Kingsley, 91, 144, 165, 166, 191, 205, 287

Woolton, Earl of, 264

World Economic Conference, 174

Worthington-Evans, Sir Laming, 80, 90, 95, 98, 127

York, Archbishop of (William Temple), 165

Young, G. M., 177 (note)

Younger, Sir George (Lord Younger), 85

Zinovieff letter, 108